Foster Care Odyssey

Foster Care Odyssey

A Black Girl's Story

Theresa Cameron

University Press of Mississippi / Jackson

Published in association with
the Center for American Places,
Santa Fe, New Mexico, and
Harrisonburg, Virginia
(www.americanplaces.org)

www.upress.state.ms.us

Library of Congress Cataloging-in-Publication Data
Cameron, Theresa.
    Foster care odyssey: a black girl's story/ by Theresa Cameron.
      p. cm.
    Includes index.
    ISBN 1-57806-420-1 (cloth: alk. paper)
      1. Foster children—New York (State)—Biography.   2. African American women—New York
    (State)—Biography.   3. Foster home care—New York (State).   I. Series.

HV883.N68 C36 2002
362.73'3'09747—dc21
[B]
                                                                    2001046667
British Library Cataloging-in-Publication Data available

Contents

Contents

Acknowledgments

This book would not have been possible without the contributions of many people. I would like to acknowledge four special people who helped make this book a reality. One prefers to remain anonymous, and the others are Margaret Wilder, Dan Harrison, and Yoomie Ahn. Each gave graciously of their time to read multiple revisions and to make suggestions that improved this work.

Gerald Markowitz made many timely and insightful comments and provided words of encouragement when my spirits were low. I also wish to acknowledge two other special friends, Anna Steiner and Sasha Valdez. Without the support of my colleagues and friends Fritz Steiner, David Pijawka, and Alvin Mushkalel, this book would not have come to fruition. I would also like to thank Toni Wynn, Brad Grant, Robert Mann, Joan Westcott, and Judy Dworkin for being my friends. And I must thank George F. Thompson, president of the Center for American Places who served as my agent, and the wonderful people at the University Press of Mississippi. To all of these people I say thank you.

Introduction

Why now, at the age of forty-six, did I write this book? What did I hope to accomplish?

Even though I now accept that my out-of-wedlock birth and subsequent abandonment were issues beyond my control, I nonetheless felt buried in shame for much of my life. Today, in casual conversations with coworkers or acquaintances, I no longer cringe when the subject of family comes up. I am frank with people and say I have no family. The reactions range from pity to acceptance, and people do not always know how to respond. Sometimes I feel sorry for them because they appear so uncomfortable. You may or may not get along with your family members, but you know they are there. However, I know absolutely nothing about my parents. Most of my friends are surprised I did not grow up shrouded in anger, but holding onto bitterness would only disrupt the course I have chosen.

I never thought my life story would be of interest to anyone. Then, one day a friend suggested I write a book about myself. "Ha, you must be joking," I thought. But she persisted, telling me what I experienced as a long-term foster child had meaning. Most books written about foster care are told from the professional's point of view. Very little has been written to convey what children experience and how they feel living among strangers. Thus, one of the main goals of my book is to let adults know their injudicious actions can have disastrous consequences for their children. Foster care may be a convenient way to deal with the children of troubled parents, but it can also hurl youngsters into an emotional abyss. Social workers, policy-makers, and parents themselves may not fully appreciate the lingering scars foster care can leave on the thousands of children who end up in the system. (According to the American Public Welfare Association, in 1996 more than 506,000 children were in foster care.) I hope my book will provide an honest, sobering account of what can happen to children when they are removed from their families.

As I began to write this book, trying to find the right words to express myself, a story slowly took shape. At times, the pain stabbed through my heart, plunging me into depression. I hated reliving those memories, but once I finished I felt an overwhelming sense of relief. Writing this book also helped me to make peace with myself and to find sorely needed serenity.

This is a memoir of my entire youth spent in a variety of foster homes in upstate New York. Like most foster children, I had no choice with whom I lived or how long I would stay. Others controlled my life. Even when I was old enough to form my own opinions and aspirations, I was never consulted on any aspect of care.

More than anything else, I wanted to be a part of a family, even if they lived in a house without a white picket fence or a two-car garage. As a foster child, I acquired many social rules with which to communicate and interact with others. My difficulties in doing so arose from a lack of emotional and financial support, as well as the familial love necessary to succeed in life. On the few occasions when those things presented themselves, I failed to fully appreciate or even to recognize when people tried to support me.

Similar to conditions many foster children currently experience, I was not raised in filth or a decrepit tenement. I also never starved, walked around in tattered rags, or camped out on a park bench. The transient nature of foster care, however, could not provide me with a sense of belonging.

Foster care was originally started as a way to provide assistance to deserving poor children, but now it offers safety and security mostly to maltreated children. I somehow slipped between the cracks because I was abandoned, not abused. Throughout my childhood, I wanted to be in a house where I had the same last name as everyone else and resembled other members of the household. Instead of feeling like a family member, I was more like a guest in other people's homes, someone who had overstayed her welcome. I was not free to be adopted because the woman who gave me life did not relinquish her custody rights. I celebrated my eighteenth birthday not because I had attained voting age, but because I was now legally my own person and no longer a ward of the state—a term that always made me feel like a number on an assembly line.

It has taken me several decades to accept there is no shame attached to my out-of-wedlock birth, my subsequent abandonment, and my status as a ward of the state. In writing this book, I have relived tender memories of days I thought I would rather forget. This process has finally enabled me to make peace with my past, the woman who abandoned me, and the imperfect child welfare system charged to look after me.

This story is about the everlasting hope of a child for a family and the ability to heal oneself with the help of a few good people. I have tried to convey the vicissitudes of the foster care system as I encountered it during the 1950s and 1960s. I invite you to travel with me through nineteen years of foster care that began in 1954, the year I was born, and ended in 1973, the year I graduated from high school and entered college.

Some of the vocabulary used in part one is from a young child's perspective. In part two, my adolescent voice becomes stronger as I developed more of an understanding about my life. By part three, my young adult's viewpoint is presented without becoming disjointed. At that stage of my life, I learned the value of listening to the voice from within, and the vocabulary used, as well as the insights made, become considerably more sophisticated.

I am a testament to all those children who have managed to come through the child welfare system. I attribute this to two things: my constant hope that life would eventually change for the better and the unwavering belief that others had in me when I lacked faith in myself.

My book is dedicated to all foster children who, for whatever reasons, have been separated from their biological families and live with surrogate families. Although this book is about the life of an African American girl in foster care, I believe it has a broad enough appeal to help anyone come to terms with a difficult past.

Names and some minor details have been changed to protect the privacy of the people involved. To tell a balanced story, I left out some of the foster children with whom I shared homes. If I had mentioned them all, the story would have become too complicated. Other parts of my history have been omitted because I either never knew all the facts or was unable to discover them.

Finally, it is my hope that one day soon it will be possible to discount the current value of assigning one's ethnicity or color to one's personal story. All of us who have survived the foster care system in the United States have had to overcome much, and it would please me greatly to be known simply as a human being rather than as the author of a black girl's story.

Foster Care Odyssey

Part One

O n e

In the Beginning

My birth certificate says I was born on January 29, 1954, in Buffalo, a medium-sized industrialized city on the shores of Lake Erie in western New York. Buffalo is the second largest city in New York State and is known as the Queen City of the Great Lakes. This official document, now a wrinkled piece of paper with faded lettering, reports the name of my mother, who at the time was a teenager from Mississippi. There is no mention of my father. I do not know if he was with my mother when I was born.

The truth behind my roots may never be known. What is the real identity of my parents? Obviously, my mother knew I existed. Did my father know that one of the sexual encounters he had with this young Negro woman from a rural southern state left her pregnant? With me? Maybe my mother never told him she was pregnant. Maybe he knew, but was unwilling or unable to accept the responsibility of fatherhood. Only his conscience, my mother, and the Almighty know the truth.

Evidently, single motherhood was too much for the woman who bore me. It must have been especially hard for her as a Negro living in a largely white community, far from her hometown in the South. Although most Negroes were Protestant, my mother was either Catholic or she had me baptized in the Catholic Church. Because New York State required that children be placed with an agency of the same religious affiliation as the parents, I ended up in the hands of Catholic Charities, a nonprofit social services agency with offices throughout the United States. This would have been a reasonably acceptable solution, except my mother walked away without making the proper arrangements to free me legally for adoption. Left in a legal limbo, Catholic Charities had no choice but to place me in foster care. There were few options available for abandoned Negro children, including me.

I wonder if there may have been extended family members from both sides who, if given the opportunity, would have taken me in. My mother probably never reached out for help. At the time, bearing children out of wedlock was still a social taboo. My mother may have become pregnant with me while living in the South and, to hide the shame to her family, traveled to another state to deliver, something unmarried women in those times frequently did. Or maybe she was a local girl who got mixed up with the wrong man.

I could spend hours speculating about this woman's life and still never know the truth. Beyond her, however, are the shadows of an extended family lost forever. I will always be curious about family members I never knew, about Fourth of July picnics or Christmas dinners missed. Once in a while, when I see pictures of family reunions, I feel a sense of emptiness, knowing I have no family albums to peruse. Sadder yet, I have no childhood photos of myself. Without a family, the normal documentation of a childhood never occurs.

Orphanages for Negro children were rare because white society never wanted to fund them and Negroes could barely make ends meet. Expecting Negroes to donate money for an orphanage was impossible. Most Negroes worked in menial, low-paying jobs. Thus, racism, as evil as it was, kept a lot of Negro children out of these human warehouses. Close family friends, although not blood related, often filled in the gaps and were quick to lend a hand when needed. To this day, thousands of people have aunts and uncles not biologically related to them, but still considered family. If my mother had come from a solid Christian background with strong family ties, chances are her people would not have left me, an infant, in the hands of white strangers.

In the Beginning

Without records to guide me and with no memory of my earliest days, I do not know what happened after my birth. Rumors suggest that when my mother was discharged from the hospital, she took me with her but subsequently deserted me in front of an orphanage. Other rumors suggest that I was turned over to Catholic Charities right away.

Regardless of why or how I was abandoned, I was a newborn without a home and therefore became a ward of New York State. Due to my tender age, I do not recall my first foster home or what the people were like. Because the nation was still in the throes of legalized segregation, it is safe to assume my first foster family was Negro. I do not know, however, if I was placed with more than one family during my first few years of life. For unclear reasons, I was not legally freed for adoption until many years later, at an age when I was less likely to be adopted. Who is to blame? Catholic Charities? My mother? The child welfare system? Institutionalized racism?

No longer angry at my birth mother for turning me over to strangers, I remain indignant, nevertheless, that she did not take the time to sign at least one important piece of paper, one that would have given me a chance to find my own little promised land. I may not have been adopted, but her actions deprived me of the chance to grow up surrounded by a loving family. I have forgiven her, but I have not forgotten what this woman potentially deprived me of. The effect of her carelessness will always be with me.

On the Road: The First
Foster Home I Remember

My memory starts to surface, around 1957, when I was three years old. One day I was left with the Chesters, a Negro couple in their mid-fifties who had become foster parents. I had a brown paper bag containing my few belongings. I have no idea what time of year it was.

The turbulence in my young life made me feel apprehensive when I was introduced to the Chesters. When Mrs. Chester first opened the door, her bronze-skinned face glowed, almost like I was a long-lost relative. She tenderly grasped my little clammy hand. "Come on in, honey, we've been waiting on you."

I sucked my thumb, stared at the floor, and in a whisper said, "Yes, ma'am."

As soon as I was safely inside, the caseworker handed Mrs. Chester a small stack of papers containing my vital statistics. The nervous-looking white woman with shortly cropped bangs peered over her shoulder a few times at her car parked outside. She said she would be back in a month to check up on me and promptly took off. It was at least a year before I can remember her next visit.

On the Road: The First Foster Home I Remember

Slowly, I discovered the Chesters had been married for many years by the time I arrived. They had already raised a family, and their three children, two sons and a daughter, lived close by. Their daughter lived in the downstairs apartment with her husband and young son.

Although the Chesters were Negroes like me, I already felt like an outsider. During my introduction to the foster children already in residence there, eight- and ten-year-old boys named Eddie and Mark, I barely opened my mouth to speak. Eddie, the older of the two, carefully studied me like a new game then asked, "What's your name?"

I felt the muscles tighten in my stomach. "Theresa."

Curious, Eddie asked, "What kind of name is that?"

Staring at my ripped black shoes with paper-thin soles, I shrugged. "I don't know."

I do not know if I had been named after anyone in particular, or if my name had been chosen to satisfy the bureaucracy at the hospital. I am not sure if Cameron is my mother's real last name.

Eddie said, "Something the matter you can't talk?"

"No." I stomped my foot and started to whine. Tears, however, never rolled down my chocolate-colored cheeks. I had learned to become stoical at a very early age.

Eddie gazed at Mark, as if he sought forgiveness. Then turned to me and pleaded, "Don't cry. We didn't mean nothing."

Mark added, "Yeah, I'm sorry, too."

Mrs. Chester intervened and said, "Boys, go clean up your rooms. Don't be hurting Theresa's feelings." Within seconds, the two boys with mocha-colored skin and close-cropped haircuts disappeared, and I clung to Mrs. Chester's side like glue. I was scared, not knowing where I was or what would happen. She took me by the hand and asked, "You OK?"

Words would not fall out of my mouth. I remained almost mute, barely able to move.

Mrs. Chester appeared frustrated. "Please say something."

I did not.

"How can I know anything about you if you don't speak?"

Stiff like a toy soldier, I stared at her without responding. She was a stranger I did not like or trust. I felt like a bad girl because the caseworker lady had removed me from one home and deposited me in another without telling me why. Nothing made sense.

Tensions eased when the front door opened and a svelte teenager with wavy, shoulder length brown hair walked in. She carried a book bag that appeared to be empty.

Mrs. Chester's face tightened. She did not look happy to see the young lady, but she said, "Lilly, come over here and meet Theresa. She'll be with us now."

Dark skinned like me, Lilly was about sixteen years old. She brushed by me and only said, "Hi" before hiking up the stairs, two at a time.

Mrs. Chester mumbled something to herself about Lilly's bad attitude. Already, I sensed trouble between the two, so I blocked out everything. I spent the rest of the afternoon seated at the kitchen table in a trancelike state. Several hours later, I broke down and drank Hawaiian Punch. It would be weeks before I finally accepted my temporary home.

Detailed memories about life with the Chester family have faded over time. I can, nonetheless, remember what they looked like. Mr. Chester had beautiful copper-colored skin with cheekbones that sagged, giving the impression he was older than his years. Because he was wafer thin, he appeared taller than he actually was. Job opportunities for Negro men in Buffalo were limited to porters, janitors, civil service, or factory work. Mr. Chester worked as a janitor for one of the local schools. Although he smelled like PineSol, he always looked sharp. Like other Negro men of his time, Mr. Chester took off his drab gray overalls and came home looking dapper in a fresh sport shirt and pressed trousers. Because he smoked cigarettes, the scent of tobacco clung to his clothes, hands, and breath, long after he had showered and changed. Regardless of how hard he worked all week long, Mr. Chester's dark eyes sparkled. Why, I do not know, but they did.

A year or two younger than her husband, Mrs. Chester was an average-sized woman, probably about five foot four inches, with bronze-colored skin. She had the hands of a surgeon, with long, slender fingers, but the skin was tough and leathery from years of housework—both for her own family and for the white people she intermittently worked for. The smell of Jergen's skin lotion was always present. She wore her long, dark wavy hair in a bun. Whenever she flashed a smile through her full lips, I noticed very white teeth, remarkable considering she rarely had money for a visit to the dentist. She used baking soda to clean her teeth. Unlike her husband, Mrs. Chester shunned tobacco.

Physical contact with the other youngsters or me was rare. Every now and then, though, the Chesters exchanged fleeting embraces with one another. Perhaps they reserved their physical contact when they were in private. Hugs and kisses were as rare in the house as the presence of white people.

Similar to other American cities, Buffalo was largely segregated. The Chesters lived in an all-Negro neighborhood. Most people owned their own homes, although they lived in abject poverty. Considering most of the homes were made of brick, a few looked like they might collapse if a strong gust of wind blew in from Lake Erie. Fortunately, Buffalo was not prone to tremors. Because it seemed as if all Negroes in Buffalo had limited financial resources, we never realized how poor we were. Public transportation was available but undependable, so people owned cars, many of which were jalopies. Car owners usually stopped to offer rides to neighbors traveling on foot. No matter how many disparaging statements have been made about the demise of the black community (and I have heard many), that is one aspect I will always remember with great fondness. Throughout hard times, Negroes always seemed to find a way to help each other.

Rent parties were another extension of self-help. The host prepared a veritable feast of fried chicken, collared greens, butter beans, potato salad, macaroni and cheese, and corn bread for the guests. Each guest was expected to drop as much money as possible inside a hat, which was then used to help the homeowner catch up on back-rent or mortgage payments. The Chesters never declined an invitation to a rent party.

Government assistance was available, although most Negroes were reluctant to take it. The tattered community may have seen better days, but the residents displayed tremendous pride in what little they owned. A few homeowners had huge piles of things piled in their yards. To outsiders, mostly whites, this was all worthless junk, but to the Negro homeowners the junk represented treasures, attachments only people with few possessions could appreciate.

On the Road: The First Foster Home I Remember

As a toddler, I believed segregation was how all people lived—that people from different races should not be combined. Like other kids my age, I got used to it. Contact with white people was restricted to rare home visits from different caseworkers and an occasional visit to the doctor for vaccinations. Of course, a number of white shop owners operated businesses in Negro neighborhoods, often charging exorbitant prices for poor-quality goods. There were virtually no Negro-owned businesses. Banks were heavily into redlining, a practice whereby they rarely lent money to minorities, including those with steady incomes and substantial assets.

All four of us foster children had different caseworkers, mostly young to middle-aged white women. The caseworkers very seldom visited, but when they did, it was never at the same time. The haphazard schedule inconvenienced Mrs. Chester, but Catholic Charities was rarely apologetic. When the caseworkers showed up, they were supposed to spend at least one hour at the house. From what I learned later on, the caseworkers had to visit with the foster parents and conduct a separate interview with the child. This hardly ever happened. Every caseworker seemed to take Mrs. Chester's word that life was just wonderful. They displayed a casual interest in their jobs and even less interest in us foster kids. Perhaps they were also uncomfortable visiting minority neighborhoods.

Slowly, the scary, confused feelings faded, but they never wore off. At that early age, I had some concept of parental abandonment, but it had not yet sunk in. I knew I had a mom who did not want me and a daddy who probably did not know I existed. Every day I wondered if she would change her mind and whisk me away from these strange people's homes. One afternoon, Mrs. Chester found me inside the kitchen, nibbling at the same sandwich she had made me earlier. She said, "You want anything else to eat?"

"No, ma'am."

"My daughter is coming over later. You feel like going to the store with her?"

"How come I don't have a mommy like her?"

Mrs. Chester flopped onto a chair next to me. The cheerful expression on her face suddenly disappeared. "Child, please don't ask me things like that."

"How come? You don't know where she is?"

"No, darling, I don't. I'm taking good care of you, aren't I?"

"Yes, ma'am."

"No reason for you to worry then."

"I was wondering where she went. You don't know?"

She stood up, grabbed an apron, and headed for the stove. "I'm going to bake a cake. Won't that be nice?"

"Yes, ma'am."

Whenever the subject of my heritage came up, Mrs. Chester ran from it, which puzzled me even further. Neither she nor anyone from Catholic Charities ever explained what happened. They treated the subject like it was a big secret that should remain hidden.

The Chesters' house consisted of two flats. Each apartment had a formal living and dining room, a kitchen, a small bathroom, and three bedrooms alongside front and back porches. Both the living and dining rooms were modestly sized, with a basic flower- print wallpaper gracing the walls. For privacy, simple shades covered the windows inside every bedroom. All the bedrooms were painted off-white, and the hardwood floors were faded and, in some places, splintered. The water-stained ceilings throughout the house were the standard eight feet high. Whenever Mother Nature cooperated, which could be iffy in the Buffalo region, tons of sunlight poured through the windows, making the home feel bright and cheery. But when dark storm clouds hung around for days, pounding the pavement with buckets of rain, sometimes snow, the house felt dreary, like something out of a Charles Dickens novel.

A scarcity of space led Eddie, Mark, and Lilly to all share a bunk bed in one bedroom. Lilly slept on the upper bunk and both small-framed boys shared the bottom. The room was otherwise sparsely furnished. Besides the bunk bed, a wobbly four-drawer dresser rested next to the door. I never understood why Lilly and I did not share a room.

Every week, Mrs. Chester scrubbed and waxed the kitchen floor with such vigor I expected royalty to make a grand entrance and dance across the floor. Despite her efforts, the linoleum always looked faded. It was cracked in several places. The kitchen walls, painted an ugly shade of green, made me think of rancid pea soup. A Formica table and four chairs covered with black vinyl sat in the middle of the room. I thought the stuffing coming out of the chairs was marshmallow, but a quick taste proved otherwise. A bowl of perfectly formed waxed fruit rested inside a plastic bowl in the middle of the kitchen table.

The kitchen seemed like it was designed for the members of a basketball team. To reach most of the cabinets, I had to stand on a stool. A ladder or stilts would have also done the job. Mr. Chester never cracked his head, but Mrs. Chester and the rest of us either had to stretch our arms almost to the breaking point or stand on something to retrieve a box of crackers or cookies.

Cockroaches also set up shop in the Chester household. Hiding in between the cracks in the floors gave them a distinct advantage over us. Like cockroaches everywhere, they demonstrated their superior capacity to reproduce and take over their environment in a matter of days. Limited funds pushed professional pest control beyond the Chesters' reach, so we coexisted with the uninvited guests.

Bored one day, the boys and I devised a game to contend with the roach overpopulation problem. Inside the kitchen, we vied to see who could outdo the other by stepping on as many roaches as possible. We acted with such exuberance it was like we had won front row tickets to see the circus.

Eddie uncovered a nest of bugs, which he claimed for his own. Standing over a few dead ones, he grinned and slapped his hand against his chest. "Hey, look here. I got me three already. And they still coming."

In a fierce battle to compete, Mark shoved Eddie aside. Acting as chief cockroach executioner, Mark stomped on at least six big ones and said, "No wait, I got more."

Not one to be left out in the cold, I joined in the fun and crushed at least three bugs. Proud of my accomplishment, I said, "Me, too. See how many I got!" I remember our joy as we proudly counted our pile of dead bugs. I felt elated to be part of something.

When Mrs. Chester finally came into the kitchen and learned about our silly little game, she erupted into a gut-wrenching laugh. We all joined in the fun and cracked up. Mrs. Chester treated us to ice cream cones as long as we promised never to tell anyone about the bug problem in her house.

Most of the house was shut off to us foster kids, an odd arrangement given the furniture was covered with thick plastic covers—the kind that crunched when you sat on them and made your behind sweat in the summertime. The living room was only used to entertain guests, mostly the Chesters' grown children and their in-laws. The off-limits part of the house was like a museum reserved for special people. I always wondered why Lilly, the boys, and I were not special. Closing off part of the house seemed like a waste of space because we all lived in cramped quarters.

The exterior was painted a light gray with forest green window trim. Flecks of paint were falling off, but a paint job was also outside of the Chesters' budget. There was barely enough lawn to separate the house from the sidewalk. A huge oak tree rested in front of the house, giving the home a grand, stately appearance, despite the massive roach problem, fading floors, and cracked windows. In back of the house were a few limp flowers struggling to survive and a postage-stamp-sized lawn that took all of five minutes to mow. The long, narrow, asphalt driveway had only one aging car parked in it. Sometimes the car worked, and sometimes it did not.

I lived with the Chester family for two years. From bits and pieces of conversations I overhead, Lilly had been removed from her young parents because she was on the wild side. Chronically truant, she refused to obey her parents, who worked long hours at a nearby factory, and hung out with the wrong crowd.

Once, Mrs. Chester and I were alone. She darned a pair of her husband's socks while I snacked on cookies. Not yet knowing it was a taboo subject, I asked, "Is Lilly my big sister?"

Mrs. Chester looked like someone who had been told a Negro had been elected president of the United States. She promptly put down her sewing needle. Stiffening her spine, she gave me a blank stare. Her friendly voice suddenly became cold. "No, she's not."

"Why not?"

"Child, stop asking me so many questions."

"What about Eddie and Mark? Are they my brothers?"

"Be quiet."

Because of our gender and age differences, the boys and I hardly ever played together. But they never bullied me. Playing with little girls was not high on their recreation list. They were rambunctious boys, with behavior typical for eight- and ten- year-olds under difficult circumstances. They should not shoulder all the blame for our lack of communication. I was afraid to become attached to two boys who I saw as brothers. Mrs. Chester warned me not to, knowing I could be taken away at a moment's notice. Foster care made me unwilling, sometimes unable, to form meaningful attachments to others. In spite of the turmoil, Eddie and Mark at least had each other. I, on the other hand, was lonely and left out. I daydreamed about Lilly, picturing her as my big sister because of our dark skin. I wanted us to be close, like Eddie and Mark, but she barely acknowledged my presence.

One winter day stands out. Eddie hurt my feelings, yet he likely never intended to. Mrs. Chester was preoccupied making dinner. The boys and I constantly battled for her attention. Sometimes we succeeded, other times not. Standing next to a large pot of greens simmering on the stove, Mrs. Chester wiped her hands on her apron. She clapped loudly and nudged us toward the door. "All of you, go outside and play."

Eddie asked, "Where?"

Mrs. Chester glanced at the open window, facing the tiny back yard full of snow. "Play in the backyard, where else?"

"It's cold."

She frowned at Eddie. "Boy, quit fussing. A little cold won't kill you."

The smell of spicy greens made Eddie's mouth water. He asked, "When we going to eat?" His brother Mark stood next to him, but said nothing. Always in Eddie's shadow, Mark rarely spoke.

Mrs. Chester stirred the pot without looking at any of us. "When you children come back, we'll sit down for a nice family dinner."

That was strange. We rarely sat down to a nice family dinner. I almost always ate alone, Eddie and Mark shared meals together, and Lilly usually had dinner while she studied. Mr. Chester, who worked odd hours, was hardly home. Dinner conversation was scarce and so was proper nutrition. My idea of fruit and vegetables was Orange Crush with potato chips. Comparing the food to today's nutritional standards, my diet was surely lacking, but I do not ever remember going to bed feeling hungry.

When Mrs. Chester snapped her finger and pointed at the door, the boys surged through the hallway to their rooms to put on their winter gear, which consisted of lightweight jackets with skimpy lining. Well-worn boots needed extra socks so their feet did not freeze. For protection from the harsh Buffalo winter, they also donned frayed gloves with ice pick holes and knit hats full of lint barely covering their ears. Mrs. Chester helped me into my pink snowsuit. Because money was tight, my snowsuit was much too big for a three-year-old. I felt apart because my snowsuit was not as nice as the one her grandson wore. I looked like I was draped in an oversized quilt.

Eddie and Mark built a snowman while I sat down and made snowballs. Mark shoveled piles of snow into one big heap. Eddie stood, towering over me. He said, "You and me ain't family."

I panicked, wondering if that was a cue to be taken away. Unable to move, I asked, "Why not?"

"Look at your skin. Me and my brother is light. You're dark."

I pulled up my sleeve, stared at my arm, feeling hurt and confused. I did not know there was something wrong. "What you talking about?"

Eddie yanked off his knit cap and moved closer. He bent down, pointed to his hair and locked eyes with me. "My hair ain't nappy like yours."

As a toddler, the uneasy disparity between "high-yeller" and darker-skinned Negroes was beyond my comprehension. Eddie's comments about our physical differences made me feel like crying, but I did not. "We're all Negroes, right?"

Watching Mark build the snowman drew Eddie's attention away. He said, "Yeah, I guess so," and walked away.

I had a flat nose, skin the color of a Hershey bar, and a head of tightly curled hair. Both boys were the color of a plain brown bag with wispy curls on their heads. As far as I knew, we were all Negro children. He made me think dark brown was bad. I felt further alienated from everyone around me.

When I overheard Eddie and Mark talk to their caseworker about a reunion with their parents, I felt crushed. Jealous, angry and hurt, I felt like kicking something, anything. No one from Catholic Charities talked to me about a family reunion. I began to think I might never have one. That night while Mrs. Chester gave me a bath, I asked, "When can I go home?"

Mrs. Chester winced as she dropped the bar of soap into the tub. "Child, what're you talking about?"

"The lady said Eddie and Mark are going home. What about me?"

Poor Mrs. Chester appeared so bewildered. I do not think she knew what to say. A few moments of clumsy silence passed when she said, "Child, you are home until you get adopted. Stop asking me questions. I got to get you cleaned up."

I liked Mrs. Chester, so I asked, "Can you adopt me?"

Now out of the tub, Mrs. Chester draped me in a towel and said, "Honey, I'm sorry but I can't."

I did not cry, but I felt afraid. "How come?"

"Cause I ain't got enough room."

"Do I have to leave now?"

Mrs. Chester held me close. "No, darling, not now."

"Then when?"

"When them people find you a good home."

I asked, "Isn't this a good home?"

"For now it is."

"What's that mean?"

"Don't go getting all worked up."

As she dried me off with a larger towel, I thought about something she had said. She said I was safe. Maybe I don't have to worry about leaving any more. Not such a bad arrangement, I thought, even if I was not adopted.

Once in a while, the boys were treated to surprise visits from their parents. The young couple dropped off small gifts, treasures their sons clung to as if they were gold. I felt sad knowing Eddie and Mark would someday leave. Although we did not always play together, I already knew I would miss them. However, I was also jealous. No one ever brought toys to me. I wondered why my mother forgot me.

An enigma, Lilly avoided all of us. I tried to catch her as she was headed out of the house one morning. I grabbed her by the hand and asked, "Can you read to me?"

Lilly, looking exasperated, replied, "Not now, but maybe some other time."

Like a little girl lost inside a big city, my voice quivered. "Nobody ever reads to me." I balled up both fists and shook my hands.

Lilly did an about face. She held my hand and spoke gently. "OK, maybe, but don't cry. I hate to see kids cry."

After Lilly left, I felt excited knowing someone would finally read to me. Although she did not turn out to be the big sister I had longed for, Lilly acquiesced and read to me, even if it was only two or three times.

Not long after school started, Lilly told Mrs. Chester she was involved in several school clubs and not to expect her home until late every afternoon. In retrospect, that may have been true. Then again, she may also have been up to no good. Honestly, no one knew how or where she spent her free time. Mrs. Chester and Lilly disagreed about almost everything. If Mrs. Chester made eggs over easy, Lilly asked for scrambled. If Mrs. Chester fried bacon strips, Lilly wanted sausage links. Lilly may have used school as an excuse to avoid the home. Unlike the boys, Lilly never received parental visits. I do not know if her parents called it quits and gave up on Lilly, or if Lilly eventually went home.

Lilly quickly developed an attraction to the opposite sex. As a pretty girl with radiant brown eyes and full sensuous lips that, when she smiled, revealed sparkling white teeth, it was not surprising boys showed interest in Lilly. When Lilly wanted to date it shoved a painful thorn in Mrs. Chester's side. Mr. Chester worked overtime a lot and he almost always deferred to his wife when it came to us foster children.

I suppose Mrs. Chester felt responsible for Lilly's behavior and feared that, if she became pregnant, the foster parent would have to face the higher-ups at Catholic Charities. Lilly had a reputation for trouble, which may or may not have been justified. I had always lived with strangers, so foster care became normal for me. If this was Lilly's first experience with surrogate parents, she probably had a hard time adjusting. Alternately, Lilly could have simply been expressing a natural adolescent behavior. Either way, Mrs. Chester came down hard on Lilly every time she had a date. Before Lilly left the house with her male companion, all of whom were Negroes, Mrs. Chester required telephone numbers, his parent's names, and his vital statistics (for example, color of clothing, height, and weight). She also threatened to kill the young man if he acted a fool. With her arms folded firmly in front of her chest, Mrs. Chester reminded all the young men that Lilly had a curfew of 10:00 P.M., not 10:02. From their grim facial expressions, I assumed they got the point.

One night, Lilly showed up around eleven-thirty, and I was awakened by all the fuss. Peeking out of my bedroom, I saw Mrs. Chester drag Lilly by her long hair through the living room. Seconds later, I watched with wide eyes as Mrs. Chester, looking rabid, smacked Lilly squarely across her cheek. The blow drew blood from the corner of Lilly's lips. Mrs. Chester shouted, "Don't you ever defy me again, missy."

When Lilly touched her chin and noticed a few drops of blood on her fingertips, she became defiant. "I'm telling my caseworker. You can't do this to me."

Mrs. Chester showed no fear. "Go right ahead and tell whoever you want. This is my house and you will follow my rules."

Lilly said nothing and stormed out of the room.

I jumped back into bed and huddled underneath the covers, worrying Mrs. Chester might not quiet down by bedtime. Sometimes, I thought Mrs. Chester was a little crazy because she reacted so harshly around Lilly.

My fears, that time and always, were unfounded. Mrs. Chester never hit me, even when I was being difficult. I tried to keep my nose clean as much as possible, afraid of getting in trouble like Lilly.

Out of curiosity or some unspoken anger, I started a small fire in the kitchen. I must have lit a match and held it next to the flowered curtains by the window. Mrs. Chester had a sharp nose, however, and within seconds she smelled the aroma of burning fabric and rushed into the kitchen. She threw a pot of water on the flames, dousing the small fire. Even though she must have seen me as I ducked out, she held the boys culpable for the fire. They got sent to bed without supper.

In contrast to other Negroes who threatened their children with God's wrath should they misbehave, Mrs. Chester, to my knowledge, never set foot inside a church. She did, however, keep a crushed velvet picture of the Last Supper in the dining room. Her adult children, particularly one of her sons, attended church regularly. Off and on, Mrs. Chester browsed through the Bible, giving me some vague notion about God, but my religious experiences were extremely limited.

A year after I arrived, Mr. Chester started to hack and cough all the time. He coughed so deeply it sounded like his lungs vibrated inside his chest. I only knew about normal childhood diseases and presumed he had the croup, like I once had. I learned his illness, emphysema, was far more serious. He quit smoking when Mrs. Chester delivered the ultimatum: Give up smoking or I'll kill you. Because he constantly coughed and spit up blood, Mr. Chester and I switched bedrooms.

I felt weird sleeping next to Mrs. Chester, a woman more like a grandmother to me. I developed a cold and I feared that I, too, would be put out because I coughed and had a bad case of the sniffles. But Mrs. Chester laughed and stroked my cheek. "Honey, there ain't nothing for you to worry about."

"You sure?"

"Yes darling, go on to sleep."

Over time, I adjusted to the new set of sleeping arrangements. Although Mrs. Chester never tucked me in or read me a bedtime story, I started to feel special by sleeping in her room. It provided me with a small sense of security, one I quickly latched onto.

Mrs. Chester constantly juggled her own schedule to look after me, her grandson, and tackle housework. Some of the white people she worked for were demanding. I thought she would fall apart from exhaustion, but she managed to perform like a wind-up toy. She kept going and going. Mr. Chester tried to keep working as a janitor, but his failing health left him unable to get out of bed some days.

As his disease worsened, his lungs wheezed and rattled and Mrs. Chester cried herself to sleep. Not knowing how or if I should comfort her, I kept my mouth shut and never asked questions. Keeping quiet was something I could do very well.

When Mr. Chester's condition worsened and he required more intensive care, Mrs. Chester gave up baby-sitting for her beloved grandson. This was the first time someone outside the family had been asked to look after him. Mrs. Chester adapted to the role of nurse's aide by dispensing medication, washing her husband's bloodied sheets, and cleaning out piles of soiled tissues from his room at least three times a day. We wanted to visit Mr. Chester, but Mrs. Chester banned us from entering his room. She said we would only get in the way. As Mr. Chester wasted away, so did she.

Life with the Chester Family Goes On

I settled into a comfortable if somewhat bumpy life with the Chesters. I finally stopped peering over my shoulders, waiting for the caseworker to take me away. Like families everywhere, the Chesters weren't perfect. But they were a family and, for the time being, they were my family. I gradually felt more relaxed, not twisted and bound up. With Mrs. Chester's admonitions, the boys stopped reminding me they were going home, and I stopped being mad because they had parents. Whenever I saw their mother drop off toy cars, I still felt cheated, but found a handy survival technique. By erecting an emotional wall around myself, the jealous feelings diminished. Sad, wild Lilly kept to herself, and I avoided her.

Although Mrs. Chester was sparing when it came to hugs and kisses, I still felt like her shining star. At dinnertime, she always loaded my plate, even if it was only macaroni and cheese or fried chicken backs. Once in a while, she served canned meat. I did not appreciate the extra helping of mystery meat but I appreciated the special attention. It's too bad they did not have a dog to wolf down the leftovers.

Fall rolled around and Mrs. Chester brought up school attendance. "You're old enough for kindergarten."

"What's kinder . . . kinder . . ."

"Darling, it's for little children like you." She explained I would attend for three hours a day, five days a week.

"What will I do?"

"You'll play games, recite the alphabet, things like that."

"Do I have to go?"

"Why, don't you want to?"

"What if they don't like me?"

"Don't say that. The kids will like you."

"Who will take me?"

"I will."

Relieved, I said, "You sure it'll be fun?"

"Yes, I'm sure."

Mrs. Chester enrolled me in a public school program, because the local Catholic school shut the door to all Negro students. Most public schools remained racially segregated. All the kids in my neighborhood went to segregated schools, so I did not feel out of place. Preschool programs like Head Start had not been established yet, and not every poor child attended kindergarten. I did not know I was among the lucky ones.

Mrs. Chester barely had extra money to spare, but she somehow squeezed out enough to buy me two new dresses. The rest of my school clothes came from the hand-me-down store, but I did not care. I was delighted I had somewhere to go every day.

The kindergarten program taught me how to count, distinguish colors, recognize the letters of the alphabet, and play with other children. I loved it when the teacher read to us. Mrs. Chester never read to me. Then again, I do not ever remember seeing her read for her own pleasure. Once in a while, when one of her children left a copy of the daily newspaper, she browsed through it. Other than the Bible, there were no books in the house.

For the first time, I was exposed to children's picture books. The poor quality did not matter. I was happy I had something colorful to look at. Although I could distinguish some letters of the alphabet, I was unable to read.

Life with the Chester Family Goes On

My kindergarten teacher helped to improve my verbal skills, which were lacking for a child my age. Despite feeling some comfort with the Chesters, I always felt like a guest, wondering when my stay would be up. No one paid much attention to me, so I never acquired good verbal or reading skills. But kindergarten seemed to fill this gap, and I started to feel better about myself. I was able to speak entire sentences.

During early evening hours, Mrs. Chester usually let me listen to the radio with her while the other foster kids stayed in their rooms studying. As a kindergarten student, I never had any homework assignments. The Chesters could not afford a television set, but it did not matter because the radio was entertaining. I felt uplifted by the spirited sounds of jazz. Now and then, Mrs. Chester and I boogied together, especially when the station played Benny Goodman's "Sing, Sing, Sing" and Duke Ellington's "Take the A Train," two of her favorite songs. Mrs. Chester was so proud some Negroes, like Duke Ellington, had their music played on the radio. Eddie and Mark poked their heads out of the bedroom and stared at us with longing in their eyes. I guess the boys wanted to enjoy the fun. Lilly, however, shunned radio time.

Now, whenever I hear the sound of swing music, I look back on those special moments. I imagine Mrs. Chester's favoritism toward me probably made the other children feel envious, but I was like a sponge, soaking up all her attention.

Until the time I lived with the Chester family, I never experienced a birthday party. In fact, I was unaware people celebrated birthdays.

One cold winter day, I sat at the kitchen table, bundled up in a sweater. Winter had been brutal that year. Mrs. Chester said, "We're having a little birthday party for you."

"Me? What for?"

"Because that's what we do on birthdays."

"What happens?"

"You get to blow out the candles on the cake. Child, haven't you ever had a birthday cake before?"

"No, ma'am."

A frown wrinkled her face. "I'll get you a nice cake with candles."

The news sent a swirl of excitement inside me. "What kind of cake?"

"What kind do you want?"

"Chocolate. Lots of icing."

The party included only Mrs. Chester, the boys, and me, but I did not care. I had a small chocolate cake with candles and "Happy Birthday Theresa" in red icing. Mrs. Chester used a small Brownie camera to take photos of me blowing out the candles and of the cake smeared across my face. Because of unexpected and sudden moves in my life, those photos remain buried in the past.

When Mr. Chester was neither tinkering with broken appliances nor shooting the breeze with his son, the garbage collector, he played games with his grandson, whom he adored. At other times, he browsed through a borrowed copy of *Reader's Digest*. The men at the plant where he worked often exchanged magazines, because they were too poor to afford their own subscriptions.

During the summer local people usually gathered on inexpensive fold-up chairs in their front yards or on the front stoops. No one had air conditioning, so it made more sense to catch the cool breeze blowing in from nearby Lake Erie. Summer in Buffalo is usually short, but the heat is stifling at times. Most women sat together, sharing stories about their families or the high prices in local stores. The men played checkers and sometimes reminisced about wartime battles.

One evening the casual conversation took an abrupt turn. The grownups talked about something serious called *Brown v. the Board of Education*. I thought some guy named Brown was in trouble at school. While some adults mentioned change for Negroes lay ahead, Mrs. Chester did not share the optimism of others. She said, "Lots of blood will be shed. You wait and see. Them crackers down south ain't gonna take integration very easily. People up here don't like it."

Another evening outside, the women talked about food prices at the local markets. Mrs. Chester folded both hands together as if she was about to pray. "Lord, I hope this King fellow can help our people get our own stores. I'm sure tired of paying top dollar when white people be paying less for the same darn thing. Now, that'll be the day." Martin Luther King Jr. was a more popular name by the day, but I still did not understand how something called civil rights would affect me.

Leaving politics and social change aside, I became fascinated by the young girls on my block who played a lively jump-rope game with two ropes that also involved rhythmical singing. This game was more appealing to me than talk about an end to segregation. It was called Double Dutch, a recreational staple inside many Negro communities. Every little girl, it seemed, knew how to play Double Dutch. Despite my young age, I begged Mrs. Chester to allow me to learn the game. At first, she said no because the game was dangerous.

She warned, "You could get hurt."

"No I won't. I'll be careful"

"What'll them people at Catholic Charities say if you get hurt?"

"Please? Pretty please?"

"Maybe, but not yet."

Gentle prodding from the neighbors eventually softened her resistance. The more experienced girls welcomed a newcomer like me, but I was so uncoordinated I fell through the ropes instead of jumping over them. I resigned myself to being a Double Dutch spectator only.

Eddie, Mark, and the other neighborhood boys frequently played stickball or marbles. Now and then, they shared baseball cards of the Negro players in the major leagues. Eddie declared, "Someday lots of Negro boys will play in the big leagues."

His brother Mark said, "You think so?"

"You bet I do."

"I'm not so sure."

Eddie had high confidence. "When they do, you and me will be watching."

The boys rarely engaged in games with the girls, swearing hopscotch and Double Dutch were prissy.

Although Mrs. Chester let me sit on the front steps during the summer, my early bedtime remained. One steamy summer evening, she nudged me with her arm while talking to a neighbor. "Go on to bed."

A bunch of neighborhood kids were outside playing, and I did not want to leave. I moped as I walked away. "Do I have to?"

"Child, you're not talking back to me, are you?"

"No, ma'am, but what if I miss something?"

She stood up and headed in my direction. "You're not missing anything but your bedtime."

"But . . ."

"No buts. If you don't go upstairs, I'll beat your butt."

"I hope I'll be OK by myself."

"Don't worry. Mr. Chester is in his room and we're all down here."

"Something could happen to me."

Behind Mrs. Chester's tiny smile, there was seriousness when she said, "Something will happen if you don't go inside."

I could not sleep, listening to all the laughter outside. Besides, the house felt like an oven and we only had one fan, now in Mr. Chester's room. Dressed in my short-sleeved light colored pajamas, I stared out the open window at the children below having fun. By the end of the day, I suppose Mrs. Chester was tapped of energy and needed time to herself, but I resented the early bedtime. To me, it was undeserved harsh discipline, and I wanted to be part of the fun. I doubt she realized how much this hurt me.

Mrs. Chester clung to the early bed schedule, but she allowed me to visit the nearby corner store by myself. Crime was rare in our neighborhood, and I was never shaken by fear as I ventured down the street alone. The store owner, an old white man with thin, gray hair and ugly black glasses, smiled as I browsed around. The first time, he said, "Hi, there. You need something?"

I kept my hand inside my pocket, holding onto my treasure. "Mister, I have a quarter."

"Want to buy candy?"

"Maybe."

"Look around and ask me if you need help."

"OK."

Most of his customers were Negroes, but he rarely smiled at them. I thought he was afraid of dark-skinned people except for me, which made me wonder why he did business in our neighborhood.

The store had a tiny lunch counter, and I spent my weekly allowance on Cherry Crush soda pop. For their french fries, most customers requested catsup, but not me. For some odd reason, I developed a taste for fries with vinegar. The old man once said I was offbeat, but he nonetheless always brought vinegar to the counter whenever I stopped in for french fries.

Searching for a way to improve his employment prospects beyond factory jobs, Calvin, the Chesters oldest son, enlisted in the Army. Stationed at a base in Texas, he squeezed in family visits at least once a year. I remember the delight on Mrs. Chester's face whenever Calvin called or sent a letter. She kept a framed color photograph of him in his dress-green Army uniform on the living room mantel. Whenever she looked at his picture, her entire face swelled with pride. Once in a while, her dark saucer-shaped eyes brimmed with tears.

Richard, the other son, worked as a trash collector. He dated several young women, but never settled down. He visited at least twice a week, usually dropping in after church service for apple pie and coffee. Following his brother's lead to escape from a lifetime of menial jobs, Richard enrolled in a community college.

Family photographs were scattered throughout the Chesters' house. Pictures from their daughter's wedding ceremony, numerous family gatherings, her son in his Army uniform, and her only grandchild took over an entire wall in the living room. One time in particular I was hit with mixed emotions by Mrs. Chester's obvious outpouring of affection for her children, but feeling slighted because my photo was not among the family collection.

After kindergarten one day, Mrs. Chester noticed I was less talkative than usual. I was on the sofa, pretending to listen to the radio. She sat down next to me, placed her palm across my forehead, and said, "Darling, what's wrong?"

I bit my thumbnail, not sure if I should tell her the truth. Instead of responding, I gazed into her mahogany eyes.

"Want me to call the doctor?"

Despite the eggplant-sized lump in my throat, I managed to spill out a few words. I pointed at the wall and frowned. "What about me? I'm not up there."

By the way Mrs. Chester cocked her head to the side and stroked her chin, I could tell I caught her off guard. Glancing at me then at the wall, she said, "Well then, let's get one of you up there." I went to bed feeling on top of the world.

Most white men supported a family on a single income. Negro men, however, were in a different category. To augment their husbands' meager wages, Negro women often worked on the side as domestics, cooks, or house cleaners for the more affluent whites in areas such as North Park. Other Negro women worked part-time as cashiers. Factory positions for all unskilled workers were still plentiful. As I got older, I learned about Negroes who migrated from the South for job opportunities in the grain plants in and around Buffalo. Living conditions were not as oppressive in New York as they were in the South.

Public housing in Buffalo was legally segregated, but the waiting list for a decent apartment was only weeks or months long, not years. There was no humiliation attached to public housing. The projects were seen as stepping-stones to private home ownership, a goal of many working-class Negro families. The projects were modest but well kept and relatively safe. Petty crimes occurred, but illicit drug use and gang warfare were unheard of. People could not afford to own guns, so fists and loud words settled most differences.

Single or divorced parents were ostracized. The neighbors castigated women who split up with their husbands. Late one afternoon as I sat on the steps, I overheard the next-door neighbors talk rudely about one young woman as she passed by, holding her son's hand.

An elderly woman rolled her eyes around as she said, "Look at her. She ain't got no man. Sure glad I ain't walking in her shoes. No wonder she don't come to church no more. Guess she can't face no one."

The other woman added, "Wonder what kind of life her son will have?"

"He got to have a man around. The boy won't grow up good without a man."

"Glad I got me a man."

Neighbors rarely spoke to the unmarried woman, and we were taught to avoid her. Her son never played with the kids on our block, even though he lived around the corner.

Apparently, men escaped blame for marital discord, because I rarely heard disparaging remarks about wife beaters or two-timers. Many couples who could not stand each other remained married, believing it was the right thing to do for their children.

Not long after I started kindergarten, Mrs. Chester treated me to a rare surprise—dance lessons at a local studio. A white man owned the studio, but he had one Negro instructor who taught all his Negro clients. Dance lessons, although segregated, made me feel like a little princess. How Mrs. Chester afforded such a luxury remains a mystery to me. Somehow, she was quite adept at stretching a dollar.

For my lessons every week, she fixed my hair in neat long braids and finished each one with a tiny pastel colored clip. She bought me a few second-hand frilly dresses, complete with crinoline slips. I was so tickled I forgot about how much crinoline made me itch. I never felt awkward in these used dresses, because the other Negro girls wore hand-me-downs as well.

After a few months, all the little girls were invited to take part in a recital. Everyone's family was welcome to attend. When I showed Mrs. Chester the invitation, she said, "Child, I'm sorry but I can't go."

Disappointed, I stormed away. I wanted so much for her to attend. I wanted to be like the other girls and have someone in the audience to be proud of me. Inside my room, I opened the closet and threw toys at my dresses.

She followed me to my room. "Mr. Chester being sick and all, I can't leave him." She stroked my head and said, "I know you don't understand, but try, OK?"

"You sure you can't come?"

"No, darling, I can't leave him. Mr. Chester is very sick."

"No one will be there to see me."

"My daughter will take you."

"Can she watch me?"

"She got her own family. We'll see."

I said, "Then I'm not going."

"Why not?"

"Cause everyone else has someone to watch them. I'll have nobody."

Mrs. Chester held me and said, "Don't be upset. We doing the best we can."

That may have been true, but to a frightened, lonely little girl, her best was not good enough. I wanted more.

Life with the Chester Family Goes On

On the night of the recital, the daughter inadvertently dropped me off at the wrong dance studio. The minute I stepped inside this strange-looking building, I knew something was wrong, yet I was too frightened to cry. Right after the manager pried my name and address out of me, his assistant telephoned Mrs. Chester, and her daughter showed up.

As she led me to her car, she said, "You're very brave."

I did not feel that way. "I was scared."

"I'm sure you were."

"I didn't know what would happen."

"I've been so busy lately, honey, I forgot to get the address."

I never made it to the recital. The excitement of dance lessons faded, and I stopped going after about six months.

Eventually, emphysema robbed so much breathing capacity from Mr. Chester's lungs that he stopped working and applied for disability. Every step he took left him wheezing and spitting up blood. Watching his slow, agonizing steps as he shuffled from his bedroom to the bathroom kept me from picking up the cigarette habit when I became an adolescent. Too bad those swayed by the smiling faces on tobacco advertisements never saw Mr. Chester.

Without Mr. Chester's income, Mrs. Chester scrambled to feed and clothe us. The monthly check from Catholic Charities was never enough, and the Chesters always dipped into their own money. When possible, their grown children pitched in, but they struggled to feed themselves.

To make extra cash, Mrs. Chester hauled me and the boys to a nearby apple orchard, a common site in this part of upstate New York. I thought the trip was strange, because we hardly ever had fresh fruit in the house. As soon as we arrived at the almost picked-apart orchard, I discovered the harvest had already passed but the trees were not entirely bare. Orchard owners invited mostly poor Negroes to pick apples bypassed in the harvest, paying them cash by the barrel. Owners sold the dented apples to food companies for applesauce and juice. Judging from the poor quality of fruit sold in Negro neighborhoods, I assumed the apples were rejects from the orchards.

Each person was given a burlap sack and payment depended upon how many bags were filled. Children were expected to fill the same-sized sacks as adults. To reach the apples at the top, men climbed up ladders propped up against the trees. Although the weather was often chilly and damp, we plucked apples from the trees with our bare hands. Mud collected around our shoes, sometimes making it hard to walk. After a day of backbreaking work, we waited in a long line to collect our money. Child labor laws were lax at the time, so no one objected to our presence in the fields. Once in a while, Mrs. Chester told me stories about her early childhood and how she worked from sunup to sundown. Apple picking was hard work. I was glad I had not been born a slave or an indentured servant.

As time passed, every move Lilly made, even when she was not being a hard head, ruffled Mrs. Chester's feathers. She chided Lilly for the slightest mistake. One day Mrs. Chester blew off a ton of steam when she found Lilly dusting the living room furniture with the "wrong" rag.

Mrs. Chester stormed over to Lilly and shouted, "What're you doing? Don't be ruining my furniture!"

Lilly's jaw dropped as she edged away from Mrs. Chester. In a quiet, respectful voice, she said, "I'm dusting. That's what you told me to do."

Still fuming, Mrs. Chester jerked the dust rag out of Lilly's hand and hurled it across the room. "You can't use a rag like this. It'll make spots on my good table."

Almost in tears, Lilly rushed to the small bedroom she shared with the boys. Mrs. Chester ran to the kitchen, where she broke down in tears. To avoid being caught in the middle, I retreated to my room, sat on the bed, and stared at the dingy ceiling. The serenity of the house was replaced by screaming, tempers with short fuses, and sometimes bawling, all of which made me feel like hiding in the closet. Times had definitely changed around this household.

At first, Eddie and Mark were left out of the fray. Both the boys and I were baffled by Mrs. Chester's change of attitude. It was like storm clouds had settled over our house, with thunder rumbling in the background all the time. We never knew when, or if, a storm would erupt.

One afternoon, Eddie came home from school, followed as always by Mark. They found me sitting in the kitchen by myself. Checking to make sure the coast was clear, Eddie asked in a soft voice, "She around?"

I shook my head that she was not, and used my finger to point upward. "Better be quiet. I think she's sick, too."

Eddie glanced at tiny clumps of mud clinging to his slacks. With a guilty look on his face, he said, "Don't tell her I got my school pants dirty. She'll be mad." A few days earlier, Mrs. Chester had sprung for new clothes for the boys when she got her monthly check from Catholic Charities.

Eddie and Mark zoomed out of the kitchen. I guessed Eddie stopped in the bathroom to rinse out the stains on his trousers.

It did not take long before Mrs. Chester lost what little patience she had left with Eddie and Mark. After the boys had dinner, she routinely helped them with their homework. One night, Eddie could not grasp the concept of long division. Enraged by his innocent blunder, Mrs. Chester grabbed a thick leather belt and whacked his hand. Anger rattled her voice. "Boy, what's the matter with you?"

"Nothing, ma'am."

"Then why can't you do your homework?"

"I don't understand it."

"You're not paying attention in class."

"But I do."

"You can't be."

"I . . ."

"Shut up when I'm talking."

"OK."

By the time Eddie stopped crying, Mrs. Chester seemed visibly shaken by her outburst. Throughout the rest of the evening, she acted like a woman bucking for sainthood, praising Eddie for trying.

From that day forward, I learned an important lesson: Be seen and not heard. I took precautions not to rock the boat around Mrs. Chester for any reason at all. She had become like two different women. Around me, she acted like I was the best of children, but around the boys and especially Lilly she behaved like they were the worst. I could do no wrong and the other children never seemed as if they could do anything right.

As Mr. Chester's health deteriorated, Mrs. Chester seemed unable to cope. He coughed harder and deeper all day and all night long. Already thin, the disease made his body resemble a skeleton. His bedroom looked like a medicine cabinet, with pill bottles all over the place. Blood-stained tissues were scattered all over his bed. I was surprised cigarettes made him so sick.

The formidable strength Mrs. Chester once displayed now withered into a surprising weakness. Most days, she cried during breakfast, was weepy over lunch, and by dinner was usually inconsolable. A woman on edge, she seemed in mourning long before Mr. Chester had actually died.

The uneasy feelings between Lilly and Mrs. Chester continued to fester. What started out as mild admonishments turned into serious threats leveled against Lilly. No matter how hard she tried, Lilly could not satisfy Mrs. Chester. Under threat of severe punishment, Lilly obeyed every order like a new recruit in basic training. Dutifully, she washed dishes, scrubbed the floor, and dusted the furniture, using the "right" rag, all to no avail. Mrs. Chester raised hell every day.

Mrs. Chester's cross feelings made the boys and me almost speechless. For three kids who hardly ever played together, the rising tensions brought us closer together, even if it was for a short time and for an awkward reason.

One morning at breakfast, Mrs. Chester was almost ready to boil. Flailing a broom in one hand, she threatened to beat Lilly with it. Obviously, Lilly feared for her safety. Without a coat on, she soared out of the house and never came home. Later on, I learned Lilly marched to the principal's office and demanded to call her caseworker. The caseworker and her teacher found Lilly's story to be credible, and she was placed in emergency group home care.

Now that Lilly was gone, I stayed away from Mrs. Chester as much as possible. I regretted that I could not escape from her anger and agony by going to school all day. I turned inward even more, hoping to avoid Mrs. Chester's wrath. We no longer listened to the radio together. My little girl giggles disappeared because I was too afraid to laugh at anything. Even the cartoon characters could not elicit a laugh from me. I was still too young to figure out the connection between her unexpected rage and Mr. Chester's steadily eroding health.

Three weeks later, I munched on sugar cookies while Mrs. Chester ironed clothes. She had recently started to do laundry for a wealthy doctor and he insisted on perfectly pressed shirts, complete with lots of starch. All of the sudden, my caseworker unexpectedly showed up. Wearing dark glasses and a knee-length gray overcoat, she seemed more like a spy than a caseworker. Steely eyed, the woman looked at Mrs. Chester and said, "Theresa is going to another home." Her voice was as sharp as her facial expression.

Once I heard the word home my eyes lit up. Like a flash of lightning, I jumped out of my seat and raced to the door. "Has my mommy come to get me?"

The stone-faced woman simply said, "No." Acting like I was invisible, she glanced at Mrs. Chester. "She's going to another foster home."

Right then and there, my world fell apart. Tears streamed down my cheeks as I dug my trembling little fingers into Mrs. Chester's leg. I refused to let go. Still sobbing, I looked up at her and pleaded, "Why? What about my school?" I was weeks away from first grade.

With her arm resting firmly on my shoulder, Mrs. Chester's normally powerful voice melted into timidity. "What's going on? Nobody ain't called me or nothing."

Negroes in those days rarely bucked the system, especially when white people were involved. They usually deferred to authority figures, even when disagreeing. Mrs. Chester, although bold when it came to Lilly, was not one to stand up to whites. Although I could not understand the gist of their conversation, I salvaged some of it. Apparently, Lilly's caseworker had spread the word about Mrs. Chester's hotheaded behavior. Perhaps Catholic Charities was truly trying to protect me, but in reality they were ripping me to shreds.

The caseworker showed no emotion as she said, "This child must live with a Catholic family. Those are the rules."

Mrs. Chester's voice cracked and her eyes became watery. "But she's lived with us for over two years. She's starting school soon."

The caseworker did not sound as if she was speaking to a woman in her mid-fifties, but rather scolding a naughty child. "Lady, did you hear what I said? Get her things ready. She's going to another home. I'll be back in an hour."

While Mrs. Chester retreated to the kitchen table, I ran into the bathroom and sobbed. Moments later, she opened the door and held me. I wrapped my arms around her neck and tears again poured down my face. Fear of the unknown gripped me hard. In between sobs, I remember saying, "Please don't let them take me. I'll be a good girl."

"Darling, there ain't nothing I can do." She hugged me and whispered in my ear, "You ain't a bad girl. There's just things you don't understand."

"I don't want to go."

"I'm sorry, but you have to."

"No. I'm staying with you."

"Please don't make this harder."

"I'll run away."

A short time later, I found myself in the back seat of an ugly gray Ford sedan, in between two paper shopping bags filled with my belongings, being driven by a brooding woman who looked like her face might crack if she smiled. As the caseworker's car passed through familiar blocks in my neighborhood, sharp tears stung the back of my eyes as I thought about Mrs. Chester and the only family I had ever known. My stomach fluttered as I realized I had to start over once again, and this time the change also involved a disruption in my education. My heart ached knowing I would probably not see the boys any more. Visions of Mrs. Chester stuck in my mind, but I stood my ground, refusing to show anyone I was scared.

After a short drive along crumbling East Side streets, the car stopped in front of a modest wood-frame house, and we got out. About to enter my second, third, or fourth foster home, I was barely six years old. The caseworker led me out of the car, but my eyes were glued behind me, searching for Mrs. Chester. I kept thinking this was a bad dream and she would come to get me.

Years later, I found out Mrs. Chester's daughter had converted to the Catholic faith and intervened with Catholic Charities for me. She promised the caseworker she would see to it that I attended Mass every Sunday and have regular religious instruction, but Catholic Charities was adamant. As long as I was under its aegis, I had to be raised in a Catholic home. No ifs, ands, or buts.

Part Two

The Sea Widens: My New Life

The caseworker with cold brown eyes opened the car door, grabbed my shopping bags, and ushered me through a chain-linked gate. I had the impression she was in a hurry to flee the neighborhood. It was summer, and dozens of Negroes were outside. A large group of women rested beneath the shade of a nearby maple tree on folding chairs while watching the children laugh and play games. The boys were engaged in a furious game of stickball and a group of little girls was preoccupied by Double Dutch. Despite the swamplike weather of early July, a wave of cold surged through my little body. All the neighbors were Negroes like me, but they were strangers. This unfamiliar neighborhood seemed remote and forbidding and, most of all, it did not feel like home.

Passing through the small but neat front yard, the caseworker tried to hold my clammy hand, but I resisted. She was my enemy, and I wanted no part of her whatsoever. Who did she think she was, a stranger trying to hold my hand? Showing no emotion, I trailed behind her and hiked up two flights of rickety stairs. Before she knocked on the front door, I spun around one more time, still hoping Mrs. Chester would save me from this nightmare. I could feel her tugging at my heart, even though she had been stingy when it came to dishing out affection. The Chester family and the boys had been my safety net, blanketing me with just enough warmth to keep me going. Being uprooted so swiftly from the only home I knew felt like punishment. Seconds later, the front door opened, and I reluctantly began another chapter in my life.

A silver-haired Negro woman answered the door and nervously introduced herself as Mrs. Woodson. She wore a sleeveless housedress in a pastel flower print, one that accentuated her flabby arms. Stockings rolled up above her knees made her look like a washer woman. I studied her oval face, which was the color of coffee mixed with cream. In the corners of her light brown eyes hung a web of crow's feet. Unlike me, she had high cheekbones along with pencil-thin lips. As soon as she extended her hand, I noted long, unpainted fingernails and cracked open skin. Mrs. Woodson glanced down at me and welcomed me inside. "Come in. I've been expecting you." She may have looked like somebody's maid, but she was articulate and well spoken.

During my five-year tenure in foster care, no one had explained the rules to me. I was clueless about how to address Mrs. Woodson. I knew she was not related to me, so using unfamiliar terms such as "granny" or "auntie" did not enter my mind. Saying the words "foster mom" felt awkward. So I said nothing and acted indifferent, while, deep down, this woman scared the heck out of me.

The system had high hopes for me, most of which I could not live up to. They expected me to adjust to sudden moves without behavior changes, to feel comfortable around strangers without crying, and to accept their choices without my input. How was I expected to thrive and to develop normally when my young life was anything but normal? Catholic Charities dictated whom I would live with and for how long. I knew the agency was supposed to be my guardian, but I wanted my own little place in the world and, at my young age, I doubted they could give that to me.

The caseworker managed to crack a slight smile when she noticed a small metal crucifix around Mrs. Woodson's thick neck. A little on the plump side, Mrs. Woodson listened to the caseworker rattle off a few details about a visitation schedule. When she presented Mrs. Woodson with a few of my vital statistics, such as the fact that I was Negro girl, I thought the caseworker must be joking. As soon as she shoved a manila envelope into Mrs. Woodson's hand, she hurried out the door without looking back.

Mrs. Woodson squeezed my shoulder, guiding me through the dimly lit hallway. "Why don't you come in so we can get acquainted?"

For the first time in almost two years, I sucked my thumb so hard I almost gagged. In a trancelike state, I followed Mrs. Woodson into her house. Once in the living room, I stood there as stiff as a board. Mrs. Woodson glanced at the wall clock and said, "The caseworker said you'd be here earlier. Want some lunch? Or a snack, maybe?"

Met only with silence, she asked again, "Look at the time. You must be hungry."

Again, I said nothing. Mrs. Woodson showed no annoyance, even though the house was as hot as an oven and I was totally uncooperative. She stood behind me, gently nudging me with her flattened palm toward the kitchen. At least she was gentler than the caseworker, who acted as if she had only minutes to deposit a bag of potatoes in front of someone's house. With my thumb still firmly lodged in my mouth, I shuffled into the kitchen and fell into an empty seat.

Humming the words to some kind of church song, Mrs. Woodson opened the refrigerator door and, within a few minutes, a small plate of cold fried chicken legs and biscuits sat on the faded yellow Formica table. My dormant appetite fell into a comatose state when I saw a few cockroaches crawling around the sink. Then Mrs. Woodson poured a glass of iced tea and sat down next to me on a chair losing its stuffing. She took a sip, then wiped the sweat pouring from her brow with a tissue.

"Come on, honey. You got to eat something."

Rocking back and forth like I was autistic, I refused to open my mouth. This behavior became a way of comforting myself. I may have looked like I was in a stupor, but the steady motion somehow eased my pain. I felt Mrs. Woodson's eyes bearing down on me. At last, I displayed an ever-so-small phony smile and said, "No ma'am. I don't want to eat." Although I had seen plenty of roaches at the Chester's, the sight of the bugs still made me want to squirm, especially around food.

Persistent, she put a chicken leg and biscuit on a small plate and gently pushed it toward me. I looked up and our eyes locked. She said, "Take a few bites."

Finally, I stopped sucking my thumb. With great anticipation, I spun my head around and looked toward the front door. "When is Mrs. Chester coming to get me?"

Immediate waves followed my innocent question. The lighthearted tone in Mrs. Woodson's voice plunged. She knitted her eyebrows together and glared at me. "She's not. This is your home from now on." She took another sip of iced tea and in a terse tone said, "Just eat something."

Figuring I had better comply, I picked at my food. But I still was not hungry. For a moment, I thought about throwing it out the open window for the brown-and-gold dog in the next yard, but changed my mind. I assumed that would not go over too well.

Mrs. Woodson was satisfied when she saw me fiddling with the food on my plate and left the room to start a load of laundry. As I munched on a biscuit, I glanced around the room. The kitchen was slightly larger than Mrs. Chester's, but not by much. Yellow curtains the color of ripe bananas covered the large window, giving the room a bright appearance. The linoleum was in better shape than Mrs. Chester's kitchen. It lacked that second-hand look and had no cracks. An off-white plastic canister set rested on a mantle piece above the stained enamel sink, which was free of dirty dishes. Although I could not yet tell time, I saw a box-shaped clock with a pear on the wall above the stove. A single roach crawled around the clock in circles. Then, with my head slanted to one side, I noticed the wall calendar had a picture of a white man with a chiseled nose, straight shoulder-length hair, and a full beard.

Mrs. Woodson passed through the kitchen and took notice of my gaping mouth. When I asked who the man was, she looked like I had asked for a cup of lye to drink with my biscuit. Her mouth hung wide open. "Child, you don't know?"

I shrugged my tiny shoulders. "No ma'am, I don't." Actually, I thought it was odd she had a picture of a white man in her house.

A worried look splashed across her face. Mrs. Woodson blessed herself several times, then raised her voice an octave or two. "That's Jesus Christ. Lord have mercy, I can't believe you didn't know. Have you ever been to church?"

"No ma'am."

"What does Catholic Charities say about that?"

"Who are they?"

As Mrs. Woodson grabbed her laundry basket and stormed away, she mumbled, "Now they'll want me to see about changing that, too. These people expect too much from an old woman like me. I can only do so much for these children."

To me, it was no big deal. Mr. and Mrs. Chester had not attended church, so I was puzzled by the fuss Mrs. Woodson had just made. I sat there feeling like I had done something bad.

Once I wiped the crumbs off my lap, I remained at the table wondering what the new routine would be like, what would be expected of me, and where I would sleep. Mrs. Woodson was busy at the washing machine, complaining about all the housework she still had to tackle. She sounded like someone who was caring for a small army.

Wandering into the living room, I saw a high ceiling but the room otherwise lacked character. A few family pictures rested on the end tables, but the room was otherwise devoid of knickknacks and other keepsakes. The only book in sight was a tattered copy of the Bible. Most of the walls were painted light blue. The small amount of wallpaper had a light texture with tiny yellow and green flowers on it. Tons of bright sunlight streamed through the six bay windows, which were remarkably clean. Not a streak in sight. The overstuffed furniture had muted patterned fabrics and scarred wood. It looked like it had seen better days. Although neat and orderly, the room felt cold and impersonal, like it had not been lived in. Even the roaches avoided the living room.

About fifteen minutes passed and Mrs. Woodson found me sitting in the living room, sucking my thumb again. I did not know what else to do, so I hung onto the edge of the couch as if I was sitting on glass. I was too afraid to get comfortable. The similarity to Mrs. Chester's living room was uncanny—both women had furnished living rooms but both rooms appeared lifeless, like the county morgue.

Mrs. Woodson lifted her chubby arm, checked her watch, and said, "Almost time for the other kids to come home. School just started the other day."

"What kids?"

"Foster children."

"Like Mrs. Chester?"

"Yes, like that."

About an hour later, two unrelated fair-skinned girls bounced through the front door. They both carried book bags and wore big smiles on their faces. When neither of the girls noticed me, Mrs. Woodson walked toward them, waving her hand. "Girls, we have someone new with us. Say hello."

The older girl, an eleven-year-old named Meekah, stopped smiling. She looked at me and uttered, "Hi."

Right behind her stood another girl, whose name I learned was Heidi. She was ten years old. Glaring at me, she barely said, "Hi." I felt like hiding or hanging out with the dog next door. Despite his loud barking, the neighbor's thick-coated dog with floppy ears acted more pleasant than Meekah or Heidi.

Sensing the unsettled feelings among us, Mrs. Woodson tried to break the ice by saying, "Come girls, let's go in the kitchen. I'll get you some cookies."

The girls flew into the kitchen and left me stranded in the living room. So much for the welcome wagon. Mrs. Woodson motioned for me to follow her, and I soon found myself sitting at the kitchen table, still feeling left out. The girls munched on the cookies with such fervor it seemed as if this was their first meal of the day. I tried to eat one of the sweet treats, but the unfamiliar cookies tasted like cardboard.

Meekah called out, "Hey little girl, don't be eating all the cookies."

Mrs. Woodson stood next to Meekah, and in an imperious voice, she commanded, "Leave her alone. I wish you'd be nice for a change."

In those days, mental health counseling to help foster families adapt to different living situations was unheard of. If it were available, I doubt Mrs. Woodson would have entered any of us, including herself, into treatment. Therapy was not very popular among Negroes, probably because most of the therapists were white and the cost was prohibitive.

The people in my community viewed therapy as a sign of weakness. Anyone who saw a psychiatrist or psychologist was considered a flake, even if the therapist was a Negro. Mrs. Woodson was an extremely proud woman who paid scant attention to the enormous stresses in her life. She would have been mortified to admit she needed help, but at times I thought we all did. These were the days before Prozac was a household name. Today, I think Mrs. Woodson would have been classified as clinically depressed. Chances are I would have been, too.

People in my working-class neighborhood treated family dysfunction by either ignoring it or praying for change. Negroes lacked faith in therapy but they were ardent supporters of the Church. A few people responded to dysfunction with alcohol, but I never saw Mr. or Mrs. Woodson take a drink in the local tavern, like so many others did from time to time. Every so often, a brawl erupted in the neighborhood among inebriated men, but the violence was never more than a bloodied nose, a cracked tooth, or a swollen fist.

Meekah made a loud sucking noise and shifted her attention back toward Heidi. I sat down and stared at the girls, who continued to talk about their new teachers and classmates. I wondered when or if they would play with me, but was too shy to ask because they acted like I was invisible.

Several months would pass before I learned Meekah, an only child, had been removed from her home because her mother died unexpectedly from heart failure and her father was in jail, serving a long sentence for armed robbery. Both of her parents were children of biracial relationships, a social concept not widely accepted. Meekah's grandmother wanted to adopt her, but social services denied the request due to the woman's age, fifty-five, the same age as Mrs. Woodson. No other relatives sought custody and Meekah now awaited a permanent home.

Heidi had been born to a German-American mother and a Negro father, who already had a wife and four children. When Heidi's mother became pregnant, her father refused to acknowledge paternity. Heidi's mother was left alone with a mixed-race baby in a largely white community. The woman tried to raise Heidi on her own, but found the task too daunting. Besides the financial burden, her family flatly rejected Heidi and her mother. Catholic Charities apparently had trouble accepting Heidi's mixed heritage as well. It refused to allow Heidi to carry her mother's last name, which was Stefanschweiger. The agency changed it to Johnson. Like Meekah, she awaited placement in a permanent home.

I remember feeling resentment that other people had the power to take away someone's name, presumably because her father was Negro. I wondered if Theresa Cameron was really my given name. Children of biracial couples were not well accepted by either Negro or white society. I suppose that's why many of these children ended up in foster care. Heidi had such light skin, a sculpted nose, and nearly perfectly straight hair that many times I really believed she was white.

By late afternoon, the box of store-brand cookies had been transformed into a pile of crumbs. Mrs. Woodson ordered the two girls to start their homework. Meekah's dark brown eyes became enlarged. She protested by saying, "We don't have none yet. School just started."

Mrs. Woodson acted like Meekah had proclaimed the sky was falling. She said, "Don't expect me to believe you don't have any. Get your books out and don't waste time daydreaming."

"But our friends are waiting for us. We're going to paint our fingernails."

Suddenly, Mrs. Woodson's round eyes surged with anger as she said, "Don't sass me girl, just go on and study. Dinner will be ready soon."

With sagging heads, both girls dragged themselves toward their room. I overheard them grumble Mrs. Woodson was sometimes mean. Because Mrs. Woodson never responded, I presumed she never caught the gist of their conversation.

Now alone in the kitchen again, I continued my reign of silence. I felt so out of place, like a mango in an apple orchard. Not having anyone's lead to follow, I remained in my seat, even though a torn piece of plastic was jabbing my rear end.

Mrs. Woodson took out a large pot, filled it with water, and hauled it to the stove. She ignored me as she peeled potatoes, readied a bunch of mustard greens, and placed a large piece of ham inside the oven. The kitchen sweltered and beads of sweat poured down my face and neck. I wanted to put on a pair of shorts and a sleeveless top, but I did not own any. Instead, I was stuck in my crinoline-lined dress, making me feel like I would melt at any moment.

Within a short time, the kitchen teemed with a delightful aroma. The grumbling sounds in my stomach reminded me I had barely eaten all day.

Despite sizzling temperatures, I felt the urge to eat something. Not a whole meal, but something. I hoped the roaches would stay away during dinner.

I heard the front door slam and feet shuffle across the floor. I looked up to see a tall, strapping man who stood nearly six foot seven inches, weighing close to three hundred pounds. He looked like a wide receiver. As he reached out to hug his wife, I saw strong and sturdy hands. He politely introduced himself to me as R. C. "What an odd name," I thought. The only R. C. I had ever heard of was Royal Crown Cola. I studied his square face and noticed honey-colored skin, a scrawny mustache, and a head full of salt and pepper hair. He reminded me of someone's grandfather. Because R. C. worked at the Bethlehem Steel plant, he wore a company charcoal gray uniform that had his name sewn above the breast pocket. Armylike black boots covered his big feet.

Half an hour later, R. C. was clad in more casual attire. Upon his return, he grabbed a can of soda and ventured into the sitting room. I watched him peruse the newspaper. With great interest, he talked out loud about the boycotts of lunch counters occurring in the South. I was slowly beginning to learn how Negroes were treated as second-class citizens and some people were fighting to change that negative perception. Judging from the fear in Mr. Woodson's voice, I sensed trouble at the boycotts. At that time, I failed to understand why Negroes got beat up for taking a seat at Woolworth's and ordering a hamburger. Moreover, I still did not know how the boycotts would affect my life, but I hoped they would.

Slowly turning the pages of the newspaper, Mr. Woodson took notice of me as I stood by the door. "Come in. Tell me about yourself."

My heart beat faster. I feared I would clam up at any moment. I obeyed his request and crept toward the table. On the way, I could feel a lump the size of an orange form in my throat. Staring at the floor, I said, "Nothing to tell."

Mr. Woodson formed a smile so warm it could melt the winter snow. Pushing the newspaper aside, he faced me and said, "Of course there's something to tell. Why don't you start by telling me your name."

"Theresa."

"Why are you with us, honey? Got family problems at home, or something? It's OK to tell old R. C."

"No sir. I don't have a family. No home either."

Mr. Woodson's eyes dropped to the floor. I could tell he was not prepared for my response. No longer smiling, he gently touched my hand and said, "I'm sorry. I . . . I didn't know."

"That's OK." I left him sitting alone at the table and returned to the kitchen. He seemed lost, and so did I.

Within minutes after my arrival, Mrs. Woodson put a plastic tablecloth on the table. She looked at me and flipped her wrist in the air. "Go inside and call the girls. Tell them we're about ready to eat. Tell Mr. Woodson to come in, too."

Like a track star, I dashed down the hallway and banged on their bedroom door. Meekah ripped open the door and handed me an evil look. "What'd you want?"

I felt like crying but I stood my ground, refusing to be intimidated. "Mrs. Woodson said it's time to eat." The minute I relayed the message, I spun around and ran back to the kitchen. These two girls seemed icier than the Buffalo winter and I immediately decided to stay out of their way. I wanted to be around the boys again. I missed Eddie's silly jokes and the made-up games we used to play.

It would be almost two years before I discovered the true roots of Meekah and Heidi's cold shoulder toward me. Another little girl around their age had temporarily lived with the Woodsons. Days before my arrival, she left to be adopted. Undoubtedly, the girls must have been envious and acted out by treating me with derision because they could not understand why no one wanted them.

Once Mrs. Woodson served the food and the rest of us were seated, including Mr. Woodson, she plopped onto a chair. Mrs. Woodson acted like someone who had been dragged through the rinse cycle. She dabbed her face with a napkin and sighed so loud I thought she might fall over. A plate of piping hot biscuits was on my left, so I reached out for a piece of bread. To my surprise, Mrs. Woodson glared at me and said, "Put that down. We haven't said grace yet."

Completely ignorant about religious manners related to mealtime, I repeated the word, "Grace." For a moment, I thought this might be some kind of game, and I went along because I was hungry.

Mr. Woodson almost fell out laughing, but when his wife handed him a dirty look, he used both hands to cover his mouth. His shoulders bounced up and down a few times. The girls showed no emotion as both of them gazed at me with weak stares. I wondered what I had said wrong.

Mrs. Woodson blessed herself, then momentarily glanced upward. She looked at me and pointed her finger. "We say a prayer to the Lord before every meal to thank Him for what we have."

I folded my hands together, like everyone else did. Mrs. Woodson prayed out loud, and when the others dug in, I did too. I ate a small slice of salty ham, put away one whole biscuit, and munched on some peppery greens. The conversation was light yet somewhat strained. The girls talked to each other but otherwise ignored the rest of us. Mr. and Mrs. Woodson both acted like nothing was out of the ordinary, yet I felt completely disconnected.

As soon as the two girls and I helped with the dirty dishes, Mrs. Woodson excused all three of us. Meekah and Heidi immediately retreated to their room and slammed the door. Mrs. Woodson showed me the small room where I would be staying. It was like an inexpensive motel room with a small bed and a single dresser but nothing else. The minute she left me alone, I ran into the bathroom, stuck my head into the toilet, and lost my dinner. I jumped on my bed and cried myself to sleep, still wearing my only dress.

Five

Riding the Waves

I was ready for the first grade, but I was scared to death about starting another school. The night before I left Mrs. Chester's home, I remember a conversation we had. I asked, "What's Cath . . . Cath . . . lic school going to be like?"

"Oh child, very different," Mrs. Chester said with a sigh. "You'll be taught by nuns. They don't take no backtalk. If you don't behave, you might get spanked."

"What's a nun?"

"You better ask them people who look after you. I think they'd know better than me."

Mrs. Woodson seemed aloof most of the time, Mr. Woodson spent a lot of time on the job, and the girls shoved a thick wedge between us, so out of self-preservation I kept my distance from everyone.

One afternoon, I sat by an opened window, staring at the dog sitting next door. Wagging his curly tail, he yapped at passersby for attention. Everyone either ignored the harmless mutt or warned him to shut up. I felt shut out like the dog. He was all by himself looking for attention, a position I could easily relate to.

As time for class drew nearer, I wondered what I would wear. Catholic schools imposed a strict requirement—all students had to wear the same uniform. Because I owned so few dresses, I felt baffled, knowing I would wear the same dress every day.

There was always an edge around Mrs. Woodson, so I kept quiet about my clothing problem. Some days, she seemed affable like Auntie Em from *The Wizard of Oz*, yet she once in a while she behaved imperiously, more like a South American dictator. I viewed her more as a caretaker than a surrogate parent. Nonetheless, I finally mustered enough courage to approach Mrs. Woodson, who stood next to the cylindrical washing machine. She cursed at the old clunker, threatening to haul it to the junkyard for a decent burial. The aging machine vibrated so loudly I thought it might blow up. While she was running drenched clothes through the rollers on top of the machine, I tugged on her skirt and asked, "What'll I wear to school?"

"A uniform, that's what all the kids wear."

"But I don't have one yet."

"What'd you wear to kindergarten?"

"My own clothes."

She said, "You sure they didn't give you any uniforms?"

"No ma'am, they didn't."

Mrs. Woodson hurled a wet pair of slacks into an empty wash basket. She said, "I'll have to call Catholic Charities. I don't have the money to buy you a uniform right now."

"Can I still go to school?"

"I don't know yet."

Not long afterward, she scampered into the kitchen and picked up the phone. I followed, hiding out in the adjacent small room. I heard her ask for my caseworker. From bits and pieces of the strained conversation, I figured out my caseworker had resigned. In an annoyed voice, Mrs. Woodson said, "I realize you're new, but the child is starting school and she doesn't have a uniform."

I watched Mrs. Woodson, holding the receiver with one hand, as she paced back and forth. "She needs a school uniform and I can't pay for it out of what you send me."

When she hung up, I felt sorry for the older woman. She seemed totally shaken by the conversation, but she never mentioned any ill feelings to me. She tapped me on the shoulder and motioned for me to follow her. "You might have to wear your dress to school for a few days. But the people at the agency will get you the right school clothes."

Someone from Catholic Charities unexpectedly showed up that afternoon with a check. Once she handed an envelope to Mrs. Woodson, the stranger took off. Could the stranger be my new caseworker?

Mrs. Woodson clapped her hands, ordering me to get ready.

I said, "Now?"

"Yes, now."

"I was going to eat some cookies."

"Don't talk back. We're going out."

"Where?"

"To buy your uniforms. Do as I say."

Half an hour later, a bus finally arrived. After a long, bumpy ride, we got out at Niagara Square to shop at the only clothing store in Buffalo that sold Catholic school uniforms. When we entered the small cluttered shop, the clerk, a mousy-looking white man with square black glasses and a beaklike nose, paid no attention to us. We were the only customers in the musty-smelling store, yet he refused to acknowledge our presence. He tidied up the place, yet it looked perfectly orderly to me. Finally, Mrs. Woodson approached him. The man lurched backward, acting as if she stood in front of him with a fully operational blowtorch. "I'd like some help picking out uniforms."

"This isn't the second-hand store you people always come looking for. That's down the next block."

Mrs. Woodson's eyes burned with fire, yet she seemed humiliated at the same time. "Sir, I'm not here for a handout. I have money." She pointed toward me and said, "This child needs school clothes. Can you help us or not?"

I guess the clerk realized Mrs. Woodson, who looked like somebody's grandmother, was not about to attack him. Yet he treated us both like we were thugs. I remained clueless as to why he appeared so fearful around an overweight, gray-haired Negro woman and a skinny little Negro girl about to enter first grade.

We purchased three navy blue jumpers, white blouses, and knee-high socks. With barely enough money left over, Mrs. Woodson stopped in a Buster Brown shoe store and bought me the required pair of black penny loafers. I liked the more colorful outfits Mrs. Chester dressed me in. These drab colors made me feel like I was on my way to a funeral instead of first grade. Walking toward the bus stop, my eyes lit up when I noticed a street vendor selling cotton candy. The sugary sweet smell made my mouth water, so I tugged on Mrs. Woodson's sleeve. I showed a winsome smile and asked, "Can I have some, please?"

Arms full of bundles, Mrs. Woodson glanced at the vendor but kept walking. She seemed to have a lot on her mind. "No, child, we have to get home."

For a moment, I thought about saying Mrs. Chester would have treated me to cotton candy, but figured I would get in trouble. I brooded, in silence, as I accompanied Mrs. Woodson to the corner bus stop.

Classes at St. Agnes Catholic School had started nearly a week earlier, but I was admitted to the first grade class anyway. I almost choked when I overheard Meekah, a seventh grader, tell Heidi, a year behind, I would be attending the same school as they.

Meekah said, "That little twerp better not expect me to hold her hand on the way to school." Until then, I had been referred to as an orphan, a ward of the state, and a little lost angel, but never as a twerp. I was not quite sure what the word meant, but from the sarcasm in Meekah's voice, I assumed it was a nasty name. Maybe Meekah acted like a bully because she was scared like me.

Mrs. Woodson frequently told us to believe we were a family unit, yet we were very unlike the other families in our neighborhood. With the exception of a few, the overwhelming majority of families were two-parent households with large, extended families. Only one other family took in foster children. I was surprised Mrs. Woodson had not befriended this family as a way of finding support. As I quickly learned, the Woodsons extended cordial gestures to their neighbors, but they had no real friends. She seemed to rub people the wrong way, yet deep down I think she wanted company.

I viewed myself as a visitor, always prepared for my next move. I lived in a house full of strangers, with tension so thick at times I felt smothered by it. All of us shouldered our own burdens, never sharing our emotional upheavals with one another. As the only one with dark complexion, a broad nose, and full lips, I felt like more of an outsider.

Mrs. Woodson glossed over the fact I rarely spoke or made eye contact when the girls were around. Heidi, for the most part, discounted me except when Meekah was around. Then she would act smart and sassy.

At dinner one evening, Mrs. Woodson buttered a roll and said, "Hey, R. C., Theresa will be going to school with the other girls."

In between a huge bite of meat loaf, Mr. Woodson casually nodded. "Sounds nice to me." He continued to pack away dinner, claiming to be famished because he had to work through lunch.

She said, "They can walk with one another."

"Sure can, can't they?"

When Meekah handed me a derisive stare, I suddenly felt sick, like I had gobbled down a pound of bacon grease. Later, inside my tiny room, loneliness overpowered me. With no one to comfort me, I sobbed myself to sleep once again.

A few hours later, I woke up drenched in sweat. I had been torn from my sound sleep by a painful nightmare. In my dream, I stood at a railway station and waited for a train. I had my hair in neat braids, wore a light blue dress with blue gingham checks, and held onto a small Raggedy Ann doll. Minutes after a train arrived, the conductor announced someone on the train wanted to see me. Of course, I assumed it was my mother, ready to take me home. As I stretched my arm out to board, the train sped away like a bullet. I was left standing there all by myself. Jittery, I tossed and turned for what felt like hours before I finally fell asleep.

Initially, I was reluctant to leave the house with Meekah and Heidi, but Mrs. Woodson insisted I had to go with them. She seemed unable to cope with the resentment brewing between us.

After school one afternoon, I scrubbed my skin with a wash cloth and hot water for more than an hour, trying to wash away the darkness. I thought lighter skin might improve my life. I only ended up with rough, puffed-up skin, so I gave up. Mrs. Woodson once mentioned bleaching creams, but I was too afraid to ask for some. I wanted mocha-colored skin like her and the girls. My dark skin felt like a curse.

Having limited formal education, Mrs. Woodson tried to shield us from disparaging remarks hurled at us from less enlightened neighbors. The community was primarily Negro but there were still pockets of whites who shared the area. Not all of them were thrilled Negroes were their next-door neighbors. I hated being called "darkie" or "nigger" when I passed by a few of these houses. The nasty names made my eyes sting with bitter tears, but I never let down my emotional barricades. I acted like the names never harmed me, but deep inside they wounded my soul.

I wanted to swear back at the bullies, but Mrs. Woodson warned us never to get into an argument with white people. Never. In fact, Mrs. Chester had given me similar advice, so I assumed both women were right. The case of Emmett Till, a young Negro teenager savagely beaten by a group of whites in Mississippi, was still fresh in people's minds. Till, a teenager from Chicago visiting with family, was alleged to have whistled at a white woman and for this he lost his life.

Whites were not the only ones who snubbed us. Some upper-crust Negro neighbors living in stately ten-room homes with shiny new cars parked in the garage were also unkind. Affluent Negroes could only buy homes in all-Negro neighborhoods. The civil rights movement was in its incipient stage and few, if any, laws existed to prevent discrimination in housing. Once, I was called "darker than the ace of spades" by a light skinned boy, sitting in front of a huge, well-maintained home. I was still too young to understand the color line that divided a lot of Negroes. Perhaps people such as me and the Woodsons reminded more educated and affluent Negroes the American dream was still beyond their reach, even if they were light skinned.

Although Mrs. Woodson had asked the girls to escort me to school, once they were out the front door and away from her sight they took off like they were fleeing from a raging fire. Their rude behavior made me feel like I was a bad girl, but at least they never punched me in the nose. I thought the girls were too ashamed to walk with me, because it was obvious none of us were related. We had vastly different shades and hair texture and different last names.

Years later, I found out some classmates had ridiculed Meekah because she lived with an old woman in a foster home. Instead of a foster home, they called it an old shoe. It took a while before I could face the shame associated with being a foster child. Besides my dark skin, which already set me apart, my personal situation made me feel more isolated. I hated being nobody's little girl.

Most Negro children in the neighborhood attended public school and viewed the few of us who went to the partially integrated Catholic school as uppity Negroes wanting to be white.

One day, I tried to explain. To a smart-mouthed little girl, I said, "I have to go there."

"Says who?"

I figured they knew I was a foster child, but I could not bring myself to speak the truth. "I can't tell you."

The stuck-up girl looked at her friends and said, "You believe that?" When they shook their heads, she said, "You a liar. You uppity, too."

"No I'm not."

"You an Uncle Tom."

"Don't say that."

"Go kiss them white people's butts and leave us alone."

Several weeks after I arrived at the Woodsons, I learned they had an older son named George. A baby girl had died shortly after birth, from some kind of congenital abnormality. George had served as an Army radio operator during the Korean War. Upon his discharge, he used his electrical training to secure a job as a repairman for the telephone company. George had his own place in the neighborhood, yet he visited his parents weekly. They spoke on the phone often. I could always tell when Mrs. Woodson was on the phone with George because her face glowed.

When I first met George, I saw a personable young man. He resembled his mother by having mocha-colored skin, yet he was tall and husky, like his father, with a bit of a spare tire around his waist. The girls ignored George, but I always greeted him as soon as he came through the front door. George always treated me with respect, but he was more interested in visiting his parents than with me. As soon as he arrived, the three of them usually retreated to the kitchen, where they drank coffee, ate cake, and talked for hours. Once in a while, I eavesdropped on their many conversations. I felt jealous because Mrs. Woodson never appeared so content in my company.

One night, George told his mother he had someone special in his life. He had met this young woman while repairing the phone system at a local factory. I could hear the gleam in Mrs. Woodson's voice as she said, "I'd love to meet her. You bring this girl over here for dinner soon."

George replied, "Sure mom, I'll set everything up." He hesitated. "What about the kids? Will they be around?"

"What am I going to do with them?"

George frowned.

"You never told this girl?"

"No, not yet."

"Son, tell her. I don't want surprises."

The blemish attached to foster care became harder to cover up.

My learning difficulties started in first grade. I had trouble under-standing phonics. All of it seemed like a foreign language that I could not grasp. When other children caught on, I felt stupid. Only later, when I discovered many children had parents who read to them, was my resentment somewhat mitigated. I was still jealous, but at least I had an inkling of why they seemed to succeed.

My teacher was an affable young nun with freckled skin and light green eyes, but she seemed agitated by her role as teacher of a class of thirty-five first-grade students. Almost daily, she dropped the chalk, tripped over her own feet, and wept. Because of her own personal troubles, this Calamity Jane could not provide me with extra attention. Perhaps she ignored me because of my race. As an alternative, she sug-gested I ask my older siblings for help. I was too embarrassed to tell her I was a foster child.

With a limited education, Mrs. Woodson had trouble deciphering phonics, too, and looked at my schoolbook as if it was scribbled in German.

One night she rested her wrinkled forehead on her palm. "I don't know about all this." Several years later, I found out Mrs. Woodson had never completed grade school. Similar to many Southern Negroes in her era, she spent more time in the fields than in the classroom.

Although she tried to help me, Mrs. Woodson was unable to clear up the misunderstandings that filled my mind. One evening, she blew off steam as I stuttered through my phonics lesson. She smacked her hand against the table so hard my pencils fell onto the floor. "If you want to get somewhere in life, you have to try harder."

"But . . ."

"No backtalk." Mrs. Woodson bent down and picked up the pencils. "Do as I say."

"But I do study."

"Then you aren't doing enough."

"I am."

"Then do more."

Her misguided words of wisdom did little to help me understand phonics. I felt like I was fighting to claw my way out of a blizzard with only a small shovel. What little self-esteem I had took a nosedive. I started to feel worse about myself.

I thought school would be a safe refuge for me, a place where I could escape from my complicated home life. At least I could spend six hours or so without Meekah around. I quickly figured out school was not the panacea I hoped it would be. Learning was difficult, and I hated to confront the possibility I was stupid.

My education was also hampered by my persistent daydreams, where I imagined myself living with my very own family, all of us with the same last name. I fantasized about a loving mother, a doting father, two sisters, and a brother. We lived in a comfortable house with a friendly dog. After dinner, we sat around the living room and sang songs. At bedtime every night, my parents read me a story and kissed me goodnight. I imagine other foster children experience the same fantasies. For children who have little or no emotional support around them, getting lost in daydreams is easier than facing reality.

During the time I lived with Mrs. Chester, I answered questions on my own. I knew my age, where I lived, and my phone number. Although I could not read, I interpreted certain letters of the alphabet and was close to spelling my own name. Not long after I was uprooted, I fumbled to answer simple questions. I stammered every time Mrs. Woodson asked me to recite my new street address. Nearly always, I rattled off incorrect responses. My forgetfulness became magnified. I left the front door open, failed to flip off light switches, and stored milk inside the closet. The sight of cockroaches around the house suddenly seemed trifling. All of my misdeeds unnerved Mrs. Woodson. She scolded me, declaring I was a naughty child. She never asked if I was having a hard time. I knew I had a caseworker, but I never developed an ounce of faith in the many people, mostly young women, who served in that capacity. I rarely saw them anyway, so I doubted I was important to them. Besides, all I wanted was my own home, and I doubted they could deliver on my most treasured wish.

I must have been terribly frightened of abandonment. If it happened once, it could happen again. Nothing felt secure anymore, and I started to act out. Daily living routines, such as bathing and eating, became drudgery. I wet the bed, refused to bathe, and only ate peanut butter crackers. Further complicating my life were Meekah and Heidi. They were not the sole cause of my unhappiness, but their insulting behavior put me further in the hole. I desperately wished they would get adopted so I could find some peace of mind.

Summer had officially ended and cooler temperatures prevailed. The harsh winter snowstorms were only weeks away. Sometimes, gloomy clouds hung around for days. I started to feel as dark as the cloudy skies. Not even Mr. Woodson's sparkling smile could warm me up.

To compensate for my lack of human connections, I developed imaginary friends. I affectionately named my favorite creation Sophie. Beautiful, with dark skin and nappy hair like me, Sophie and I became best friends. I left space in my bed for her. When Mrs. Woodson noticed me sitting on half my chair at the dinner table, she asked why. I replied, "For my friend, Sophie."

Mrs. Woodson acted as if I had loose marbles in my brain. In a condescending tone, she said, "There is no Sophie sitting next to you."

I smiled. "Yes there is."

"No there is not."

"You can't see her. Only I can."

"Don't ever say that around anyone."

I said, "Why not?"

"They'll think you're crazy or something."

"I'm not crazy."

"I don't want the people at the place saying I did this to you."

"She's my friend, for real."

"Stop it, I said."

Riding the Waves

I overheard Mrs. Woodson talking to her husband inside the kitchen. "I wish this child's mother would come for her. She's talking to people who don't exist. I'm worried."

Mr. Woodson said, "Be easy on her."

"Why? She's acting crazy."

"The kid is having a hard time."

"I'm doing all I can, but I guess it'll never be enough."

When I went to bed, I briefly wondered about my mother, something I rarely did. Who was she? Did she ever think of me? Did I look like her? Why did she leave me? Because I had no memories of her, not even a picture, I can honestly say I did not miss her. I had no idea who to miss. To me, she was only a name on my birth certificate. She could have been anybody. I hated her for stranding me in this human purgatory.

Growing up in the nuclear age was no big deal. The Cold War sounded like the weather in Buffalo. The Iron Curtain was the wall I put up between me and the rest of the world. Fear of the bomb was beyond my sheltered environment. I was more afraid I would never have a home.

On the day of my first air raid drill, a loud gong sounded. The nuns herded us, single file with our fingers on our lips, into the clothes closet. We were ordered to sit down and take cover. I lost my cool, honestly believing the building was under attack. I let out a shriek and so did the kids sitting next to me. In a matter of seconds, the once quiet clothes closet was a pandemonium of frightened, screaming children begging for their mothers. The nuns tried to restore calm by swearing this was only a drill and not the real thing. But they said nuclear war could erupt at any time. If that should happen, they warned, take cover in the basement. Ugh, just what I wanted—to hide along with a bunch of rats. I hoped the bomb would never be dropped.

Completely baffled as well as scared by the air raid drill, I rushed home constantly staring at the sky in search of war planes. I hoped war wouldn't break out, at least until I got home. By the time I reached the front door, I was drenched in sweat despite the chilly temperatures outside. I must have looked like I had seen a ghost because Mrs. Woodson asked me what was wrong.

My teeth still chattered. I managed to blurt out, "War. The nuns said war could happen."

Mrs. Woodson approached me and felt my forehead to see if I was warm. "What're you talking about? There's no war going on."

"The nun said there might be a nu . . . nu . . . nuclear war."

"No there isn't."

"You sure?"

"Yes, I'm sure. We got more important things to worry about."

"But the nuns said we should run to the basement when war starts. How will we know? What'll we do?"

"There's no war, nuclear or otherwise. Stop fussing. You'll live longer."

Mrs. Woodson had smooth, almost straight hair. She had trouble adjusting to my more African features, especially my tightly curled hair. She attempted to roll my hair out in her sponge curlers, but my hair resisted her efforts. She bought a jar of Dixie Peach Pomade and plopped a big wad of the gooey cream onto my hair, without massaging it into my scalp. So, I walked around with hair that looked like it had been dunked in grease. My hair still remained tightly curled. The results left Mrs. Woodson flabbergasted. I explained I knew how to braid my own hair but my statement was met with a frown.

Somehow, she scraped together enough money every few weeks to send me to a hairdresser so I could have my nappy hair straightened. In those days, lye was used and I hated the excruciating pain I had to endure so my hair could look less Negro. No matter how the hairdressers tried to tame my tightly curled hair, they never could undo the work of Mother Nature.

One day a man with pale skin knocked on our front door. I heard him tell Mrs. Woodson he was here to deliver the coal. "That's odd," I thought, "It's already cold." So I ran to the door and asked Mrs. Woodson, "Why is he here to deliver cold?"

The man cracked up laughing, but Mrs. Woodson remained as imperturbable as ever. She nudged me away and said, "Go back to your homework."

"It's Saturday and I don't have any."

"Well then, do something. Leave us alone."

Riding the Waves

I watched the man unload his truck and heard the coal as it barreled down the chute leading to the basement. The man knocked on the front door again. This time, his face was covered with soot, giving him a dark appearance. As he stood there waiting for payment, he took out a handkerchief and wiped the black soot from his face. His skin became light again. I ran into the bathroom, wondering if perhaps I had soot on my face, too. I tried to wipe the chocolate color of my skin with a rag, but nothing happened. I was most angry with my mother not for abandoning me, but for having dark skin. No matter how hard I tried to feel good about myself, I almost always failed. Everyone seemed to treat me differently because of my dark skin.

As Halloween approached, I wanted to go trick-or-treating. Mrs. Chester had taken me, and like most children, I was eager to collect a huge supply of sweet treats. My sad face turned to a smile when Mrs. Woodson told me George had volunteered to take me through the neighborhood on Halloween. She took me to the Woolworth's store downtown to buy a witch's costume and a plastic pumpkin to collect my goodies. Mr. Woodson came home from work with a real pumpkin. I giggled as he scooped out the insides and carved a funny face.

On Halloween night, George led me through the neighborhood, holding my hand. I was impressed by the colorful decorations on all the homes. It seemed everyone displayed cardboard cutouts of skeletons, ghouls, and witches. Most young kids were also accompanied by adults, presumably their parents or older siblings. I was glad George made it possible for me to celebrate Halloween, but it also made me sad because I knew the special moment I shared with him would soon be over. George would make a good father, but he was not my father. I went home feeling sad, even though I had collected at least a month's worth of candy.

With most days cold and raw, Mrs. Woodson fixed us a hot breakfast every morning. I was used to corn flakes, cold biscuits, or plain toast. She usually cooked a variety of hot cereals, including grits, oatmeal, and cream of wheat. I had trouble digesting oatmeal. I couldn't stomach the taste of the hot, mushy cereal, no matter how hard I tried. As a rule, Mrs. Woodson rarely stayed in the kitchen while we ate breakfast, so I usually disposed of my cereal instead of eating it. Heidi was revolted by cream of wheat, so we covered for each other while shoveling cereal down the drain.

Ever since I arrived, my appetite had become hit-or-miss. Some days I packed away all of my meals, but on others I barely touched the food. Mrs. Woodson had a responsibility to make sure I was fed, but at times she took the role of foster mother far too seriously.

One morning I woke up feeling sick to my stomach. Because I was expected at the breakfast table, I took my usual seat and pretended to be happy. Mrs. Woodson removed a pot from the stove and heaped a pile of oatmeal into my bowl. I was too afraid to tell her I felt nauseous, fearful I would be accused of lying.

I stared at the bowl of wax fruit next to the salt and pepper shakers, feeling beads of sweat crawl down my face and neck. I forced myself to take a few bites but could not swallow the oatmeal. I gagged, then vomited all over my plate. Mrs. Woodson thought my sickness was intentional. She waved her clenched fist in my face and went nuts. The girls sat there with wide eyes and their mouths agape. Eyes ablaze, Mrs. Woodson yelled, "I made this oatmeal so you could have a hot breakfast before school. You're going to eat it." She grabbed a few of my braids and shoved my face into the plate of vomit. Angry, I wanted to hurl the plate against the wall, but I was also disgraced. Because I was so adept at controlling my feelings, teardrops never fell. I avoided Mrs. Woodson's glare and ran into the bathroom, where I cleaned myself up. I left for school without saying good-bye.

Later on that day, Mrs. Woodson mellowed out, but she never apologized or asked why I could barely stand up. I was still under the weather with a stomach virus and I fell asleep without eating dinner.

Several days later, Mrs. Woodson figured out the girls did not escort me to school. She expressed no surprise, nor did she scold them for it. Just as well. I was happier without them around. The neighborhood was safe. Strangers of any race were not treated with suspicion. Child abductions by disgruntled family members or strangers were almost unheard of. If there was any drug dealing, it was done behind closed doors. No one, except the police, carried weapons. The neighbors, they kept a watchful eye on school children walking to nearby St. Agnes Catholic School. I never once felt afraid. Besides, I had Sophie to accompany me.

Riding the Waves

One fall afternoon, shortly after school, I heard a knock at the front door. Mrs. Woodson flew out of the kitchen, where she was preparing dinner, and opened the front door. I was ecstatic when I heard Mrs. Chester's voice. "Wow," I thought, "I'm going home." I dashed through the living room and grabbed onto Mrs. Chester's leg with such force I almost knocked the unsuspecting woman off balance. I could hardly speak because I was so excited. The only words to fall out of my mouth were, "Mrs. Chester, Mrs. Chester!"

The ends of Mrs. Woodson's lips curled downward. She glared at Mrs. Chester with something like disdain burning in her dark brown eyes. Not surprisingly, she acted out of character by not asking Mrs. Chester to come in. Mrs. Chester obviously picked up on the icy reception. Backing away from me, she met Mrs. Woodson's cool stare. She hesitated for a moment, then said, "Hi, I . . . I only stopped by with some toys for my baby. I thought it would be OK."

Mrs. Woodson acted as if Mrs. Chester had arrived with a bottle of scotch for me instead of a new doll. She took the gift from her hand and impudently waved it in Mrs. Chester's face. She said, "How will I explain this to the other children?"

"But . . ."

"Now, they'll be wanting something, too."

"I . . ."

Strong-willed Mrs. Woodson said, "I don't have money to buy them presents. You above all, should know it's hard being a foster parent."

I could tell Mrs. Chester was totally dumbfounded. Her voice cracked a bit as she said, "Please tell her I still think about her. I didn't mean to cause trouble. Please, forgive me."

"The only thing you can do is stay out of her life."

I felt like an object in a bidding war, not like a child. Psychologists say all children need to form an attachment to either their parents or caretakers. It was clear I still had a solid attachment to Mrs. Chester. Now I can look back and see perhaps Mrs. Woodson was jealous because I had not formed a similar attachment to her. I doubt the girls had either. Foster care, no matter how well intended it may be, cannot take the place of a stable family. This was true when I was in foster care and is true now.

Riding the Waves

Mrs. Chester slowly edged toward the front door. The sparkle she came in with had quickly faded to gloom. Without looking at me, she muttered, "I better go now. Sorry if I made trouble."

I stood by the door, feeling once again dismantled by my emotions. On the one hand, I wanted to run after Mrs. Chester and beg her to take me home. But common sense took control and I said nothing. Tears formed in my eyes, but I stood there as stiff as a board while I fought to hold back my tears. Mrs. Woodson threw the doll at me. "Don't you go telling the girls about this. If you do, I'll take it away from you."

With clammy hands, I held onto the small doll and raced upstairs to my room. Once inside, I hurled the doll against the wall with such fury I caused the small plastic nose to fall off. I ripped the doll in shreds and stuffed it underneath my bed.

Alone, I stared out the window into the vast night skies, teeming with bright stars. I pretended Sophie was next to me. I sat on the edge of my bed and said, "Maybe you and me can run away some time. We could go someplace and find us a regular home. We could still be best friends, too." Of course, I knew no one would respond, but talking out loud to Sophie eased my pain. In a short time, I felt drowsy and fell into bed. For a change, I slept through the night without experiencing another nightmare or wetting the bed.

The next day was Saturday. As I moped through a breakfast of biscuits and sausage, I suppose Mrs. Woodson felt sorry for me. She offered to take me to Woolworth's for a new doll. Begrudgingly, I agreed. Once inside the bustling store, I glanced around at the dolls available for sale. There were all kinds of dolls—-dolls that wore diapers, dolls that cried, and dolls that had long straight hair that you could comb. After a thorough search, I tugged on Mrs. Woodson's dress and asked, "How come they don't have Negro dolls with hair like mine?"

Mrs. Woodson rubbed her temples as if she had a headache. "Honey, there are no Negro dolls here or anywhere."

"No place?"

"Pick out something."

"I don't like these."

"That's all there is."

Riding the Waves

To satisfy Mrs. Woodson, I picked out a pink-faced rubber doll about the size of a ruler. The doll, however, had no meaning for me. I would have preferred to cuddle with the doll Mrs. Chester gave me, but it had been hauled away by the trash collector. I left the store wondering why nobody sold dolls looking like me.

S i x

Growing up with the Woodsons

Ever so slowly, I accepted the change of venue and new routine. The girls still balked at walking with me to school. I began to pretend they did not exist. Now that I had thicker skin, I stopped feeling sick whenever Meekah called me a twerp. The stigma associated with foster care and the uncertainty of life had to eat away at her soul, too.

At dinnertime, Mrs. Woodson acted like the Negro version of the mother in *Leave it to Beaver*. Sometimes, I was convinced we were a happy family. After saying grace before dinner, everyone started to pass the plates. Often, I sat there and watched Mrs. Woodson fill my plate, usually with turnip or collard greens, potatoes, and meat, but as long as the girls were around I had little appetite. A chilly silence surrounded the dinner table in spite of Mrs. Woodson's efforts to melt the ice.

Mrs. Woodson talked to us about the growing boycotts at Southern lunch counters. The news was everywhere. I was still confused about Jim Crow, but I trusted I would never meet him face to face.

As I got older, I saw racism in Buffalo, too, but in hindsight it was not as pervasive as it was in the South. There were no "colored only" signs at public facilities, nor were we forced to sit in the rear of the bus. One time, I remember asking Mrs. Woodson, "What's civil rice?"

For a rare moment, the ends of her lips curled upward and she showed some teeth. She almost smiled but managed to control herself. "It's called civil rights. People like Dr. King are working to make a better life for us. You, me, and all of us Negroes."

"Oh." I wondered if Dr. King could do something about finding me a home.

After school one day, Meekah boasted only dark-skinned Negroes such as me would have problems. She announced light-skinned girls such as she and Heidi were more accepted by society. I did not know whether to believe her or not. I knew most Negroes, including those with light skin, were not respected by whites. They were treated like second-class citizens, like those of us with dark skin. I assumed that was how the world existed.

I became friendly with the dog next door, despite Mrs. Woodson's vehement objections. The first time she saw me approach the dog, who was sound asleep behind the front gate, she yanked my arm and shouted, "Don't, that stupid beast will bite you."

"No, he won't. I want to say hi. Please, can I?"

"Are you deaf? I said stay away from this creature."

Mrs. Woodson's loud voice caught the dog's attention. He lifted his head off the ground, then wagged his furry tail. Seconds later, he curled up in a ball and returned to sleep.

One morning a few days later, the dog's owner waved at me as I passed by on my way to school. I stopped and asked, "Mister, where's the dog?" The neighbor had come outside to pick up a bottle of fresh milk that had been delivered. A lanky man with copper-colored skin grinned, and said, "I'll call him out. It rained last night so we brought him inside."

Next thing I know, the dog with droopy ears bounded out the front door and briskly wagged his tail. He surged toward me, standing behind the front gate, and immediately slobbered all over my hand. I started to laugh. The man said, "Dog's name is Boomer. You like him?"

"Yes sir, I do."

"Why don't you ask if you can get a dog?"

I knew right away Mrs. Woodson would never go for the idea. She was the only adult I knew who disliked Lassie. I lowered my eyes and said, "Thank you for letting me play with Boomer. Can I do this again?"

"Sure, anytime."

Before leaving, I stroked Boomer's big head one more time. During my walk to school, I thought of approaching Mrs. Woodson about a dog, but by the time I reached the schoolyard, that idea was gone. I decided not to ask because I knew she would say no. I wanted someone who would be happy to see me every day, even if that someone was a mutt.

Because I was a young child, Mrs. Woodson steered me to wear dark-colored clothing. "Don't wear red or something bright."

"How come?"

"Cause I said so."

"A girl at school wears a red coat."

"Red isn't appropriate for dark-skinned children."

"Do you know why?"

"If you don't quit asking so many questions, I'll send you to your room."

What choice did I have except to believe her? I never knew my African ancestors glorified the color red. I doubt she knew either. I always looked ready for a wake.

In addition to buying black, blue, and charcoal gray all the time, Mrs. Woodson also purchased clothing two or three sizes too large. The stipend from Catholic Charities was not enough to outfit us properly.

She said, "You're still growing."

"But the clothes don't fit."

"They will sooner or later."

"Next time can I get clothes my size?"

"Buying clothes too big makes the outfits last longer."

"I look like I'm wearing a tent."

"Don't get smart with me. You'll wear what I buy you."

Every Friday, Mr. Woodson brought home his salary from the plant. A lot of employers paid in cash, a practice that created havoc for a few neighborhood families. Some men dished out their money on alcohol or the numbers, a flourishing underground network of gambling common in working-class neighborhoods. Quite a few men and women squeezed out a living in those days running illegal numbers. Police took money under the table to look the other way. Numbers runners collected bets and delivered the cash to a bookie. Despite Mrs. Woodson's straightforward ways, I remember a few times when a stranger knocked at the door and she quietly handed him a slip of paper with a few bucks. If she caught me looking, she always claimed it was the paperboy, yet we never had home delivery of the *Buffalo News*.

Mr. Woodson always brought home every dime he earned. Many Negroes, including the Woodsons, did not maintain checking accounts because banks did not welcome their business either. In addition to racism, older people who had lived through the Depression refused to trust banks.

Mr. Woodson left the bill paying to his wife, and she probably would have had trouble balancing a checking account. Mrs. Woodson either paid cash at the local drug store (a common practice at the time) or bought money orders at the nearest post office. On the first of the month, an unusual number of white men walked through the neighborhood—landlords showing up to collect the rent.

Catholic Charities paid Mrs. Woodson at the end of the month. How much money she received remains unclear because she never spoke about the payments. Mrs. Woodson stretched the monthly check to buy food, clothing, toiletries, and other necessities for three children. There was almost no money left over for items such as books, toys, or recreation. On the few occasions when she did treat us to a night at the ice skating rink or a movie, she paid with her own money.

For medical care, each of us girls had our own Medicaid cards. I hated the disgrace associated with Medicaid. Whenever Mrs. Woodson accompanied me to a doctor's office, the receptionist usually handed us dirty looks when we presented the Medicaid card. The card made me feel like I was from the gutter. In addition to the subservient feelings connected to Medicaid, only a few providers accepted it.

Mrs. Woodson and I often had to travel on two or three buses to reach a dentist who accepted Medicaid. And at the providers who accepted it, the wait for service sometimes took all day. After sitting for hours in shabby waiting rooms, we were treated by doctors and dentists whose competency was sometimes questionable.

Growing up with the Woodsons

Once, Mrs. Woodson took me to a dentist because I had a toothache. The squat man had sideburns like Elvis Presley and showed no manners. He ordered me into a chair, and his breath almost knocked me out. In addition to his crude behavior, he also tried to extract the wrong tooth. He never apologized for the mistake, but he was one of only a handful of dentists in Buffalo who accepted Medicaid. To this day, I still despise going to the dentist.

Besides the scarcity of Medicaid dentists, only a few doctors practiced in our neighborhood. Mrs. Woodson took us to Dr. Pastorini, a middle-aged white woman, one of the few to accept Medicaid. She treated us with respect, even when the waiting room was filled with sick patients.

Gastric upsets, caused by dairy consumption, frequently left me with diarrhea. Dr. Pastorini examined me and consulted with Mrs. Woodson. "She might be allergic to milk."

"What kind of gibberish is that?"

"Some people, especially Negroes, can't digest milk."

The headstrong Mrs. Woodson brushed off the doctor's recommendations. "Nonsense."

Frustrated, Dr. Pastorini said, "It'd help Theresa if she ate fewer dairy products."

"Every child needs milk. What kind of doctor are you?"

"A doctor who cares about her patients."

On the way out, Mrs. Woodson mumbled, "Doctor don't know what she's talking about."

Mrs. Woodson took the bus three mornings a week to a downtown store that sold day-old bread. Whenever we needed new clothes, she shopped at the Woolworth's in downtown or at second-hand stores. Every clothing item she picked was purchased through a layaway plan.

Sometimes, it took a few months before Mrs. Woodson could settle the entire lay-away bill. Heidi and Meekah protested that they had to wear cheap clothing. Those comments probably made Mrs. Woodson feel bad because she did the best she could, given the circumstances. I was too young to complain but old enough to notice her uneasiness.

The local grocery store disposed of dented cans by selling them at a discount. Mrs. Woodson stocked her pantry with dozens of cans of vegetables where the Jolly Green Giant looked as if he had been behead-ed. She pored through the Sunday paper only for the coupons. On occa-sion, neighborhood churches handed out government surplus food sup-plies, and people waited on long lines to bring home cans of mystery meat, salty cheese, and overly thick peanut butter.

Mrs. Woodson could not handle the shame associated with govern-ment handouts. She slipped a neighbor a few dollars to pick up the free food. No wonder they gave that stuff away. I thought Boomer's dog food looked more appealing than the stuff the government doled out. But Mrs. Woodson never passed up a bargain. Never.

Food was not wasted, either. We ate leftover after leftover, including when the food was dry as dust. When I got tired of eating the same thing day after day, I cheated by hiding food inside the pockets of my slacks. After dinner, I hurried next door and shared my leftovers with Boomer. The dog never complained. I kept up this charade for almost two years until I was caught red-handed. Needless to say, Mrs. Woodson was not happy, but more than anger, I think she was ashamed.

Back then, a meatless diet was viewed as a sign of poverty, and Mrs. Woodson scraped up enough money to feed us meat with every meal. She usually bought chicken backs, overly fatty chopped meat, and paper-thin pork chops. In addition to fresh meat, she bought canned meat products, including Spam and Vienna sausages. To make the canned meat more appealing, she cooked it with potatoes and greens. It still tasted like mush, but there was nothing else to eat. Fresh fruits and vegetables, except for potatoes and greens, were beyond our reach. On occasion, Mrs. Woodson bought applesauce, canned peaches, and fruit cocktail, but that was the extent of my exposure to fruit.

I grew up feeling sorry for Mrs. Woodson. I had no idea how hard she struggled to serve three meals a day and keep a roof, albeit a leaky one, over our heads. She was like a cheerleader trying to rally the crowd around a losing team, but the burden on her shoulders was a heavy one.

Mr. Woodson was hardly ever home. The plant was often shorthanded and he worked double shifts at least twice a week. Work inside a factory may have been drudgery but it paid a living wage. Negro men, in particular, flocked to the factories because the salary, although not much, was enough to keep them and their families afloat. Opportunities, even for Negroes with an education, were limited.

George's family visits were like clockwork. He showed up every Wednesday evening and Sunday afternoon. Once in a while, he brought sweet rolls and scrumptious cherry Danish from Pokorney's, the only Polish bakery still in the neighborhood. George was thoughtful—he arrived with enough rolls for all of us—-but Mrs. Woodson never doled out the treats until her son had gone home. Both George and Mr. Woodson spoke kindly to me, but beyond that I had little to do with either of them. Once in a while, George brought his new girlfriend around, but I have little recollection of this woman, except she was pretty and quiet. Still, I loved the sweets George brought with him.

I battled through first grade. Phonics still confounded me. I had trouble with spelling, and I was completely taken aback by religion classes, which I never had before. I was not sure I could believe everything taught in the classroom. When the nun said God was everywhere, I felt puzzled. I asked, "Does God come to Negro neighborhoods, too?"

The nun almost dropped her rosary beads. Her cheeks became fire-engine red. She stormed toward me and raised her hand as if to swat me. "Don't say such a thing."

"I only wanted to know."

"Wait until your parents find out."

"I don't have any."

She ignored what I said, but she was still mad. "Young lady, God is everywhere. Don't you people understand anything?"

During recess one day, one of my classmates, a young white boy with dimples and pretty blue eyes, asked me why he never saw me in church on Sunday. Unmoved by his question, I continued to munch on my cookies. I took a sip of milk and said, "Cause we don't go."

"Why not?"

"I don't know."

"My mommy says God will punish you if you don't go to church every Sunday. Aren't you afraid?"

I was more worried about living my life as a vagabond. I still had only a vague concept of God. Since I had no religious background, I was nonplussed by the concepts associated with religion. "Afraid? What for?"

The little boy had confusion splashed all over his chubby face. "I do what mom says so nothing bad will happen to me."

The minute I arrived home from school, I found Mrs. Woodson, mopping the kitchen floor. The harsh scent of ammonia made my nose twitch. Still holding my schoolbooks, I asked, "When are we going to church?"

Mrs. Woodson stopped dead in her tracks. She plunked the mop into the bucket of soapy water, held her arms akimbo, and looked at me with a cool stare. "Did the nuns ask you that?"

"No, but some little boy did. He said God would get me if I didn't go to church. Are we going?"

"I don't know."

"Something bad could happen."

"I better take you this weekend. Surprised no one asked you sooner."

If it was so important for me to be raised a Catholic, why wasn't Catholic Charities more actively involved in my religious upbringing? Why was I uprooted from the Chesters, the only home I ever knew, because the family was not Catholic? The Chesters may have been poor, but I was not mistreated. I wonder how different my life would have been had the Chesters been able to adopt me.

At dawn the following Sunday morning, Mrs. Woodson barged into my room and flipped on the overhead light. She rapped her hand against the wall and made a loud noise. "Get up. We're going to church." The service was not scheduled to begin until ten o'clock.

The sudden glare made me squint. The minute I rubbed my eyes, I rolled over and gazed out the window. Huge buckets of rain poured out of the dark gray skies. I pointed to the window. "It's raining out. Can't we go some other time?"

"No. I don't want those people complaining I don't take you to church. Go fix yourself."

"Can I eat first?"

"No, not unless there's time. It's already getting late. And I don't want to make a bad impression on these people."

Dragging myself out of bed and down the hall toward the bathroom, I stopped in front of Meekah's room and overheard muffled voices. I assumed the girls would be joining us. Just what I needed to start my day. As soon as I was dressed, I found Mrs. Woodson inside the kitchen clad in an old, faded housedress. She poured six teaspoons of sugar into a cup of instant coffee. Taking a sip, she studied me up and down. "I hope these people appreciate what I'm doing for you children."

I sensed she was waiting for a reply, but what could I say? I stood there with my eyes glued to the floor. The sound of rain beating against the house was so loud I looked up to see if the roof leaked. This time it had not. When I started to back out of the kitchen, Mrs. Woodson asked, "You hungry?"

I nodded. She pointed to a plate of cold biscuits resting on the edge of the table. I reached out and took one. Two bites later, Meekah waltzed into the kitchen and held her hand over her stomach. "I'm famished."

The minute Mrs. Woodson caught a glimpse of Meekah's evil eye the haggard old woman's face became contorted with anger. Mrs. Woodson jerked herself up and approached Meekah. "I'm sick and tired of you mistreating this child. You stop your nonsense this minute." She jabbed her finger in Meekah's face. "I'm warning you, missy. This is my house and you better listen to me. Or else." The harshness in Mrs. Woodson's voice frightened me.

Meekah's voice dropped as she stared at the floor. "Yes, ma'am." She took a cold biscuit and hurried out of the kitchen without saying another word.

I thought about calling Mrs. Woodson my savior, but I kept my thoughts private. Instead, I politely took a seat at the kitchen table where I finished a biscuit and a glass of milk. Maybe some of the bad times were about to end. For a change, I ignored the cramps caused by the milk.

Everyone was dressed in his or her best clothes. Mr. Woodson had on a worn tweed jacket with wrinkled charcoal gray slacks and a mismatched striped tie, making him look frumpy. Mrs. Woodson, dressed in a plain blue dress with white beads around her neck and a white pair of gloves, said, "R. C., Go back and put on something presentable. You look like a hobo."

"But," Mr. Woodson protested.

"But nothing. We got to make a good impression."

"There's no time."

Mrs. Woodson sighed with annoyance.

All of us girls had on new Woolworth's dresses with black patent-leather purses. This church business was a first for me, and I was shocked that people took it so seriously. Before leaving, Mrs. Woodson urged us to don our raincoats. Under her breath, I heard Meekah swear Mrs. Woodson was making her crazy. Once we were outside, the rains had eased up a bit but the skies were still dreary. I would rather have stayed home.

To everyone's surprise, Mr. Woodson's ten-year-old Chevy Impala started right away. The car usually failed to turn over in the rain.

Most of the worshippers at St. Joan of Arc Church were white. The ushers ignored us, so Mrs. Woodson took the lead and seated us in a front pew. I noticed a few of my classmates sitting with their families. As a rule, I never told anyone I was a foster child. I imagined these children assumed I sat with my family. I avoided their stares and waited until the service began.

Mr. Woodson must have been bored by the service because I noticed his head bob around a few times. Whenever he drifted off, Mrs. Woodson quickly jabbed her arm in his side, startling him. The girls wore such sour faces it seemed like they had been punished. When the service was over, I wanted to race out the door despite the cold, damp weather. Mrs. Woodson politely acknowledged a few of the neighbors, but otherwise she did not engage in casual conversation. The girls stuck to themselves, and Mr. Woodson looked lost. I hid behind Mrs. Woodson as we walked out, hoping to avoid my classmates. As luck would have it, we left before I ran into anyone I knew. I felt relieved when we piled into the car and drove home.

I found the service entirely too long. Moreover, it was in Latin, a language as hard to decipher as phonics. I was uncomfortable listening to a sermon too advanced for a six-year-old, especially one who was new to religion. I spent a lot of time kneeling and I could not grasp all the concepts associated with the Mass. If God was all-loving, as the priest had said during his sermon, why was I in such dire straits? At the age of six, how many sins, venial or mortal, could I have committed? I knew that not all the worshippers adhered to the Church's teachings because some white kids still called me nigger. Thankfully, we did not attend another service for more than six months.

Growing up with the Woodsons

Not long after our first visit to Mass, Mrs. Woodson announced we were going to adhere to the Catholic Church's prohibition against eating meat on Fridays. Initially, I had no reaction one way or another. I did not care for canned meat or some of the other less costly meat dishes Mrs. Woodson served such as tenderloin, liver, or chicken gizzards. Fish sticks and fried fish fillets came as a welcomed relief.

One Friday afternoon, I came home from school feeling hungry. I had found a hair in my tuna salad sandwich that day and lost my appetite. Without thinking, I fixed myself a plate of cold meat loaf along with a slice of buttered white bread. As I sat munching on my snack, Mrs. Woodson showed up and almost had a coronary. She pointed to my plate as if I was eating poison and shouted, "What're you doing!"

I had snacked prior to dinner several times before, so I was confused why she reacted so harshly. I could barely swallow my food. With a full mouth, I mumbled, "I was eating something."

"Don't you know the Church says no meat on Fridays?"

"I'm sorry, but I was hungry."

Mrs. Woodson gave me the evil eye. "Don't ever eat meat again on Friday. I'll have to take you to confession for this."

"How come?"

"Because. That's why."

When she stormed out of the kitchen, I felt worried. Would I be punished for eating a hunk of meat loaf on Friday? I never intended to offend anyone, much less put myself on the path toward hell. From that day on, I never went near a piece of meat on Friday, even after the Catholic Church gave the go-ahead to do so. I figured it was safer to eat the fish sticks.

By late November winter had descended upon Buffalo. Temperatures hovered around freezing most days, and snow already blanketed the ground. Fierce winds from nearby Lake Erie whipped across the city, making it hard to walk some days. The snow usually stayed around until spring, but the constant activity from so many smokestacks gave the snow a sooty color. That, along with days of gray skies made the whole city feel dreary.

Growing up with the Woodsons

Once we ate a light breakfast on Saturday mornings, duty called. In spite of Mrs. Woodson's cleanliness, the smokestacks billowed out enough soot to make regular scrubbing a necessity. So Mrs. Woodson hauled out cans, bottles, and jars of cleaning products along with mops, buckets, sponges, brooms, scrub brushes, and dust rags. Did we eat canned meat at least three days a week to free up money for other important items—bleach, ammonia, furniture polish, floor wax, and scouring pads? The kitchen soon resembled a janitor's closet. Mrs. Woodson delegated the chores, giving each of us a time frame in which to finish. For the next several hours, we worked hard cleaning the house.

Mrs. Woodson's previous threats of bodily harm leveled against Meekah must have done the trick because the girl's icy feelings toward me had warmed up slightly. It was not a miracle but, for the most part, Meekah left me alone. We learned how to coexist peacefully, yet we continued to keep our distance. The new arrangement suited us both.

One particular Saturday morning, I leaned against the counter and studied the kitchen, wondering how we could possibly make it any cleaner. Meekah came in with a rag draped around her head. "You could eat breakfast off the floors around here."

I replied, "Yeah, only if you don't mind Mr. Clean on your biscuits."

Meekah derisively tossed a sponge onto the counter and folded her arms in front of her chest. "The woman is trying to kill us. I wish I'd get adopted soon so I could live like a normal person."

"Me, too."

Some people grew up surrounded by the smell of fresh flowers. I grew up with the distinct aroma of Lemon Pledge. The furniture was polished to such an incredible sheen I could see my image by looking at the coffee table. I think a psychiatrist would have easily labeled Mrs. Woodson as having an obsessive/compulsive disorder. She admitted to her strange affliction by saying her favorite shopping place was the dry goods store, particularly the section with all of the cleaners, steel-wool pads, mops, and sponges. She acknowledged sneaking in sometimes to look at the new house-cleaning products. I told my imaginary friend Sophie that Mrs. Woodson was the one with the loose screws.

As the holiday season approached, I felt bluer than usual. The long, harsh Buffalo winter dampened my spirits further. Due to the cold weather, Boomer, the dog next door, spent most of the time indoors. From time to time, I stopped by the neighbor's house on my way from school to visit with him, even though Mrs. Woodson had urged me not to. She still swore I would contract rabies. Unlike the people I lived with, Boomer was the only one who consistently showed excitement whenever I was around. I relied on his disarming good cheer to make me smile.

My shaky truce with Meekah held up. Every so often, the girls braved the cold winds with me as we headed to school. I maintained a close relationship with Sophie. She was still my best friend. Nothing could change that.

At Christmas time, neighbors strung lights in their windows. Boomer's owners set up a plastic Santa with the eight reindeer in their front yard. Others displayed Nativity scenes. The Polish-American man who owned the bakery sold freshly cut trees from the parking lot alongside his property. Many Negroes, however, could not afford the cost of a real tree. Mrs. Woodson bought an artificial tree from Woolworth's. She decorated the homely green tree with a set of tacky ornaments and hung a cardboard picture of Santa Claus on the front door while we were at school. I was sorry she neglected to include us. I had enjoyed decorating the tree when I lived with Mrs. Chester.

One evening before Christmas, I ran into Meekah on my way out of the bathroom. She waved then followed me to my room. "Can I come in?"

This was a first, but I quickly agreed. "OK, I guess."

Meekah sat on the edge of my bed. "You still believe in Santa?"

"No, do you? That's kid stuff."

"Nah, I stopped believing in that a long time ago. Right after I left my mom. I wanted to know if you did."

I asked, "What do you think it'll be like?"

"What? Christmas?"

"I don't know how much the old lady can do for us."

"I never expect anything. This way I won't be disappointed."

For the first time ever, Meekah smiled at me. She jostled me good-naturedly before leaving. On the way out, she flashed a quick grin. "Thanks for letting me in."

"OK."

Like Meekah had warned me, Christmas was lukewarm for all of us. Catholic Charities never handed over extra money for gifts. Mrs. Woodson shuffled her bills around to squeeze out enough money to buy us a few presents. As always, she bought the gifts from Woolworth's and, on Christmas morning, I feigned delight with the new doll, puzzles, mittens, and a coloring book she selected for me. The only gift I wanted was my own home.

School continued to feel like a forced labor camp. I made little progress with phonics. My spelling was atrocious. Arithmetic almost killed me. The only subject where I showed any interest was geography. I enjoyed the lessons about far-away places. Foreign lands and exotic people seemed more inviting than my staid life in Buffalo.

By the time spring rolled around, I felt like I was headed for the graveyard. I failed almost all my classes, including religion. That just about sent the nuns into a special prayer session. My teacher's last words that day were, "You people don't seem to get it, do you?"

Not surprisingly, on the last day of school I was handed the expected news I would have to repeat first grade. With a pounding heart, I ran home as fast as my feet would carry me. Boomer was in the yard. He yapped for my attention but I ignored him and raced upstairs to my room. I could not believe I had failed the first grade. Too ashamed to speak to anyone, I was also afraid that, if the local children found out, they would tease me endlessly about my failure. So, I hid in my room, refusing to come out.

After nightfall, Mrs. Woodson rapped lightly on my door. I was curled up in my bed in a fetal position, sucking my thumb. Because I was unresponsive, Mrs. Woodson entered. She held a small tray containing a ham sandwich and a glass of milk. She rested the tray on my windowsill. I could tell from the look on her face that she felt sorry for me. "I guess I wasn't much help. Maybe next year will be better."

Seven

Getting By However I Could

By the spring of 1963, I was almost finished with the second grade. Repeating the first grade had crushed my already frail ego, but I held my head high and did my best. Luck was on my side because I did not end up with the same first-grade teacher. Rumors swirled around the school the young freckle-faced nun had collapsed in front of her class and ended up in a mental institution with a nervous breakdown. Sometimes, I thought I might have one, too. My new teacher, who was also a nun, seemed more relaxed around young children. Also, she was never cantankerous and did not refer to me as "you people." I assumed this young woman was wise to my background, because she once acknowledged I had a hard time. Now and then, she spent extra time helping me to understand my lessons, yet all my teachers, including her, were impervious to the fact I was barely able to read. I passed the first two grades and ended up in third grade with severe reading problems.

Because I was mortified to speak with total honesty, I had a distinct disadvantage. This was the shameful secret I was forced to live with. To admit the truth meant opening myself up to further ridicule, which I was not prepared to do. I had memorized certain letters of the alphabet so I was able to fake my way through school, but I hated being in this position. Teachers at my school had very low expectations of Negro students anyway. To exacerbate my poor reading skills, there was never enough money left over from each month's Catholic Charities check to buy me any reading workbooks or to pay for a private tutor. Moreover, the Woodsons were not into reading either. So, I had little to practice with except for what was written on the food boxes or the street signs.

One evening at dinner, I asked Mrs. Woodson if I could apply for a library card. As my legal guardian, she had to give permission for a card. There was a public library in the predominantly white neighborhood next to ours. I figured this would help me improve my reading skills and ultimately help me get over my social isolation.

Once she swallowed the food in her mouth, Mrs. Woodson acted as if I had asked for a shot of whiskey. "What do you want that for?"

"No reason. All the kids in school go to the library."

"It comes out of my pocket if you lose books," Mrs. Woodson said, looking worried.

"I won't lose any," I said.

"I don't have that kind of money."

"But all the kids go to the library."

"You sure you want to go over there?"

"Yes ma'am." I gathered she was about to say no. I dropped my head, lowered my eyes, and murmured, "I'm sorry, I . . .I . . . just wanted . . ."

"Wait and see."

"OK."

Later, Mrs. Woodson rapped on my door. Perhaps she worried about my safety traveling to and from a predominantly white neighborhood on my own, so she said no. "I'm responsible for you. I can't have you traipsing all over creation to read some books. Maybe next year, but not now."

I was let down, but not surprised. After all the lights had been turned out, I stretched out in bed, ready to fall asleep. I tried to roll over, but my body felt like it weighed a ton. I thought all four walls were about to cave in on me. I needed additional help to complete school, but I could not count on anyone to guide me safely through these turbulent waters. I would have to guide myself to safer ground. I assumed that, if I had access to the public library, at least I could practice reading on my own. I do not know if Mrs. Woodson believed I might get lynched for walking into a white area or if she failed to understand the gravity of my situation. For the first time in almost a year, I wet the bed that night.

In the second grade, I learned I would participate in the Catholic sacrament First Communion. During this ceremony, a child receives the body and blood of Jesus Christ (the bread and the wine) for the first time. For Catholic families, First Communion is a joyous event, one regarded highly along with birthdays and anniversaries. Because I had little indoctrination to the Catholic Church, I never shared my classmates' elation with First Communion. I doubted it would significantly change my life. As far as I was concerned, it was something I had to go through.

Shortly before my First Communion, sister told us about confession. "Confession," she said, "is when you tell God about your sins and ask for forgiveness."

"How come?" I asked.

My question caught the nun off guard. "How come?" she said in a raised voice. "How come?"

I was immediately sorry I asked.

"Everyone sins and has to ask God for forgiveness. Everyone, including you."

I wondered what bad things I had done.

I must have had a quizzical look on my face because the nun waved her finger at me and said, "Don't act like you've never sinned before. You'll be doing a lot of penance, young lady."

Penance? What was that? Mrs. Woodson never mentioned it. To avoid trouble, I went along with the nun. "Yes, ma'am, I've sinned." I had a few more questions, but I thought it best not to ask.

Thoughts swirled around my mind about what misdeeds to tell the priest. I planned to confess about the times I fibbed and said I liked Mrs. Woodson's cooking, the time I told her I took a bath when I had not, and the day I said I cleaned my room when I had swept the dust and debris under my bed.

On the morning of our First Confession, the nun instructed us about the proper procedure. "Be quiet and don't talk loud. You don't want everyone to know what bad things you did. When you're done, say your penance and wait inside the vestibule. And don't talk. I'll be watching."

Outside the classroom, she ordered us into a straight line, then we made the short walk to the church with our hands folded. Dimly lit and very quiet, the church made me nervous. It was not a place in which I spent much time.

"Don't forget to say the confessional prayer I taught you in religion class," the nun said. "It's very important."

The nun broke us into small groups and lined us up outside the confessional box. She offered few additional details about what would happen next. At the end of the line, I started to sweat, wondering what type of punishment I would receive. Would it be a beating? A verbal scolding? Each child in front of me spent about five minutes inside the small booth covered by a dark curtain. The solemn-faced nun patrolled the church to make sure no one skipped penance. No one did.

By the time my turn came, I could barely stand up. I slid into the small confessional box and knelt down. My stomach fluttered. Then I heard a sliding sound followed by a deep voice.

After saying a short prayer, the priest asked, "Are you ready to confess your sins?"

"Yes," my tiny voice squeaked.

"Go ahead," he said. The priest sounded firm but not harsh. That was comforting.

"Bless me Father, for I have sinned," I said, remembering the prayer I was to recite.

The space was so tiny I felt closed in. In addition to fear of an unknown ritual and what punishment was soon to come my way, I suddenly had to use the bathroom. I got right into my sins, revealing the times I lied about Mrs. Woodson's cooking and so on. Then I asked for forgiveness. Because I did not want to return to confession any time soon, I swore I would never misbehave again. Never.

The priest told me to recite a number of prayers. I said, "Anything else?" I thought for sure I would get a beating for lying.

"No, my child, that's it. Say your penance and try hard not to sin."

"OK, I promise."

So, that was it. I left the confessional box sweating like I was inside an oven. Relieved my punishment was only to say some prayers, I rushed to the pew and got to work. Once outside the church, I felt glad it was over. I had gotten myself worked up over nothing.

During a dress rehearsal for our First Communion, we lined up. The nun in charge proceeded as if she was directing a room full of inmates, rather than young boys and girls.

The drillmaster said, "Walk straight. Don't turn around. Keep your heads up."

When she saw a little boy falter, she smacked the back of his head and said, "Move it."

Not once did she explain the special rite to us. Communion felt more like punishment than a special initiation. The head nun with ice-cold eyes pulled me out of line and said, "Recite the Communion prayer."

"Me?"

"Are you deaf?"

"No ma'am."

When I floundered, trying to figure out the correct words, the nun raised her arm and slapped me across the face so hard I lost my balance. From the opened mouths of the other kids, I imagined they were terrified, too. Although my eyes swelled with tears, I showed absolutely no emotion. The nun shoved me back in line and said, "You'll never get to heaven unless you can recite a prayer properly."

Heaven? I was more worried about life here on Earth. I was surprised she reacted so harshly to my innocent mishap.

Corporal punishment is banned in most school systems. When I grew up, however, it was common for the nuns to throw erasers, chalk, books, or other classroom items at ill-behaved children. On occasion, they smacked students for trivial offenses, such as not understanding a lesson or wetting their pants.

First Communion also created another kind of headache in my house. Mrs. Woodson had been instructed by the school to buy me a special white dress, one used only for this event. As always, she operated on a shoestring budget and had no extra money. Orders at the plant had been flat over the past few months, and Mr. Woodson was rarely called to work overtime. Out of desperation, Mrs. Woodson phoned my caseworker at Catholic Charities to petition her for a extra money, but the caseworker familiar with my case had unexpectedly resigned more than four months earlier. Amazingly, I had not been assigned a new caseworker. Mrs. Woodson's request was met by only a weak promise of help, but nothing ever materialized. I did not meet the new caseworker until nine months later, and this woman only lasted six months before quitting.

To buy my First Communion dress, Mrs. Woodson borrowed from Peter to pay Paul. She used to keep cash stuffed inside different envelopes hidden behind the bread box. One was for the mortgage, one was for utilities, and one was for food. The envelope for emergency expenses had been empty since the oil burner broke down the previous year. She snatched a few dollars from the food envelope and bought me the required white crinoline dress along with a pair of white patent-leather shoes and a white veil. To compensate, we ate Spam and Vienna sausages for almost two weeks solid. Our morning orange juice was replaced with watered down fruit drink or powdered beverages that tasted foul.

On the day of my First Communion, I felt like a doll on display. Only a few of the neighborhood kids attended Catholic school, so most of them did not know why I was dressed all in frilly white. Because the school was close, Mrs. Woodson accompanied me, but she wore a house-dress and a pair of open toed slippers. I think she came with me only to make sure I kept my dress clean. Knowing how she could stretch a dollar-fifty out of a dollar, I guessed she had plans to hock the dress for cash in a second-hand store once the ceremony was over.

When we arrived, I immediately wanted to disappear into the small booth known as the confessional. All the parents and siblings were dressed in nice suits and fancy dresses. Mrs. Woodson stood out like a sore thumb, because she was the only one of a handful of Negroes in the church and also because she was inadequately dressed. No one made any attempt to talk to her.

After the long service, I met Mrs. Woodson outside. I wanted to cry because all the other children were lined up with friends and relatives in front of smiling parents who eagerly snapped photos with Polaroid cameras. Some families planned to celebrate with elaborate parties. I walked home in silence with Mrs. Woodson, glad to be away from the crowds. I imagined everyone talked about us behind our backs. The minute I got home, I took the dress off and stuffed it in my closet. Although this was supposed to be my special day, I received no cards or congratulatory words. Perhaps this was punishment for not attending church regularly, I thought.

From time to time, I performed light errands for some of the neighbors, such as fetching milk from the store, raking leaves, or carrying out the garbage. I offered my services as a way to make money because my pockets were always empty. After a few weeks, I had earned more than five dollars, a tidy sum I hid underneath my bed. One afternoon, Mrs. Woodson noticed me accepting payment of twenty-five cents for raking the leaves in our neighbor's front yard. She rushed over and said, "Don't take money for this."

"How come?"

"Because you do it out of the goodness of your heart. You may need help some day and have no money to pay for it."

Although resentful at first, I adopted her philosophy and performed the errands without charging a fee. I did accept payment in the form of milk and cookies. As an adult, I am grateful for the strong work ethic she instilled in me.

Mrs. Woodson scrimped and saved that year. Somehow, she stashed aside enough money to buy a new television set. She called Meekah, the ever-elusive Heidi, and me into the kitchen. Heidi always followed in Meekah's footsteps, rarely initiating conversation with me or anyone else. If we happened to run into each other, a salutary greeting fell out of her mouth but nothing more. I lifted my eyebrows as I caught Meekah's anxious stare. I presumed Mrs. Woodson was about to saddle us with additional housework chores. I almost fell over when she announced we could spend one hour every evening watching television.

"But," she said, "you girls are going to have to share. We only have one set and I don't want you to fight over it. And nobody gets to look at TV unless homework is done."

I traded excited glances with Meekah who said, "Yes ma'am. We won't fight. That's a promise."

Mrs. Woodson waved her finger at the three of us and said, "And keep my living room clean. If you make any messes, then no more TV. Understand?"

Meekah and Heidi were in their early teens and going through the opposite-sex phase. Mrs. Woodson, who wielded old-fashioned ways, put a damper on the girls' burgeoning interest in boys. Every time a boy called the house, Mrs. Woodson subjected him to a tortuous round of questions: What's your name? Where do you live? What's your mother's name? How old are you? Where are you going? What time will you be back? The FBI should have taken lessons from her in the art of interrogation. She ended each conversation threatening to inflict severe bodily harm if either girl ended up pregnant. Many boys never called back.

Because Mr. Woodson was hardly at home, my memories of him are very sketchy. Most evenings, he arrived home after we had already eaten dinner. Sometimes, he worked past midnight and I would go days without seeing him. Many times, he amused himself by playing solitaire or attending a football game with his son George. He loved eating a bowl of Jell-O mixed with fruit cocktail, which Mrs. Woodson served him every night after he ate a hefty dinner. Once in a while, he chatted with Boomer's owner next door, but he mostly kept to himself. On Friday evenings, when most of the local men got paid, they shared a few beers at the local tavern, but Mr. Woodson never joined them.

Mr. Woodson had aspired to become a violinist. As a young child growing up in Harlem during the 1920s, he learned how to play the violin, unusual for a Negro child in those days. His mother worked as a housekeeper for a man who played in an orchestra. As a favor to Mr. Woodson's mother for keeping his apartment so clean and orderly, the musician gave R. C. private music lessons. The man used his influence to open doors for R. C., but during that era orchestras did not welcome Negroes as musicians. Mr. Woodson's dreams faded when he joined the Army and was shipped overseas to fight in World War II. When he returned, he made the rounds to various orchestras looking for a break, but the door was always slammed in his face. With no other alternative, the only work he secured was in a factory in Buffalo.

School ended in June. Despite the fact I had passed the second grade, I moped around the house because I wanted to attend a sleep-away camp like many of my classmates had planned to do that summer. I needed a new adventure to perk up my sagging spirits, but I doubted

Mrs. Woodson had the extra money to send me to camp. For entertainment, Mrs. Woodson occasionally took me to a decaying neighborhood park. It only had a few sets of swings, a seesaw with chipped wood, a slide that was not smooth, and slightly rusty monkey bars. I never had an ounce of fun because Mrs. Woodson usually brought me to the park when it was empty. As a child, I naturally wanted playmates my own age; however, Mrs. Woodson resisted my efforts to reach out to neighborhood kids. Like me, it seems very possible Mrs. Woodson avoided questions, too. It had to be obvious we were unrelated.

Erie County held a fair every year, and Mrs. Woodson once treated me to a few rides, a hot dog, and cotton candy, but I spent most of my spare time hanging around the house. Mrs. Woodson got antsy whenever I was out of her sight. I think she was overly protective because she had a fear of retaliation from Catholic Charities, even though we rarely heard from them.

One evening in late June, Mrs. Woodson made a surprise announcement at dinner. Without smiling, she looked around the table and said, "Girls, we're going to visit my people in Cortland this summer."

I almost choked on a sip of Kool-Aid. Once I cleared my throat, I asked, "How come?" Until that point, Mrs. Woodson had rarely talked about any of her family members, except for George. The Woodsons seemed unlike a lot of the other Negroes in my neighborhood, many of whom had large, extended families that included aunts, uncles, grandparents, cousins, second cousins and long-time friends who were considered as family.

Mrs. Woodson acted surprised and wrinkled her brow. "I have a sister and a few nephews who live there. That's how come."

"Where is Cor . . . Cortl . . . Cortland?"

"About three hours from here."

"How are we going to get there?"

"Mr. Woodson will take us in the car."

"Oh. Is George coming?"

"No, he has to work."

Both Meekah and Heidi had sour faces, so I assumed they were not pleased by the announcement. But I looked forward to a new experience. The thought of spending another monotonous summer in Buffalo made me sick. Although Negroes were not legally prevented from using public recreation facilities such as the local pool or library, we were not especially welcomed in these places either. How could we mistake the sneers for smiles? I was thrilled at the prospect of leaving Buffalo for the very first time.

On the drive to Cortland, I stared out the window at the rolling hills. All the trees were in full bloom. Everything was green, a rich verdant green. I was mesmerized by all the cars, trucks, and buses that passed by us on the New York State Thruway. It was the height of the tourist season. Although I was now eight years old, this was the first time I had ever seen highway traffic. This was a whole new world.

Mrs. Woodson's older sister Patty lived on a ten-acre dairy farm outside of Cortland. Both on in their years, Patty and Joe stubbornly clung to the family's prized farm. It had been in Joe's family for over a hundred years. His ancestors, once slaves, escaped via the Underground Railroad. They settled in upstate New York, where they found jobs as farm hands. Through years of hard work, they stashed enough money aside to buy their own farm. By this point, Patty and Joe's four sons had grown up and had their own families. Two of their children lived in the area. It was expected they would take over the farm when their parents retired.

Over the course of our two-week stay, I had a surprisingly pleasant time. For a change, I was able to sleep past seven o'clock. Joe even took me fishing a few times, although I was revolted by the idea of putting worms on the fishhook. I never caught a thing, but that did not matter. I had fun. I was also tickled when Joe let me milk one of the cows. Every time one of the cows let out a loud "moo" I fell out laughing. The experience was so rewarding to me I volunteered to help out with chores around the farm, such as feeding animals or stacking hay in the barn, despite the blistering summer heat. (Upstate New York could freeze like the Arctic in winter, but the summer heat was sometimes brutal and oppressive.) My emotional balloon was quickly deflated when Meekah told me all the cows, including the one I called Mary, were slaughtered for meat. I assumed they were family pets like Boomer. For the duration of my stay, I refused to eat meat and I viewed Joe and Patty as executioners.

Getting By However I Could

One evening, I remember snippets of a conversation that intrigued me. The adults gabbed and sipped iced tea inside the kitchen while I crashed in the living room. The girls were outside on the porch. I heard Mrs. Woodson ask, "Anyone you know going to that march in Washington?"

Patty said, "I hear it's going to be a big one."

Lots of Negroes in my neighborhood are going," Mrs. Woodson said. "Got a bus leaving from Buffalo. Too bad I waited so long to make plans. Now it's too late."

Joe replied, "We ain't got the time nor the money. My old car won't hardly make it to Syracuse."

"Sure wish we could go," Patty said, "but this farm keeps us tied here. Our spirits will be there."

Mrs. Woodson's voice filled with worry. "I hope Dr. King can do something to change life for us. I hope these children won't have to work as hard as we do."

Joe added, "You got that right."

On the day we left for home, I thanked Joe and Patty for their kindness. They tried to hug me but I shied away. Affection was not a part of my life. Although I enjoyed my visit, I continued to believe Joe and Patty were murderers because they killed cows. As we pulled off onto the driveway, I flashed a phony smile and waved good-bye. I only started to eat meat again when Mrs. Woodson assured me it came from the store and not from the cows.

As time for the march on Washington approached, my neighborhood overflowed with excitement. You could see a craving for change in people's faces and hear hope for better days in their voices. Everyone rooted for Dr. King. He was our hero. A man from the local Negro church recruited George to hand out free pictures of Dr. King, which most people, including Mrs. Woodson, proudly displayed in their homes. I was sad we were not going, but I was unaware the march would make history.

On the afternoon of the march, George came over. All of us huddled inside the stuffy living room, glued to the television set. The window was wide open but the air was stagnant. I glanced out the window and there was not a soul in sight, a rarity in my neighborhood on a hot, sunny afternoon. We were flabbergasted by the hundreds of thousands of people who showed up in Washington. Negroes from every corner of the United States were there. I was surprised to see a substantial number of white people there, too. It gave me a renewed sense of hope that perhaps change was possible and I might live to see it.

As Dr. King delivered his historic speech, we became spellbound by his fiery passion. We sat there, completely speechless. I felt chills tingle all over my body, in spite of the sizzling heat. Mrs. Woodson's hands trembled as Dr. King spoke about change. George sat on the edge of the sofa and gripped his hands together. I saw Mr. Woodson's light brown face glisten with sweat. If Dr. King could not open doors for us, then I suspected we would always find them closed. At the end of his fiery speech, we all were too choked up to talk. As Mrs. Woodson's shoulders heaved, tears crawled down her cheeks. George and Mr. Woodson took turns hugging Mrs. Woodson. The girls and I had watery eyes, but we held in our emotions.

That night, I went to bed at nine o'clock as usual, but I could not sleep. The weather had been a sticky mix of intense heat and humidity. Without a fan to keep me cool, I sat up in bed and stared at the star-filled heavens, believing that I, too, would be "free at last" someday—free from foster care and maybe even free from segregation.

By the time I entered third grade, I was no longer a bony little girl with skinny legs. I ate three meals a day, but they were not very nutritious. Sometimes, we could only afford to eat macaroni and cheese or dumplings. As a result, I put on a few pounds. I did not have a roly-poly figure, but I was slightly plump. For a welcome change, Mrs. Woodson stopped making me have my hair straightened. I was thrilled to return to braids.

My third-grade teacher was not a nun but a young Negro woman with nut-brown skin named Mrs. Gooding. Initially, I was relieved someone colored would be my teacher. I assumed Dr. King's predictions had come to fruition. Maybe change was really in store for Negroes. My joy was short-lived, however. My teacher, whom I sarcastically nick-named Mrs. Goodtimes, was colder than the Buffalo winter. Every time her eyes shot daggers at me, which was often, I cringed. At every available opportunity, she poked fun at me, mocking my braided hairstyle, my chocolate skin color, and my awkwardness. Whenever she spoke to me, she addressed me as if I was a moron by using a slow, exaggerated voice. The small yet significant gains I worked hard to achieve in the second grade were quickly wiped out by her pompous and downright cruel behavior. I started to wet the bed almost every night, had trouble sleeping, and lost my appetite. I could barely crawl out of bed in the morning.

For the first time ever, I thought about dying; I was only nine years old. Death must have provide me with some peace of mind. I considered running away. I knew Canada was not far away. Maybe it could be a promised land for me, as it had been for runaway slaves. As soon as I realized I would get caught, though, I gave up that idea.

I thought about pleading with Mrs. Woodson to help me, but I doubted she would believe another Negro woman could make my life so utterly miserable. More importantly, Mrs. Woodson was not a demonstrative person, and she rarely challenged anyone. I began to fantasize again, and confided in Sophie because I knew she would listen. I felt as if I was losing my grip on reality.

I had developed a keen interest in basketball and followed my favorite teams, in particular the New York Knicks, all the way through the NBA finals. On occasion, I watched *The Twilight Zone*, but Rod Serling's eerie programs ripped me away from my studies. To shield myself from my teacher's mockery, I began to work overtime to understand my lessons. I sat at the kitchen table night after night, poring over my books, and I gave up watching television, except on weekends.

During class, I never raised my hand, even when I knew the answer. I was terrified the wicked witch would belittle me; when she did, some of my classmates would usually join in. Even her son, who was not very smart, derided me.

I failed almost all of my classes, and my frail self-esteem felt like shards of glass strewn about a dump site. I will never forget when the teacher boldly announced I had failed another test. She held up my paper with a big red F scrawled across the top and waved it in front of my face. I mustered up every ounce of my self-control to avoid biting her hand. Instead, I surged out of the room and headed straight to the girl's bathroom, where the floodgates finally opened. For the first time, I bawled in public for more than fifteen minutes, when I was interrupted by another teacher, who must have heard my sobs and came in to investigate. She squeezed my hand and gently asked, "What's wrong, honey?"

I should have told the truth, but I assumed doing so would only make matters worse for me. So I got a grip on myself and fed her a lie. I said that I felt sick. She moistened a few paper towels and told me to wash my face. Then she accompanied me to the principal's office, where they called Mrs. Woodson and asked her to pick me up because I appeared to be very ill.

On the walk home, Mrs. Woodson asked, "Should I get you to a doctor? You don't look so good."

"No ma'am, I'll be OK."

"But the teacher said you were sick."

"I was, but now I'm better."

"You sure?"

"Yes."

The minute I walked through the front door, I sprinted toward my room with such speed I stumbled up the stairs. I scraped and bruised my knee but the pain was insignificant compared to the emotional upheaval I had experienced. I thought about slashing my wrists with a pair of scissors but was stopped by my intense fear of blood. Experts assert suicide is uncommon in children, but I definitely had suicidal thoughts. I saw death as one way out of my unhappy life.

The television set opened up the troubled world around me. I remember sitting on the sofa, drenched in fear, watching news footage of policemen in the South breaking up civil rights marches with fire hoses. I could hardly believe the cops used attack dogs on everyday people peacefully protesting for change. I thought about Boomer next door, and he was such a well-mannered dog. This was my first exposure to viscous dogs and I was frightened by what I saw. Sometimes having access to the television was more troubling than enjoyable.

In November 1963, Negroes dealt with another shattering blow. The principal came over the loudspeaker at school and made an unexpected announcement: "President Kennedy is dead."

Although JFK was not revered by Negroes in the same way as Dr. King, Negroes had faith he would support civil rights legislation. JFK's sudden death temporarily damaged that dream. Some people in my neighborhood wept openly about the president's death. They worried another president might not favor the changes sought by Dr. King and his followers. It turned out better than anyone could have imagined when President Johnson took office.

Christmas approached, but my dismal experiences at school robbed me of any holiday spirit. I stopped visiting Boomer. Mrs. Woodson, as always, attempted to make a nice holiday for us, but my heart was not in it. I was stuck in a quagmire. Meekah even asked me what was wrong, but I still did not trust her so I kept my sadness to myself. Heidi, as always, was in her own world.

In late January, as my birthday approached, I asked Mrs. Woodson, "Why don't we celebrate mine like Meekah and Heidi?" Heidi celebrated her birthday in June and Meekah's was in October. On both occasions, Mrs. Woodson bought each of them a special cake from the Polish bakery and one small present. Some years, Mrs. Woodson threw birthday parties for the girls. Every year on my birthday, she would bake me an unappetizing cake and give me a card.

Mrs. Woodson said, "Since your birthday is so close to Christmas, I have no money left."

"Nothing?"

She said, "I buy you an extra present at Christmas time to make for your birthday being in January."

On the surface, I accepted her reasoning, but deep down I believed she did not like me. Without a store-bought cake, I saw my birthday as another meaningless day.

Every child at school was welcomed to bring in a bag of candy to share with the class on his or her birthday. When I told Mrs. Woodson, she balked and said, "I can't be buying that much candy."

"The other kids do."

"I don't have that kind of money."

That may have been true, but once in a while I thought she harbored an unexplained grudge against me. Again, the color issue came up. Meekah and Heidi, both fair-skinned, appeared to receive benefits I was denied. I grew up resenting my dark brown skin and viewed it as an evil curse.

Toward the end of the third grade, my teacher suggested that I be left back again. The principal noticed my failures, and my teacher told her I was retarded and should be placed in a special school. I was ordered to undergo a series of tests administered at another Catholic school. Even Mrs. Woodson agreed with the teacher's assessment and concluded I was retarded. To everyone's surprise, including my own, the tests revealed I was not the village idiot. They showed above-average intelligence, and a learning disorder that would eventually become known as dyslexia. Treatments then were primitive, and I continued to have trouble in school. But at least I knew I was not stupid. I think my teacher was shocked to find out I was not totally inept. Over the last few weeks of the school year, she ended her sadistic game of making me the laughingstock of the class. I was overjoyed when school was over and I found out Mrs. Goodtimes had been transferred to another school.

At the end of summer, a Negro family named Mead purchased one of the last white-owned houses on the block. White flight had invaded the east side of Buffalo, as it had spread throughout most cities in the country. The neighborhood was now almost exclusively Negro, with the exception of a few elderly adults who chose to remain, one of whom was Mr. Pokorney from the bakery, who I later discovered was married to a Negro woman. My community was still very proud of itself, but most people eked out a living on meager salaries, barely surviving from one paycheck to the next. The social taboo against single motherhood and welfare had lightened, too. Divorce was rare, but it was no longer considered a disgrace.

Regardless of the social changes resulting from the civil rights movement, poverty, unemployment, and overcrowded and inferior schools were still pervasive throughout black neighborhoods in Buffalo. The loss of unskilled factory jobs compounded the despair because so many blacks relied on that form of employment. Homes slowly deteriorated and fell into disrepair. More litter was strewn about the streets. Some people stopped sweeping the sidewalks in front of their homes. Abandoned cars popped up around the neighborhood, creating an unsightly mess. Stray dogs and cats roamed the streets, foraging for food. The city also added to the neglect. Garbage was not picked up as often and streets gutted by the snow-removal trucks were hardly ever repaired. Bit by bit, the neighborhood slipped into decline at a time when most of us were holding onto Dr. King's dream for a better life.

Mrs. Mead unexpectedly showed up one day to introduce herself. Mrs. Woodson must have been in a good mood because she invited her in for a cup of coffee. I sat at the kitchen table working on my reading. Mrs. Mead said, "I was in college but I married Mr. Mead. I dropped out when I got pregnant. Some day I'm going back."

Mrs. Woodson said, "What for? You got a family now."

Mrs. Mead replied, "I want to become a teacher."

While Mrs. Mead drank her coffee, she must have seen the puzzled look on my face. She said, "You need help with your homework?"

I practically jumped all over the woman and snatched her offer right away. Because she lived down the block, Mrs. Woodson said, "It'll be OK for you go there a few times after school."

Shortly after I started the fourth grade, a letter from Catholic Charities addressed to me arrived. Although the envelope had my name on it, Mrs. Woodson opened it first. She always intercepted and read the few pieces I received, or she insisted I read my mail out loud to her. Mrs. Woodson knocked on my door, and I said, "Come in."

I had put down my books and taken off my shoes.

Mrs. Woodson said, "You got a letter from Catholic Charities."

Assuming it was nothing to worry about, I shrugged my shoulders and started to remove my socks. What could it be, I wondered, besides another official notice my caseworker had resigned?

I replied, "Did you read it?"

"Yes, I did."

"What'd they say?"

"You are legally free for adoption. I thought you'd want to know."

Lots of mixed-up feelings gyrated through my mind. I knew both Meekah and Heidi had been freed for adoption years ago, although they still waited for permanent homes. I figured I had a greater chance of being struck by lightning than of finding a family who wanted to adopt me. I felt sweat dripping down my neck. I threw up a defensive wall to protect myself. "Thank you."

"That's all you have to say?"

"Yes ma'am."

Mrs. Woodson stormed out of the room, behaving like a hurt little girl. She often got into these states where she refused to speak. Now and then, she held her tongue for days at a time. Why did she leave in a huff?

Adoption agencies often threw up impediments for Negroes who wanted to adopt. Some of the many reasons given to prohibit Negroes from adopting included: We did not make enough money. We did not have the extra room. We were too old. Adoption subsidies were rare, and if they were available, Negro families most often failed to qualify. Home ownership was also a qualification. For those who had the financial means to buy a home, finding a good one was almost impossible. Prior to the fair housing laws of the 1960s, Negro families had no legal means of redress to fight realtors who refused to show them decent houses. As a result of lopsided adoption policies and the insidious effects of racism, loving, stable families who could have provided homes to children in my situation were summarily rejected by both public and private adoption agencies.

Throughout the fourth grade, I studied with Mrs. Mead. The extra attention paid off in the classroom. I was not an A student, but my grades picked up and I was more comfortable reading. I rejected Mrs. Gooding's claims I was stupid and would never amount to anything except a domestic or a clerk at the five-and-dime.

Mrs. Mead had two children of her own—a teenage son named John and a daughter my age named Cassandra, whom everyone called Sandy. Over time, I relaxed my guard just a tad and became friendly with Sandy. She attempted to teach me how to play Double Dutch, but I was clumsy so we both agreed I should try something else. As an alternative, we walked around the working-class neighborhood together. We passed modest one story, wood-frame homes on tiny squares of property. A coat of fresh paint could have improved the appearance of some of these slightly shabby homes. Used sedans were parked inside one-car driveways. Lawns were generally manicured but several begged to be mowed.

When we tired of walking, we stayed in her room and read stories. The Meads' house was loaded with books of all kinds. I was astonished when I saw Sandy read books written by Negroes.

One afternoon, while we were drinking sugary-sweet lemonade in her kitchen, Sandy said, "Why can't I ever come to your house?"

I could hardly swallow, so I prepared myself to lie. Mrs. Woodson never allowed me or the girls to entertain at home. She never offered any reasons, but we did not challenge her. Perhaps Mrs. Woodson was trying to protect herself from humiliation. A number of the neighborhood kids belittled us because we lived with someone older, someone they viewed as a grandmother figure. In those days, few children were brought up by their grandparents. In addition to Mrs. Woodson's unyielding ways, I was loath to admit I was ashamed of her. She often went outside in a housedress or wore her hair in sponge curlers draped with a hairnet. I thought she looked so low class and I felt embarrassed by her, but I would never admit my true feelings to anyone except Sophie. So I danced around the point and said, "Well, I'll ask and see if it's OK. I'll let you know."

I enjoyed Sandy's company, but our relationship never moved beyond casual. The fear Catholic Charities might move me to another home loomed inside my head. I had to shield myself from any potential loss. Gradually, Sandy and I drifted apart. About a year later, the Meads sold their house and moved to the Midwest. I heard Mr. Mead took a job in Chicago. I never saw them again.

Mrs. Mead filled a significant void in my life, and I remain grateful to this day for all the help she provided me. I imagine she pursued her dreams and finished college. If she ever became a teacher, I firmly believe she was wonderful at it.

By the end of the fourth grade, the world around me was in a whirlwind. Change was everywhere. Instead of being referred to as Negroes, the term "black" had become popular. Black power and self-defense "by any means necessary" were advocated not only by the Black Panthers but also by Malcolm X. In February 1965, Malcolm X was assassinated. On top of this popular leader's loss and the chaos that ensued, the inequities associated with the bloody war in Vietnam were like festering wounds as well.

Getting By However I Could

Where I lived, young men usually had no way avoid the draft because they could not afford college. The same was true for white men who came from working-class or poverty-stricken areas. Those barely out of high school were drafted and shipped off to fight an ugly war in a far-away place. Lots of people in my community were caught up with the civil rights movement. They wanted to eat an entire meal, not accept scraps handed to them. Consequently, they were unable to see the war in Vietnam had a damaging effect on thousands of young black men without ways to beat the draft. Black people claimed protesting the war was white man's work.

Some young men and women wore their hair in large Afros and wore African-styled clothing. Some of them adhered to the separatist policies of the Black Panthers. The Panthers may have used a radical approach to spread their message, but, like Malcolm X, they essentially wanted equality. They were tired of police brutality, discrimination, and inferior treatment.

The girls and I wanted to switch our hairstyles to the popular Afro, but Mrs. Woodson promptly said no. She insisted only radicals wore Afros and we were not radicals. Moreover, she acted as if the Black Panthers were axe murderers. Whenever the black revolutionaries Angela Davis and Huey Newton appeared on television, she immediately changed the channel. She preferred we model ourselves after Donna Reed, someone she said was more suitable. I think the Black Panthers frightened Mrs. Woodson because they were not obsequious around white people the way she was.

I was caught up in the changing environment, too, yet I was unsure how to adapt to the world in which I lived. Mostly, I felt blue and sunk further into depression. It was hard to feel excitement about black power when I felt so powerless over my own life.

My sad feelings were exacerbated when I found out Boomer had been run over by a taxi driver who was speeding down the block. When Boomer's owner told me the bad news, I could feel tears form in my eyes. I held them back and simply said, "I'm sorry."

That mutt's death sliced pain through my heart. He was not even my dog, but I had grown to appreciate him for what he could do best—wildly flap his tail every time he saw me. From that point on, I turned the other way whenever I passed by the empty doghouse in his front yard. Boomer's owner said they were so broken up by the dog's death they could not see themselves getting another pet, and for the rest of my time with the Woodsons, they never did.

My relationship with Mrs. Woodson continued to be adversarial. She insisted again and again I should refer to her as mom. She had the same feud with the girls, and they must have caved in at some point because they called her mom. To keep the peace, I tried to comply, but every time I uttered the M word, I stammered. Eventually, I gave up because I could not play along with what I viewed as a foolish game. I knew Mrs. Woodson was not my mother, and I had trouble pretending she was. On occasion, I had thoughts about adoption and what it would be like to live with the Woodsons on a permanent basis, but I abandoned that idea. I doubted I would ever feel like this was my home. In an odd way, I had grown used to the nomadic lifestyle, and I no longer believed I would ever find a permanent home.

As my depression expanded, so did my need for solitude. I had trouble facing anyone. I retreated to the basement, despite the presence of rats, and took over a household chore no one wanted: I volunteered to iron everyone's clothes. Mr. Woodson always insisted on wearing only starched shirts to work, and I willingly complied. From a neighbor who operated a laundry service for affluent Buffalo residents, I learned how to starch a shirt to the point it felt like cardboard. The aging woman invited me to her home and offered me a snack of milk and cookies. Like a schoolteacher explaining a new subject, she stood in front of her washing machine. "Child, first thing is to get yourself a box of plain white starch available in the grocery store."

"What does it look like?"

"Honey, it's white stuff inside a blue box. Don't be worrying about what it looks like. Go down the aisle with all them washing products. You'll see what I'm talking about."

"What's next?"

"Toss in a good-sized chunk of the starch to the washing machine. Make sure to leave out the clothes that don't need starching. Lord have mercy, child, one day this doctor's undershorts got mixed up with the shirts. He nearly liked to have a heart attack."

I paid close attention to her instructions, knowing that if I messed up, Mrs. Woodson wouldn't be too pleased with me. I assumed R. C. would be annoyed, too, should I screw up his shirts. I asked, "What should I do when the rinse cycle is over?"

The laundry lady said, "Hang all the shirts out to dry. Then, sprinkle the shirts with water and roll them inside a damp towel. Ask Mrs. Woodson if she got some old towels. When you're done, store them stuffed towels in the refrigerator until time to press them. To make the shirts extra crispy, apply a steaming hot iron. A good hot iron gives you the best results."

When Mrs. Woodson first saw me place towels full of her husband's shirts in the fridge, she looked at me almost cross-eyed. She had never heard of this method. Mrs. Woodson only used spray starch. After I had starched his shirts for a few weeks, Mr. Woodson asked me to cut down on the starch because he claimed some of his shirts started to feel too stiff and made his neck itch.

Mrs. Woodson said I was weird because I derived pleasure from ironing, but this routine task kept my mind off my unhappiness. Using the dank basement also afforded me the privacy I sorely missed. Except for the rats scurrying from one hiding place to the next, I was alone. Like many kids did when their parents were out, I blasted the radio and listened to loud rock music, something Mrs. Woodson never permitted. I also liked the popular Motown sound, and I enjoyed belting out a few tunes with Diana Ross and the Supremes, Martha and the Vandellas, Smokey Robinson, and the Spinners. On days when I was introspective, I listened to the more sedate folk sounds of Peter, Paul, and Mary and Simon and Garfunkel. I sometimes thought Paul Simon wrote the song "Sounds of Silence" just for me. I wanted so much to belong, but with whom?

My fifth-grade teacher showed an interest in me. Sister Sophia, a middle-aged nun with striking green eyes and an easy smile, was one of the few teachers who insisted I could do better. Sister Sophia told me to believe in myself. She acknowledged my difficulties, but made me believe I was still capable of learning. She encouraged me to participate in after- school activities, which I had thus far avoided. I think Sister Sophia assumed I shied away from school clubs because of my race, but that was not an issue. I was more concerned the other students would make fun of me because I had no family.

I finally agreed to join the basketball team. My body was awkward, yet I managed to hold my own. I was a decent player with a good eye for the ball. Our competition was local Catholic schools, and we played about two games a week over a three-month period. We were strongly encouraged to invite our families to each game. I asked Mrs. Woodson, but every time she came up with excuses. Proud of my accomplishments, I was depressed no one in the audience rooted specially for me. The team made me feel wanted, but those good feelings shriveled up as soon as I left the gym. My life felt like a jigsaw puzzle, one with pieces never seeming to fit.

After a game one evening, I ambled home along the darkened streets thinking about my birth mother. All of a sudden, I clamped my teeth together. I felt the anger twisting my insides apart. I was enraged she had walked out without signing anything. She had abandoned me for a reason, but I refused to forgive what she had done.

Eight

The End of the Line

As fifth grade wound down, Mrs. Woodson said, "Girls, I have something to tell you." From her sour face, I thought we were being kicked out. "You're going to summer camp this year."

I had wanted to attend a summer camp for years, but nothing ever came of my requests. Catholic Charities had a limited budget for summer recreation for its foster care program. This summer, however, would be different. A young black doctor who recently set up practice in Buffalo had made a sizable donation to Catholic Charities so all foster children could attend a two-week summer camp. Due to our age differences, the girls and I were assigned to different camps in the Catskill region.

The sprawling camp was a mix of old, shaky wooden cabins and outdoor tents. We had a choice to sleep inside or outside. Sleeping outside did not appeal to me, so I went inside to check out the living arrangements. In front of me were barracks-style bunk beds made of aging wood. Boards were missing in a few places across the wide floor. I smacked one of the paper-thin mattresses and a huge cloud of dust spread into the air. The showers and toilets were outdoors. The cavernous cafeteria-style dining hall had one long table for the campers and a few smaller ones for staff. A military-style kitchen with pots the size of buckets was off to the side.

The End of the Line

I met a young woman counselor, who I presumed was in her early twenties. Penny had dazzling green eyes, dirty blond hair, and a smile so warm it easily melted my nervous feelings. She must have realized from my timorous behavior I needed a friend. Until she extended herself, I had spent much of my time at camp alone. Most days, I walked around the lake or sought refuge in the nearby woods, avoiding all group activities. Hungry mosquitoes feasted on my skin, making me itch most of the day. To pass the time, I collected rocks and studied the distinct features of each one. I was glad when Penny showed an interest in me.

A college student at Syracuse University, Penny was like an angel to me. She was so kind and gentle I momentarily let down my guard. We spent long hours talking about foster care, Mrs. Woodson, and my uncertain future. For a brief time, I felt like I had a big sister. At the end of my two-week stay, I felt sad to leave her, but Penny and I exchanged addresses. We promised to stay in touch.

I wrote her a long letter as soon as I returned home. Little did I know my new friendship was threatened from the time I received my first letter. Mrs. Woodson frowned at me as she handed me Penny's missive. "Who's this from?"

"Penny, a friend I made at camp. She said we could write letters to each other."

"Read it to me. What does she say? Nice girls share their letters with their parents."

I felt violated. "But the letter is for me."

Mrs. Woodson pouted. "I said open it."

And so I read the letter, line by line, out loud to Mrs. Woodson. I left out the part where Penny asked how I was getting along with Mrs. Woodson. Mostly, she wrote about school and how much she enjoyed the university.

Mrs. Woodson asked, "Is this girl in college?"

I nodded that she was.

"You be careful. What's a smart girl want with you anyway?"

Mrs. Woodson's disapproval did not deter me from writing to Penny. I told Penny what had happened and not to mention Mrs. Woodson by name in future letters. When I asked Mrs. Woodson for a stamp, she said no. So I carried my envelope to school, and a nun agreed to mail it for me.

The End of the Line

Once in a while, Penny called me. Because the only phone was inside the kitchen, Mrs. Woodson took a seat at the table every time I received a call. My conversations were extremely limited. After I hung up, Mrs. Woodson always asked, "What did she say?" I wonder how she would have reacted if I had received a call from a boy.

Perhaps Mrs. Woodson was jealous of my relationship with Penny. I admired Penny in a way I had never felt about Mrs. Woodson. In fairness to Mrs. Woodson, though, my relationship with Penny was on a different plane. The two women clearly had different roles in my life.

Penny offered me kind words and understanding. More importantly, she accepted me as I was. Conversely, Penny was not the one to impose discipline, a harsh reality in every young person's life. Mrs. Woodson stretched the monthly stipend to last for thirty days. She shopped, cooked, and maintained order around the house. With all her imperfections, Mrs. Woodson could never be compensated for the guidance and values she instilled in us. No one, including me, ever thanked her.

Had Penny and I lived together, I imagine our relationship would have been different. We would have seen each other's flaws and perhaps I would not have elevated her on such a pedestal. Over time, Penny and I gradually drifted apart. But I was thankful our lives had crossed and for the little bit of solace she had given me.

I was far from comfortable with my life, but I accepted I had nowhere else to go. Neither the girls nor I had found permanent homes. Long-term foster care looked like it was our only option, but I still held out for a miracle. I secretly maintained my imaginary friendship with Sophie, who had changed little over time. Mrs. Woodson, when she heard me talking to Sophie, stopped poking fun at me and no longer insisted I was touched upstairs. Sometimes, I even prayed. I kept hoping and trusting, for better days had to be ahead.

Mrs. Woodson finally signed for a library card, which I put to good use at once. The public library became my second home, a place I visited several times a week. Her paranoia about me losing books prevented me from ever checking any out, but I perused lots of material while I was there. I became fascinated with the *National Geographic,* dreaming about the exotic lands in the magazine. I also devoured books and magazines about houses and sports, imagining myself living in one of those fancy homes with the stately columns out front. But my house would be more than something to look at. It would be filled with gregarious people, tail-wagging fluffy dogs, and lots of love and caring. Every so often, I became so caught up in my daydreams that I spent hours in the library without reading a thing. Contrary to Mrs. Woodson's fears, I was never lynched. In fact, no one seemed to notice me as I came and went from the library.

In the sixth grade my marks improved a little bit, and I no longer failed any of my classes. I had to study for hours every night, but the blood, sweat, and tears seemed to pay off. For a change, I temporarily let go of the feeling I was a nobody. I believed there must be life after foster care.

The growing civil rights movement stirred a number of social changes, yet I imagined it would take bulldozers to knock down people's attitudes toward blacks. Many of my teachers and classmates treated me in a cordial manner, but few of them showed any real faith in me. Consequently, some black students did not produce much and developed a lackadaisical attitude toward school. With virtually no guidance to carry me along, I reached deep down inside for the courage to keep moving ahead.

My art teacher noticed I had a good eye for drawing. She suggested I practice at home. Armed with this unusual compliment, I took up the advice. When Mrs. Woodson saw me drawing at the table one afternoon, I thought she was about to have a fit. I could almost see the steam seep from her pores. She grabbed one of my drawings, waved it in the air, and said, "What're you doing this for? You're supposed to be doing homework."

"But this is homework. My teacher said I should practice my drawing."

"How many black people do you know who make a living by drawing?" Mrs. Woodson pushed my sketches aside and said, "Don't let those nuns put this gibberish into your head. Drawing won't get you a job."

"But . . ."

"No more of this." She snatched my papers and tossed them into the trash before walking away.

Yet another of my dreams was hammered on. I told my teacher what happened, but her reaction was lukewarm. She insisted Mrs. Woodson knew best. To this day, I regret I never had more faith in myself. With proper training and education, who knows what sort of artist I might have become? I might even have become an architect.

That same school year, I let down my guard a little more and tried out for the glee club. Bored at home, I needed an outlet for my energy, and the nun in charge invited me to join. When I sang at practice no one cupped their hands over their ears, so I guessed my voice wasn't that bad. Mrs. Woodson discouraged me from singing at home, but I was undeterred. I needed to feel as if I could do something right, even if I was not the next Aretha Franklin.

The school planned a special talent show for parents and family members to attend a few months later. I was supposed to sing along with a boy who played the guitar. Walking onto the stage, I choked when I saw a large room packed with a full audience. There were probably a hundred people there. I could hardly move and was completely unable to sing. My heart pounded so fast I thought I might faint. I flew off the stage. The nun in charge tried to console me by explaining how lots of people are afraid to perform in front of crowds. She suggested I join my parents in the audience. When I told her I did not have any, she looked as if she might cry. I said, "Don't be upset." I assured her I was capable of getting home by myself.

Late one winter afternoon, an emotional earthquake unexpectedly shook my world. The weather had been particularly fierce. Snowstorm after snowstorm blanketed the city. The near-zero temperature readings made Buffalo feel like it was permanently frozen. For days at a time, the winds howled, forcing the windows to shake and rattle. The icy winds seeped through the cracks in the window frames, making the house feel like an igloo even when the oil burner was on full blast. If I had to be abandoned, I was sorry not to be left in a warmer climate.

Mrs. Woodson stood by the stove preparing a dinner of fried chicken, corn bread, and turnip greens when the telephone rang. I was at the table, trying to study. I also wanted to take advantage of the warmth in the kitchen. The minute Mrs. Woodson greeted the caller, I knew something was wrong, gravely wrong. Mrs. Woodson dropped the phone and buried her face inside her hands. She sobbed so loudly Mr. Woodson, who had been in the driveway shoveling snow, must have heard her. He appeared in the kitchen within seconds, still clad in boots, hat, and winter coat.

In between her piercing wails, Mrs. Woodson's voice cracked dozens of times until she finally blurted out the police had called to say George had been killed. A stranded motorist caught his attention. He stopped to offer help but was hit by a tractor-trailer that skidded on a patch of black ice and spun out of control. George died instantly from massive internal injuries.

For the next few days, the girls and I prepared our own meals. We stayed out of Mrs. Woodson's way as much as possible, realizing she was heart-broken. Mr. Woodson had to make all the funeral arrangements because his wife could not stop crying. George's death hit her like a train. She was simply unable to cope.

Once Mr. Woodson returned to his factory job, Mrs. Woodson was left alone. Prior to George's death, she had spent most of her day shopping or cleaning house. Although she never admitted it, Mrs. Woodson became hooked on one of the soap operas. I suppose the afternoon drama series kept her mind focused on something else besides the loss of her son.

Now that George was gone, she operated on a very short fuse. Every little mistake we made caused a major uproar. She scolded me for trivial matters, including not finishing all the food on my plate. She slammed down the phone whenever one of Meekah's boyfriends called. She became incensed when I asked her for money to buy starch. I had asked her to pick up a can when she went shopping, but she forgot. She threw a few quarters at me and demanded I buy it myself.

I felt sorry for Mrs. Woodson, realizing she agonized from this terrible loss. Most evenings, when I cleaned up after dinner, she sat at the table with a blank look covering her face, staring into space. While I sat at the kitchen table completing my lessons, I could hear Mrs. Woodson's pitiful wails coming from the living room. Each morning when I showed up for breakfast, Mrs. Woodson was already there, sitting at the table with puffy eyes. She stayed in the same pair of pajamas for days at a time. It seemed as if she stopped eating altogether and filled up only on coffee. She barely spoke to anyone, and the girls and I fixed our own breakfast. Meekah and Heidi otherwise stayed in their room as much as possible. It seemed as if we all felt locked inside Mrs. Woodson's sad storm. She had given up on living and we were unsure how to react.

George had been a stranger to me, but I knew how much the Woodsons loved him. The three had been a very close family. He was a good son, too. Without fail, he remembered his parents' birthdays, wedding anniversary, and special holidays by showering them with cards and gifts. Often, he dropped by just to chat.

As I watched Mrs. Woodson reel from George's death, it dawned on me how different I was from other people. Because I had never been that close to anyone, I had trouble accepting death could make someone so absolutely despondent. I also had doubts death could get to me in the way it had ripped Mrs. Woodson apart. As a child, I had always wanted to share my emotions. I daydreamed about having heart-to-heart family talks with a caring adult like the television character Beaver did with his mom and dad. The powerful fear of separation always stifled my true feelings, and I never opened up to anyone except Boomer the dog and Sophie.

By the time spring arrived, Mrs. Woodson slowly crawled out of mourning. She took a more active role in meal preparation. Perhaps she noticed we girls had all dropped a few pounds. The atmosphere at dinner was still cold, but at least she no longer wore pajamas all the time.

Out of the blue at school one day, a nun approached me about weekly piano lessons, all for fifty cents per session. I was shocked by her offer, because I had never expressed an interest in music. That same nun, whom I had for math class the previous year, knew I struggled to make sense of long division and fractions. Could there be a connection between music and my trouble with classes, one I overlooked? The nun suggested I should consider *all* my career options when thinking about the future. I had not yet mastered the art of reading between the lines, so I missed her empty-headed point. In retrospect, perhaps she thought she was doing me a favor by teaching me to sing and play the piano rather than encouraging me to use my mind to make a living.

The End of the Line

Out of curiosity I agreed, but told her my allowance was only one dollar per week and I was not ready to part with half of it for piano lessons. All the lessons were held in the school auditorium. Once I had taken a few lessons, the nun picked out a new a song to work on. I was disgusted when she belted out the word "darkie" with tremendous vigor. I felt like shredding the sheet music, but I was so afraid of my own shadow I did not speak up. My teacher must have noticed the change in my behavior—every time she sang the word "darkie" my eyes dropped to the floor and my voice became tinged with sorrow. As an alternate, she substituted the word "colored" in place of darkie, yet the change did nothing to appease my hurt feelings. I thought she had the sensitivity of a rock, and the following week, I quit studying the piano. I was fifty cents richer and my stronger self-esteem remained intact.

One sunny afternoon in late March, I was on my way from the public library when I stopped inside a luncheonette for an order of french fries and vinegar, my old favorite. On my way out, I ran into a handsome, young black man who looked like he was about eighteen. We exchanged curious glances, but since I failed to recognize him I kept walking. Then I heard my name and spun around. The young man turned out to be Eddie, one of the foster boys who shared the Chesters' home with me. Eddie broke out into an ear-to-ear grin and shook my hand. "Hey, remember me? I'm Eddie. We used to live with Mrs. Chester over on Elm Street."

"Yeah! Hi! How are you?" I felt a smile coming on, but kept a lid on my emotions, limiting my enthusiasm to a modest grin.

Eddie must have picked up on the distance I kept from people. He stepped back a few feet and said, "My brother and I went back home. I got into the college here in Buffalo. Won a scholarship. . . . So, how are you? One day, Mrs. Chester said you were gone, but never told us what happened. Mark and I always wondered what became of you."

I hated to dredge up old wounds, but I liked Eddie and I wanted him to know the truth. When I explained the nature of the move, Eddie hung his head down and grabbed my hand. "Hey, I'm sorry."

I changed the subject. I had no intention of crying in front of Eddie. "How's your little brother?"

"Mark. He's good. He's into running track. Me and him are still real tight."

I checked my watch and realized I had to get home for dinner. I had not told Mrs. Woodson I would be late. Because she was always on edge, I wanted to avoid a hassle when I walked through the door. Also, I was still jealous Eddie had a close relationship with his younger brother. "I have to go home now. It was nice seeing you again."

Eddie gently touched my elbow and said, "Hey, why don't you and me and my brother get together some time? We can maybe have lunch or something."

I actually liked the idea of having lunch with these two young guys. I felt we shared a unique bond. I asked Eddie for his phone number and said, "I'll give you a call. I have to check in with Mrs. Woodson first." Whenever a boy was involved, the girls and I had to first secure her permission.

Eddie never attempted to hug me. Instead, he grinned and gave me a high five. "I'm sure Mark would like to see you, too. I'll wait for you to call."

For the next few days, I looked for the courage to ask Mrs. Woodson for permission to see Eddie and Mark. Every time I thought about asking her, my stomach became jittery and my legs felt like rubber. She was still touchy most of the time, so I held out for the right moment. Realizing no time was ever the right time, I pushed aside my anxiety and popped the question: "Um, um, can I please call this boy named Eddie?"

Mrs. Woodson grilled me with those same old questions: "Who is Eddie? Where does he live? What's his mother's name? What does he want to see you for? How old is he? Where did you meet this young man?"

I was caught off guard because my pending date with Eddie was not really a date. I had no romantic interest in him. I simply wanted to reconnect with him and Mark. I counted to ten and then said, "He's this boy who I used to live with when I was with the Chesters. I ran into him the other day. He suggested that him, his brother, and me get together for lunch."

Mrs. Woodson acted as if I had asked to have lunch with an inmate on death row. "You can't go out with strange boys. Who knows what will happen?"

"But . . ." My voice tapered off when I noticed she stood next to me with her hands firmly planted on her hips, looking like she was ready for a battle. "You're right. I won't go. Sorry I asked."

Mrs. Woodson waved her finger at me and held her stare. "No strange boys."

Inside my room, I took from my pocket the piece of paper that contained Eddie's phone number. I crumbled it and tossed it out the window. I was so mad I could feel my hands tremble. How could she do this to me? I should have lied and met Eddie and Mark anyway, but I figured that, if Mrs. Woodson found out I went behind her back, I would be in big trouble. I never ran into Eddie again and was sorry I never told him why.

Besides the emotional upheaval young girls faced, my body was beginning to change. Mrs. Woodson seemed unprepared to deal with my budding maturity. She acted as if I was damned.

I also was out of touch with changes associated with adolescence. My breasts and hips had become fuller. One day when no one was around, Mrs. Woodson quietly handed me a few bras and ordered me to wear them. Although I could have used a demonstration on technique, I figured out how to wear these odd- looking garments. I felt strangled by a bra but I offered no resistance when Mrs. Woodson insisted all young girls had to wear them. Thank God she did not expect me to squeeze myself into a girdle like she did.

To complicate matters, I started to menstruate. Because I knew nothing about this bodily function, I assumed I was dying. I had once contracted a kidney infection and I presumed this was the cause of the blood in my underpants. Without anyone to confide in, I kept my flow shrouded in secrecy. I stuffed a thick wad of toilet paper in my drawers without knowing sanitary napkins could have done the job. My secret was safe until Mrs. Woodson found me doubled over in pain. I was still in the dark about the monthly flow, so I thought the end was near. Nothing, not even dairy products, had ever made me feel this bad. When I failed to show up for dinner one evening, Mrs. Woodson came to my room. She found me keeled over in bed, in tears.

"I'm dying. I think we better get the doctor."

"What's wrong?"

"My stomach hurts and I have blood in my panties."

Mrs. Woodson let out a sigh of relief. "Wait, I'll get you some aspirin."

Still in the dark, I asked, "Why am I so sick?"

"You'll get that way every month. Take aspirin when you don't feel so good. And I'll get you some napkins when I go to the store tomorrow."

"We have already napkins on the table."

Mrs. Woodson flashed a weak smile. "No, not them." In a tone barely above a whisper, she said, "They're called Kotex."

Moments later, she returned with two aspirin and a glass of water. She dashed out of my room without offering me an explanation of why I would feel so crummy each month. I thought about asking Meekah, but opted not to.

When I woke up the next morning, I discovered a blue box and a weird-looking elastic belt resting next to my bed along with a booklet entitled "Menstruation." I read the book, then figured out the art of wearing a sanitary napkin. The thick pad made it feel as if I had a small mattress stuck in between my legs. At breakfast, Mrs. Woodson averted her glance every time I tried to make eye contact. We never discussed menstruation. To uncover the truth, I stopped at the public library a few days later and looked up menstruation. I felt bad Mrs. Woodson treated it with such ignorance.

Just when I thought life had finally calmed down, another unexpected blow occurred, one that shattered lots of lives besides my own. I no longer believed menstruation would kill me. I was doing reasonably well in school. Mrs. Woodson was better and so was the weather. Another brutal winter had finally ended.

On April 4, 1968, we were all stunned by the news that Dr. Martin Luther King Jr. had been assassinated at the Lorraine Hotel in Memphis. We watched the news coverage of Dr. King's death. Perhaps Mrs. Woodson took the news harder because of George's recent loss, but she cried so hard she finally fled the room. The girls and I sat with our mouths agape as we continued to watch the horrifying news. I could hardly believe Dr. King was gone, really gone. He fought so hard and for so long to improve the lives of black people, which included me. In an instant, an assassin's bullet took away a beloved man from all of us.

The End of the Line

Over the next few days, chaos abounded in black neighborhoods of many cities. I was saddened by Dr. King's loss, but I was equally dismayed by the violence. Black people had tons of bottled-up anger from years of segregation, closed doors, and treatment as second-class citizens. Buffalo was relatively calm in comparison to Detroit in 1967 and Watts in 1965. The people in my community all mourned Dr. King's loss and felt angered by the man who shot him. For days on end, it seemed everyone congregated on their stoops and talked about the killing with their neighbors.

A week later, a special memorial service was planned for Dr. King at one of the Baptist churches in Buffalo. Mrs. Woodson gathered us together and we all attended this very sad service. I was left with the feeling Dr. King's death would eventually open up doors for children in my position. It was no longer a matter of if, but when.

Toward the end of dinner one evening, shortly after school ended, Mrs. Woodson said, "We're going to see my people again in Cortland."

I had gotten over the shock of cows going to the slaughterhouse and actually looked forward to the visit. Anything to get out of Buffalo for a while. I asked, "When do we leave?"

"First of July. R. C. has been tired lately. I think he needs a good rest." Mrs. Woodson wiped the perspiration from her face with a napkin. She waited until her husband walked away from the table. Staring at me, she said cautiously, "Don't go near the cows when we get there." She dropped her head and lowered her voice. "You know, if you have your thing."

Over the years, Mrs. Woodson had filled my head with lots of old wives' tales. She avoided black cats, never left the house on Friday the 13th, and thought the full moon made people crazy. But the warning about the cows and my "thing" thoroughly confused me.

"Why? What did I do?"

Mrs. Woodson tightly wrapped her arms around her waist. She stood next to me and cautioned me to "stay away from the cows if you have your period. You might cause the milk to spoil. Do as I say."

Again, I associated menstruation with a curse. I could not make the connection between my period and spoiled milk, but I knew I should heed her warnings, however puzzling they might be.

And so we arrived at the farm outside of Cortland on a bright, sunny afternoon after an uneventful three-hour drive from Buffalo. Prior to our departure, sixteen-year old Meekah told me she and Heidi preferred to stay in Buffalo with their friends, but Mrs. Woodson wouldn't even listen to their request. The girls seemed detached and uninterested in spending two weeks around a farm.

As we made our way into the large wooden farmhouse, Mrs. Woodson's sister Patty and her husband Joe graciously greeted us and told us to make ourselves feel at home. Because I did not have my period, I asked Joe if I could help with the cows. Mrs. Woodson gave me the evil eye and I returned it with a nod, confirming I was momentarily safe.

Over the previous few months, Mr. Woodson had dropped a few pounds. He no longer had the build of a football player. He also tired more easily and backed off when Joe suggested they go fishing at five o'clock the next morning. Mrs. Woodson nagged her husband to see a doctor, but he repeatedly said no every time she opened her mouth. At sixty years old, I surmised the backbreaking work at the plant wore him down.

One morning, Mr. Woodson woke up completely unable to move his left arm. His speech was slightly slurred and Mrs. Woodson panicked. Joe volunteered to drive Mr. and Mrs. Woodson to the big hospital in Syracuse, about a half-hour drive north on Interstate 81. Patty stayed to supervise me and the girls.

That evening I heard the car pull into the driveway. I noticed Mr. Woodson was not in the car. I could tell from the dazed look on Mrs. Woodson's face I would be greeted with bad news. In somber tones, Mrs. Woodson explained her husband had to remain in the hospital overnight for a few diagnostic tests because the doctor suspected he had a malignant brain tumor. The diagnosis was confirmed the next day, and we cut our trip short. Joe offered to drive us home, but Mr. Woodson swore he was well enough to get behind the wheel. We drove back to Buffalo weighed down by an uncomfortable silence. Another neurologist in Buffalo immediately confirmed the malignancy. The doctor advised Mr. Woodson to stop working and suggested a course of chemotherapy, because the tumor was inoperable. I overheard Mrs. Woodson say chemotherapy was only a way to buy more time. She had been told her husband only had six months to a year to live. The news, coming less than a year after her son died, just about totaled her.

As I learned more about other people and their families, I thought more about my own roots. My mother and father must have relatives out there somewhere. Were they from close-knit, loving families? What would their people do if they knew about me? Would any of them welcome me into their homes?

Talking to Mrs. Woodson about tracing my background was out of the question. Even if her husband had not been gravely ill, she would have raised a fit knowing what was swirling around in my head. On my own, I poked around the local grapevine. Black neighborhoods during the 1960s were self-contained; that is, residence was limited to certain neighborhoods. They also had their own underground network of communication. Everyone seemed to know something about someone else. When I finally found an address of a woman named Rose Cameron, I started to shiver. What would I say, I wondered? As I got ready to leave the Woodsons', I suddenly chickened out.

After several weeks of hemming and hawing, I swallowed my fears and I rode the bus to another run-down section of Buffalo. I knocked on this woman's front door. A part of me had hoped this Rose Cameron lived in a well-kept house with a thriving flower garden out front. When she opened the door, I felt a knot the size of a bowling ball crash in my stomach. In my fantasy, I wanted to be greeted by a warm, exuberant woman who was surrounded by a loving family. That was not to be the case. This plump woman was dressed in a tattered housedress and torn slippers. It was obvious she did not wear a bra. Dark circles the size of shopping bags sat underneath her eyes. Bits of lint collected in her tightly curled hair. Her skin was so ashy it gave her a gray appearance. She looked like she had not been out of the house in a long time.

From my position at the front door, the apartment looked as if a tornado had blown through it. Clothing was strewn across cheap furniture. The stale smell of tobacco soured the air. A large ashtray on a crooked coffee table overflowed with cigarette butts. Cockroaches scurried across the light-colored walls. Huge chunks of paint hung from the ceiling. What a rat's nest she lived in!

Once we exchanged tentative glances, the woman grumbled, "What you want?" I probably woke her up from a sound sleep.

I felt my knees start to buckle. To avoid stammering when I opened my mouth, I slowly counted to ten. "My . . . my . . ."

The woman pointed her finger at me and roared, "What is it? I be sleeping."

"My name is Theresa. Does that mean anything to you?"

The woman looked at me like I had three eyes. "It sure don't." Without saying another word, she slammed the door in my face, and I took off.

The entire exchange lasted no more than four minutes. I carefully studied her puffy face to check for similarities. Beyond the same dark colored skin, we bore no resemblance to one another. Slowly making my way home, I wondered what I would have done if that woman had answered yes. Merely looking at her haggard appearance and filthy apartment made me feel sick. Obviously, life had been unkind to her; still, it did not mitigate my pain. I may have been unhappy living in foster homes, but I doubt living with this woman would have brought new meaning to my life.

If this woman was in fact my biological mother, caseworkers would not have fought to return me to a woman who could not even care for herself. I shuddered at the idea. As hard as it was for me to be a ward of the state, I now realize my life could have been considerably worse. Giving birth to a child does not make you a parent. Returning to Mrs. Woodson's house was no longer such a bleak prospect.

Mr. Woodson headed downhill, despite several rounds of chemotherapy. His job at the plant provided him with adequate medical insurance so he did not have to resort to the less-than-promising care given at the public hospital. Mr. Woodson was now thin as a rail, his skin had a gray tint to it, and he looked haggard all the time. His deteriorating condition reminded me of Mr. Chester, whom I guessed had long since passed on. I regretted Mr. Woodson, a decent human being who worked hard all his life, was stricken with such a horrible illness.

I thought Mrs. Woodson would have fallen apart by now. On the contrary, she held up remarkably well. She tended to all her husband's needs with the efficiency of a highly paid nurse. She cooked all his favorite foods, even though his appetite had greatly diminished. She asked me to continue to iron his shirts, claiming it would make Mr. Woodson feel better. How could I say no?

I suppose the very real possibility her husband would be gone in a matter of months caused Mrs. Woodson to reconsider her commitment to the Catholic Church. She started to attend Sunday Mass. She insisted the girls and I accompany her but Meekah and Heidi resisted. Mrs. Woodson did not have the strength to argue with them, so she backed down. I accompanied her a few times, but after a few weeks Mrs. Woodson stopped going altogether. So did I.

I was in the seventh grade and doing fairly well in school. I felt as if I always had to try harder than my classmates, but I managed to eke out decent grades. For the first time, one of my teachers, a middle-aged nun named Sister Joan Marie, said, "You need to believe in yourself."

"I know, but it's not easy."

"If you don't believe in yourself, nobody else will either."

Once in a while, I stayed after school and talked with Sister Joan Marie about my private life. She was genuinely sympathetic, and I appreciated the open ear she offered me. I was glad someone had taken the time to find out more about me and why I was so aloof. She said, "It's almost time to fill out high school applications."

"What're you saying?"

"Pick up your grades so you get into a good school."

I was delighted she had faith in me and believed I could make something of myself.

Every fall, Mr. Woodson had tinkered with the furnace to ready it for the winter. But not this year. Mrs. Woodson cautiously approached me. "Can you help me with the furnace this year? I've never gone down there before."

"I'm not sure what to do, but I'll try."

"Be careful of the rats down there."

I still shuddered at the idea of working among vermin, but I had a job to do and that was that.

The holiday season was bleak. Mr. Woodson looked like a skeleton and could hardly get out of bed. The spreading cancer had seriously damaged many of his brain functions. He lost control over his bodily functions and wore adult diapers, which Mrs. Woodson dutifully changed every few hours. She spoon-fed him hot soup for lunch and dinner. When the cancer ravaged his eyesight, he went blind. He had trouble remembering the date. No matter how difficult her life had become, Mrs. Woodson never once complained while caring for her husband. Her relatives in Cortland offered to stay with her for a while to help out, but she flatly turned down their offer.

She did, however, accept an overture made by the parish priest. Through the local grapevine, he had heard of Mrs. Woodson's troubles. He took the girls and me on a number of outings, telling us Mrs. Woodson needed a little time to herself. Actually, the priest's intervention introduced me to some of the cultural activities, namely museum exhibitions, storytelling, and music concerts, I never knew were available in Buffalo. The girls seemed to resent the priest, but I enjoyed the time spent away from home.

It was clear the end was near. Mr. Woodson's bedroom had the antiseptic smell of a hospital. The priest came over more often to get us out of the house. Mrs. Woodson's energy seemed all but drained. Even she had a gaunt appearance most of the time. I was uncomfortable being surrounded by death.

Mrs. Woodson decorated her fake spruce tree that year and cooked a turkey dinner on Christmas. Knowing she was not in the holiday spirit, I believe she tried to make Christmas enjoyable for us. Meekah, Heidi, and I pretended to enjoy ourselves, but the mood inside the house was incredibly low-spirited. Although it was never acknowledged, I knew this would be Mr. Woodson's last Christmas.

The end came two weeks later. Mr. Woodson died at home in his sleep. He had received his final wish—not to die in the hospital. Although Mr. Woodson's death had been expected, Mrs. Woodson sobbed like a baby when the ambulance drove away that morning with her husband's body. She looked at me with devastation splashed across her face, spread her hands apart, and in the most pitiful voice I had ever heard, she said, "What am I going to do?"

I should have reached out to console her, but I stood there, feeling out of sorts. Dealing with difficult emotions was not one of my strong points. I stammered for a second, then said, "I . . . I . . . don't know. Would you like to sit down?"

Mrs. Woodson's entire body shook, and sad tears streamed down her puffy cheeks. I was so sorry her son had died. He would have been the strong support she so desperately needed. All I could offer her was a tis-

The End of the Line

sue. Later that evening Patty and Joe arrived from Cortland, and they stayed for the next week.

Although Mrs. Woodson had initially been devastated by the loss, she managed to pull herself together enough to handle her husband's affairs. Mr. Woodson had a small life insurance policy he purchased through his employer. Mrs. Woodson was the beneficiary and she collected twenty-five thousand dollars.

One evening at dinner, Mrs. Woodson said, "I'm going to look for a new house. This one has too many memories. I can't stay here any more."

I could feel panic surge through my body. "Where are we going?"

"Don't know yet. I'm going around with some real estate lady tomorrow."

I was scared about making another major change. I had grown used to my school and the surrounding neighborhood. The idea of starting over again made me shiver, but what choice did I have?

At the end of a three-week search, Mrs. Woodson settled on a decent two-story, three-bedroom, wood-frame house with a nice backyard in a predominantly white neighborhood called Polonia, several miles away. A few other blacks lived in the area, but the for sale signs on our new block went up shortly after we moved in. I felt awful people seemed so fearful of us.

I was devastated I had to move away from my few friends at my school. I had also grown attached to some of the teachers. Although I exchanged phone numbers with two or three of the girls, I knew things would never be the same.

Despite Mrs. Woodson's earlier warnings that I should do errands for the neighbors without charge, I had nonetheless developed my own small business within the old neighborhood. Among the jobs I performed were baby-sitting, mowing lawns, and grocery shopping. I took in about ten dollars per week, keeping my prices low because I knew and respected these people. I lamented the fact my only source of income would soon dry up.

Knowing I would have to start the eighth grade in one new school, then change again a year later to begin high school, left me feeling like I was standing next to a cliff. My world felt turned upside down again. I should have been used to change by now, but this relocation hit me harder than the ones before.

As moving day drew closer, I overheard a conversation between Meekah and Mrs. Woodson that disturbed me. Mrs. Woodson reminded Meekah she would soon turn eighteen. Once foster children reached eighteen years of age, they were no longer under the auspices of the state. In this case, Catholic Charities had alerted Mrs. Woodson by telling her payments for Meekah would end in another two months. Mrs. Woodson told Meekah she could not afford to put a roof over her head for free. She offered to give Meekah a room in her new house if she had a way to pay rent, but Meekah declined. Two weeks after Meekah had moved out, Heidi disappeared. Mrs. Woodson alerted Heidi's caseworker but evidently no one bothered to look for her because she was already seventeen. That was the last I saw either of them.

Mrs. Woodson asked Catholic Charities for more foster children. Because of her age (she was now in her sixties), I assumed her offer would be declined. A week later, two young black boys, ages four and six, were brought to our doorstep. The fair-skinned boys with short hair and big ears seemed stunned upon their arrival, and immediately retreated to the bedroom they would share. Looking at these two little lost souls made me feel as if I was staring at myself. I could easily relate to their bewildered feelings. From my lengthy tenure in foster care, I felt as if I had become a pro.

I expected Mrs. Woodson would have trouble relating to young children again, but she seemed right at home among these boys. The tensions in the household arose from our now thorny relationship. As I grew older, I became more assertive and less willing to accept everything told to me. Mrs. Woodson resisted, and we were at each other's throats almost all the time.

To escape the ill feelings at home, I spent much of my summer at the library. I read books on subjects I previously had no interest in. For years, I had stared out my window at the stars glistening in the dark skies. Now I decided it was time to read about astronomy, and I devoured every astronomy book in the children's section that summer. I was able to recognize a large number of constellations and, for a fleeting moment, considered becoming an astronomer, but soon changed my mind when I found out how many math classes would be required. Math was not my best subject, so I shifted my focus to housing.

I started browsing through books that contained various pictures of homes, all different kinds: brick houses, wood-frame houses, adobe-style homes, town houses, apartment buildings, and mansions. I enjoyed studying the fine details, which every home no matter how large or small, seemed to have. As a result of my growing interest, I took walking tours through different parts of Buffalo to look at houses. Some kids my age were fascinated with music and the opposite sex, but not me. Housing mesmerized me and it eventually led to my career choice of urban planning.

Mrs. Woodson, who had grown suspicious of my outings, put me through the second-degree one day when I came home late for dinner. Convinced I was secretly dating a boy without her approval, I had to work double time to convince her I had been walking around looking at homes.

Adapting to a new school almost did me in. I asked Mrs. Woodson to allow me to finish my last year of grammar school in my old neighborhood. I was shocked when she got up the nerve to ask, but the principal said that, because I was now living in another parish, I had to attend the school there. The dividing lines among parishes made no sense to me. I believed the school administrator was being unfair. Nobody seemed to be concerned that breaking into a new school almost put me over the edge.

To make matters worse, some of the white students in my new school pounced on me with nasty names such as "jungle bunny" and the proverbial "nigger." My skin had grown thick; nevertheless, the names still hurt every time I heard them. I no longer harbored anger at the narrow-minded people who showered me with bad names. On the contrary, I felt sorry for them because they behaved so ignorantly and were full of hostility. Whenever I heard the N word, I simply turned my head and kept walking. Even though the growing black consciousness movement preached racial pride, deep down, however, nasty names still made me want to cry.

Like the rest of society, the Catholic Church was also in the midst of change. Fewer young women entered the convent, causing significant gaps in the educational system. Thus, the Church recruited more lay teachers. The nuns now dressed differently. With the Pope's approval, nuns wore their regular clothes, conservatively styled, of course. By the late 1960s, you could only tell they were nuns by the veil they wore on their heads and the crucifix around their neck. Nuns also began to receive a modest salary.

The End of the Line

My growing independence rocked the boat with Mrs. Woodson. I had also taken an interest in the new foster boys and stood up for them when I felt Mrs. Woodson treated them in dictatorial ways. She insisted they clean their room almost daily, banned television except on weekends, and limited playtime to one hour a day. The results of my more assertive behavior caused Mrs. Woodson and I to be at odds all the time. As a result, I became even more introverted at school. I had a lot of bottled-up steam, but no safe way to release it. So I held it. One of my teachers noticed the changes in my behavior and asked me to stay after school one afternoon.

In the privacy of an empty classroom, the nun asked, "Is there anything I can help you with?"

I stood there motionless for a few seconds. The nun motioned for me to sit down, and I did. I chewed on my upper lip. "Yes, I have problems at home."

For the next half-hour, I leaked a little bit about my unhappy home life. I told the nun I had trouble concentrating and worried I might fail again. She asked me for my caseworker's name. I had no idea whatsoever, because it had been almost a year since I last had a visit. I presumed the previous caseworker had already resigned.

The aftermath led to my removal from Mrs. Woodson's home, but it did not happen without a struggle. My caseworker had to hustle to find another foster home for a thirteen-year-old black girl, not an easy task in a primarily white city. During a conversation in her office, the caseworker looked at me with a smirk on her face. I had to be a cadaver not to notice she was annoyed. "I don't know what you want me to do."

What did she expect me to say? Of course, I knew the slim opportunities available to me, but I had to get away from Mrs. Woodson. "I need help. Isn't that your job?"

The caseworker frowned. Hastily, she grabbed a couple of file folders, then shoved them across her ugly steel-frame desk. "I'll have to do a lot of checking to find you something. Are you sure you can't stay put? That would make my life a lot easier."

I could almost feel her sizzle when I said, "No, I can't."

Immediately, however, I had second thoughts. Should I stay? Should I go? Perhaps I had been impetuous. I wanted stability in my life, but there was something inside me urging me to leave. I was not ready for more confrontations with Mrs. Woodson nor was I prepared to deal with conflict. What would I do now? I had already asked my rarely seen caseworker for another placement. If I decided to stay and my relationship with Mrs. Woodson deteriorated further, would Catholic Charities bail me out again? No, I had to leave.

As expected, the caseworker's search for another foster home turned up nothing, so she resorted to plan B: sending me to a local group home run by Catholic Charities. And so after almost seven years with Mrs. Woodson, another chapter in my topsy-turvy life was about to close.

Part Three

Bouncing Around
as an Adolescent

Not surprisingly, my caseworker had to hustle to find new quarters for me. "I've been on the phone for days, hounding people to give you a break. It's not easy finding a place for someone your age."

I asked, "So what did you find?"

"A group home."

"What kind?"

"It's called Flourette Hall, and it's run by the Catholic Church."

For the past seven years, I had my own room, so I was not thrilled about sharing a room. The idea of living among strangers, however, was no big deal, because I had done it for such a long time. The life of an outsider was the only life I had ever known.

On the day of my big move, I woke up with the sun, wondering what my new life would be like. The weather had been hot and sticky over the past few days, and I was drained from sleeping in a room that felt like an oven. The mounting anxiety about another move left me tossing and turning most of the night. Thinking about the group home, I hoped it would be an improvement over the general discord I had found over the past fourteen years. Unlike some children in foster homes, I was not brutalized. I never had to shove a chair in front of my door to keep out a molester. I never had to fight off a drunken foster parent. However, I often felt like the captain of a ship steering through stormy seas, searching for good winds and a safe harbor. I ventured inside many different ports but I was continually lost. The sea was so wide, my boat so small.

On my way out of the house, I passed through the kitchen looking for Mrs. Woodson. We remained far apart, but I felt obliged to thank her. Although I resisted my feelings, I knew I would miss the old woman. She probably had feelings about my departure as well. After all, our lives had intertwined for seven years. I had mixed feelings about leaving. I looked forward to relief from the emotional chaos that surrounded me. No matter how hard she tried, Mrs. Woodson could never accept the rebellious stage that accompanied adolescence. She flew into uncontrollable rages whenever I made any efforts, even feeble ones, to assert myself. It seemed as if Mrs. Woodson interpreted my adolescent urges to be independent as a knife in her back. Learning how to deal with my typical teenage behavior was beyond her ability. I believed it was best to move on.

Alternately, I had grown accustomed to the sometimes highly neurotic routine at Mrs. Woodson's house, and I was antsy about leaving. I knew it was almost impossible for me to feel secure anywhere and with anyone, but at least Mrs. Woodson's home afforded me some stability.

Mrs. Woodson, wearing a tattered white housedress dappled with big blue polka dots, sat at the kitchen table hovering over a mug of hot coffee. I gingerly took a seat next to her and noticed her shoulders sagged more than usual. She looked at me with sad eyes. "You don't have to go."

I said, "I think I should."

"I got room for you here."

I took one big swallow. "Catholic Charities found a space for me."

Unexpectedly, Mrs. Woodson's voice cracked. "I'll be all alone now. All by myself with these two boys. What am I going to do?"

I sensed she was asking me not to leave, but by this time, I had already made up my mind. Despite feelings drowned by a tidal wave of confusion, it was clear my time with Mrs. Woodson had to end. Surprisingly,

I felt incredibly guilty about leaving her. She seemed so weak and vulnerable, not the tyrant she often behaved like. "I came to say thank you."

Sniffling, she said, "OK."

"If you want me to come back and help around the house, I will."

My offer mitigated her anxiety, because she cracked a faint smile. Leaning back in her chair, she sighed with relief. "The Lord has spoken so I guess you have to go. But this old lady will sure appreciate any help you can give me."

Because neither of us was very affectionate, we made no effort to hug one another. I stood up and waved good-bye. As I left the kitchen, I noticed Mrs. Woodson as she dabbed her eyes with a tissue. I was alone at the door, ready to go. My eyes filled up, and no matter how hard I tried, I could not prevent a few droplets of regret from crawling down my cheeks. I was surprised I was so moved.

A caseworker with long, straight brown hair and round sunglasses showed up. The woman's appearance reminded me of Natalie Wood. All of my possessions fit inside two paper shopping bags. Passing through the front yard, I turned around one more time to catch a last glimpse of the two-story yellow house. Then, I hopped into the back seat of the Ford wagon parked out front, and off we drove.

Because Mrs. Woodson had recently moved into the area, I was unfamiliar with most of the neighbors hanging around outside. I did not even know the next-door neighbors' names. I actually missed some of the residents from the old neighborhood, but this community held little special meaning to me. This time, it was much easier for me to walk away. Only a few shards of emotional anguish dug into me, quite unlike the day when I left Mrs. Chester's home. In an odd way, this felt like an overdue divorce, but, although ready to leave, I was also scared to death about moving on.

During the long drive through the crowded midday streets, the caseworker kept her eyes glued to the road. As usual, the skies were stained with the thick gray smoke belching out of the few factories that had not abandoned Buffalo. A gigantic steel plant, one of the main employers the city, had packed up shop the year before, causing many unskilled workers to lose their steady jobs. The caseworker never once turned around to discuss arrangements for my new living situation. Just as well. I supposed she was still frustrated. I had nothing to say to her either. She had only been my caseworker for a few months, and I had no feelings about her, either good or bad. This woman was simply one more in a long line of caseworkers, none of whom had ever accomplished what I thought they were supposed to do. At the age of fifteen, I no longer believed I would be adopted. Like a telescope focused on the heavens, my mind converged on my eighteenth birthday, when I would be liberated from the still struggling child welfare bureaucracy, a stubborn system resistant to change and deeply scarred by racism and ineptitude.

After plowing through stop-and-go traffic in a hot, uncomfortable car, we cruised through North Park, a very chic neighborhood full of expensive-looking brick homes with two-car garages. Everyone's lawn was immaculate, and the streets were clean and without potholes. Shiny new cars bearing names such as Mercedes-Benz and BMW were parked along the impeccably neat streets. Unlike my old neighborhoods, not a soul congregated on the street corners. This place looked like a ghost town. The car slowed down. I thought the caseworker was either lost or delirious from the heat. I doubted my new group home, especially one for a black girl, was in a posh community such as this. When the caseworker finally stopped the car, my mouth hung open so wide I could have caught flies. Without turning around, the caseworker said, "This is it."

Through the back window, I stared at the regal-looking brick building in front of me called Flourette Hall. The lush green lawn and hedges looked as if they had been watered regularly and trimmed recently. Each ground floor window contained a flower box filled with bright red geraniums. Clutching my two shopping bags, I slowly followed the caseworker along a narrow pathway made of hand-carved stone pieces that ended in front of a six-foot-high wrought iron gate. My knees felt as jittery as my stomach, but I knew there was no going back. Although I had to press forward, I wondered where I would find the strength to continue my journey. I felt like I was quickly running out of gas and had no way to secure replenishments.

The caseworker rang the front doorbell and, within seconds, a tall, sturdy-looking gray-haired woman in a beehive hairstyle answered. She introduced herself as Miss Abigail Booke, the secretary, and quickly welcomed us inside. Not surprisingly, my caseworker handed Miss Booke a packet of papers and was gone in a flash. I assumed the envelope contained my vital documents. Once alone, Miss Booke, who wore cat-eye glasses and enough hair spray to hold together at least ten well-teased wigs, led me on a tour of the home. In a sugary sweet voice, the elderly woman said, "Welcome, dear, to Flourette Hall. We try to make this as homelike as possible. If you have any questions, now's the time to ask."

The reality of my situation surged through me, and I felt numbed with fear. Another home, another set of rules, and more people to learn how to get along with. I wanted to break down in tears, but I refused to show weakness, especially in front of others.

Miss Booke again asked, "Dear, do you have any questions?"

I tried to keep my lips from quivering. "No ma'am, not yet." As the secretary continued the tour, I studied the layout of the home. The first floor contained a large institutional kitchen. Besides two gigantic refrigerators and a freezer the size of a walk-in closet, there was a stove that looked liked it was capable of handling enough pots to cook dinner for the Buffalo Bills.

Nestled to the left was a dining room with six large dark walnut tables, each with claw feet and eight chairs. "Quite elegant," I thought. Redwood wainscoting adorned the dining room and hallway. A large oriental rug rested on the red oak floor. The fancy floors were adorned with chestnut inlaid patterns in the corners. The dining parlor reminded me of photos I had seen in magazines of corporate boardrooms. This was far from the stark image I expected of a group home.

Several framed portraits of Jesus Christ hung from the beige walls, and a large crucifix rested above the mantel near the dining room table. Cabinets covered with mahogany held dozens of canned goods with items ranging from crunchy peanut butter to creamed corn and, to my chagrin, Spam. Tacked onto a bulletin board was a handwritten work · schedule including a variety of chores such as food preparation, dishwashing, and vacuuming. Miss Booke pursed her pencil-thin lips and said, "Check the schedule each day, because all the girls are expected to pitch in. Don't forget, because the sisters don't like it when girls neglect their duties."

Bouncing Around as an Adolescent

Because I had looked at the work schedule, I was shocked when Miss Booke introduced me to Hassie, a middle-aged black woman who served as the cook, and Rosario, an Italian-American who worked as the housekeeper. Both women worked only during the week. Miss Booke told me all the girls were on their own during the weekends.

Behind the dining room, there was a fairly roomy living room that held two beige, crushed velvet sofas with huge fluffy pillows, several side chairs, a big television set, and a glass- top coffee table covered with at least a dozen religious magazines. This was the family room, but it seemed more like a waiting room inside a hospital. I was relieved to see the furniture free from vinyl covers. I hated sitting on vinyl during the hot steamy summers. Evidently, Miss Booke must have seen me staring at a large black-and-white photo of a nun with very wrinkled skin, because she tapped me on the shoulder. She blessed herself, then said, "That's Sister Flourette. She founded this place."

"Does she still work here?"

"No, I'm afraid not." Miss Booke glanced upward, blessed herself again and said, "Sister Flourette is with God right now. She was called away two years ago. We felt it would be an appropriate tribute to keep a picture of her. She loved this place and all the girls she helped to look after."

"Oh."

"Come on dear, I'll introduce you to the other girls."

This was the moment I dreaded. I hated introductions to new people, because they usually plied me with questions I did not want to answer. Trailing behind Miss Booke up a long flight of carpeted stairs, I listened as she related more details about Flourette Hall. While I was daydreaming about the name Flourette, which reminded me of the stuff used in toothpaste, the secretary said, "There are twenty-four girls here, ranging in age from twelve to seventeen. All our girls attend school and some hold part-time jobs."

As if she were a school marm, Miss Booke said, "We don't like lazy girls around here."

I assumed it might be a good idea for me to consider working, especially because it was summer. School was at least two months away.

Bouncing Around as an Adolescent

It was late in the afternoon and I was overwhelmed. Miss Booke, however, was still as cheery as ever. "Not all the girls are home right now. So, we'll knock on doors to see who's around."

After two unanswered knocks, a young white girl with stringy blonde hair, a button nose, and vivid blue eyes finally responded to Miss Booke's knock. She wore denim bell-bottoms and a tie-dyed T-shirt. In true hippie-like fashion, she said, "Oh cool, someone new. My name is Kathy." The young girl spun around like a baton twirler and pointed to her roommate sitting on top of her bed. This girl gave me the peace sign, but never got up to greet me.

All I could muster was, "Nice to meet you."

Unlike the flower child, I encountered a detached response from each occupant of the next seven rooms. None of the girls seemed overly friendly, yet none displayed any hostility. I doubted race alone was the cause for the icy reception. At least six of the other girls were black or of mixed race. I assumed adolescent behavior played a part. Cliques are as common among teenagers as acne and heartfelt crushes.

Three girls shared each bedroom, so I was extra nervous when Miss Booke knocked on the door to my new room. The secretary smiled so much I felt worried. She said, "I talked to the girls about you."

I hoped they would be kind to me. As soon as the door opened, I could feel butterflies dancing around my stomach. Good thing I hadn't eaten all day. One girl, a very pale-faced teenager with prominent acne on her cheeks, opened the door and said, "Hi. Come in." The other one, a skinny mixed-race girl with honey-colored skin and willowy dark hair pulled back into a ponytail, said nothing, but she flashed a quick smile. I assumed that meant hello.

Miss Booke rested her arm on my shoulder and said, "Girls, I want you to meet Theresa. She's the new roommate I told you about."

The girl who resembled a cadaver glanced at the floor, then mumbled, "I'm Tammy." Seconds later, the mixed-race girl added, "Hi, I'm Grace."

Miss Booke said, "OK, girls. I'll leave you alone. I'm sure you'll want to get acquainted."

The minute the older woman walked out of the room, Grace nodded toward a single bed by the window. She was polite but not terribly friendly. "You sleep over there. That dresser and desk next to the bed is yours.

There's a bathroom down the hall. We all share that." I dropped onto the bed and finally let go of my shopping bags. The pounding in my heart had lessened by now, and I stopped feeling as if I would pass out.

Over the next half hour, Grace filled me in on details about Flourette Hall that Miss Booke neglected to mention. Some girls were at the group home due to parental incest or physical abuse. One girl had an incomplete spinal cord injury that had resulted from her mother's rage. She threw the little girl down the stairs one evening when she discovered her husband's affair. The girl had trouble walking and got around using a walker. Because the home was not handicapped accessible, she had her own small room on the first floor, next to the rooms occupied by the resident nuns. Tammy said, "One girl ran away from home to go to Woodstock. After she got home, still stoned, her parents shipped her here. They hoped the nuns could straighten her out."

Without showing a glimmer of emotion, Grace stared straight ahead and said, "I'm here because my mother died, my father is in jail, and nobody else wants me."

Tammy chimed in. "My father couldn't keep his hands off me, and my mother couldn't do much to stop him. I told one of my teachers, so the state sent me here. The social worker said I can't live in the same house as my father, but my mother is such a devout Catholic she refuses to get divorced. What about you?"

Around now, my mouth was dry as Death Valley. The tiny window fan only circulated the hot air around the room. I asked Grace for a sip of her soda, then shared some of my past with both girls. Grace shook her head from side to side. "That's too bad. I know what it feels like to be unwanted. All my mother's people say I'm too much trouble. Let them kiss my ass. She spent her life taking care of her people."

Tammy threw in her empathy, too. "Can you believe my two younger sisters are still at home? I see them every so often, but mostly my parents act like I don't exist. The hell with them."

By the end of our conversation, I found out every girl at the home had a sad story. A group of mostly older Catholic nuns, with few or no parenting skills, was supposed to fill in the gap in our lives.

To keep my mind occupied, I glanced around, making a mental note of the details in our room. It was about twenty by twenty feet and looked like a room inside a hospital or nursing home. The plain white walls were empty except for the crucifix required in each bedroom. Rolling her eyes around, Grace said the head nun frowned upon posters, unless they were of religious figures. Only small portable radios were allowed, and music had to be played very low, or else the nuns confiscated the radios. The only window in our room contained dark green, drab drapes that reminded me of an army depot instead of a teenager's room.

With the awkward introductions over, it was time to settle in. I unpacked my shopping bags and placed my scanty supply of clothes inside my dresser. Because I lived the life of a vagabond, I never held onto any mementos. The nature of foster care didn't allow my roots to grow too deeply in any one place.

Within minutes, both shopping bags were emptied. For a few seconds, I felt my heart jump around before deciding what to do next. As I mentioned, I had always had my own room. Considering bedtime was hours away, I dreaded having to disrobe in front of Grace and Tammy. I expected shyness would force me to change in the bathroom.

Because Tammy and Grace were scheduled to set the table for dinner, I had a few minutes to myself. I still felt like an overnight guest at an exclusive hotel. The entire experience seemed surreal, like a scene from an episode of *The Outer Limits*. I fantasized I was an alien visitor from another planet, trying desperately to fit in with the Earth's population. Staring at the sparkling white ceiling, I became mesmerized by the smooth, even surface. I wondered if I would ever fit in anywhere. I decided I would never become close to my roommates, fearing that at any time they or I could be taken away.

Just then, a knock at the door jolted me out of my emotional torment. I flew off the bed and responded. I was startled to see a grim-faced nun, arms firmly folded in front of her, staring down at me like I was a naughty child. In a flash, my hands started to tremble. Hiding them behind my back, I said, "Yes, may I help you?"

The stone-faced nun, wearing funeral colors, said, "I'm Sister Petrina, head of the order. Have you been given a tour yet?"

"Yes ma'am."

"Good." Sister Petrina shoved her massive frame past me and planted both hands on her wide hips. She stared at me with deep penetrating eyes and said, "Dinner is promptly at six o'clock. If you're late, you don't get dinner. Only the girls who work are excused. Every girl has chores. Someone will talk to you about yours. Bedtime is strictly at ten o'clock. No exceptions, except for those who work. We go to Mass every morning in the chapel next door. The girls aren't required to go, but you're welcome to join us. Uh . . . what did you say your name was, dear?"

"Theresa."

The nun scratched her chin and said, "Yes, after St. Theresa. I hope you pray to your patron saint."

I pretended to be happy by showing a fatuous grin. She reminded me of a drill sergeant. Without thinking, I almost saluted. I finally said, "I understand, sister."

"You better." Sister Petrina imperiously moved closer to me. She jabbed her finger in my direction and issued a stern warning, one that almost made me gasp. "And no boyfriends allowed. The sisters keep a close eye on all of you. Don't try sneaking around. Our girls *will not* become pregnant. I hope you understand."

"Yes, I do." Up until now, I had never experienced a typical schoolgirl crush. Once I digested this lecture, any romantic thoughts I may have had evaporated.

As soon as the nun marched out of my room, I raced down the hall to the bathroom. Filling a sink with cold water, I dunked my head in. My mouth still felt like crud, so I let water from the faucet pour right into my mouth. When I felt normal again, I retreated to my room. I hoped my contact with Sister Petrina would be minimal.

Most of the girls returned by late afternoon, and the hallway buzzed with activity. Some girls chatted, while others belted out words from the latest hits or cracked silly jokes. I wanted to blend in, but I was too timid to approach anyone. So I sat in my room until about two minutes before six o'clock. On the way to the dining hall, I acknowledged some of the girls by nodding my head as our eyes met, but it seemed almost impossible to penetrate the shields of the obviously well-established cliques.

My appetite was about the size of a nickel. To exacerbate my uneasiness, the dining hall felt like a steam bath. Hassie, the black cook, looked like she was about to wilt. For all its outward opulent appearance, Flourette Hall lacked air-conditioning. I was surprised to see the oven in use. Salads seemed more fitting for this time of year.

Staring at Hassie as the cantankerous Sister Petrina bossed her around the kitchen, I felt uneasy. Hassie referred to the nun by her proper name, but Sister Petrina referred to Hassie a few times as "girl." Hassie had to be at least forty-five years old.

Because there were no assigned seats, I took an empty chair near Kathy, the blonde girl with the button nose who I had met earlier. Her bright blue eyes now seemed much darker. She shrugged when I sat down, but otherwise showed no reaction. Within minutes, every chair surrounding the four large, rectangular tables was occupied. Tammy, Grace, and two other girls appeared, carrying huge ceramic bowls filled with piping hot food. Just what I needed on a day that felt like Miami in July. Once we were all seated, from out of nowhere Sister Petrina appeared at the front of my table. Her chunky face glimmered with sweat. She clapped her hands so loudly it sounded as if she was applauding for the Pope. Bowing her head, she folded her hands together and said, "Bless us, oh Lord, for these thy gifts which we are about to receive, from thy bounty, through Christ our Lord. Amen."

Without saying a word, the nun walked away. The pressure was gone, and the air inside the room became incredibly light. I forced myself to a meager helping of meat loaf, mashed potatoes, and freshly steamed carrots, but mostly I picked at my food. For the next twenty minutes or so, tables full of adolescent girls stuffed their faces, and gabbed about the latest fashions and their favorite movie stars. Every time a man's name popped up at my table, all the girls surreptitiously glanced around as if they expected fifty lashes with a whip. Throughout dinner, most of the girls displayed politeness toward me, but it was clear I was the square peg. Jell-O with fruit salad, not on my top ten list, was on the menu so I never bothered to wait for dessert. I excused myself, even though no one seemed to have heard me. I bolted up the stairs and jumped into bed, still completely dressed.

Later that night, I heard Tammy and Grace enter our room. I surmised they had spent the evening in the family room watching television. No one was allowed outside after dark, unless the nuns saw written permission from someone's parents. Tammy turned out the lights, and I felt safe blanketed by darkness. I wished it could have lasted forever. But as the night wore on and I was still wide awake, I pleaded with God to take me. From time to time, I had suicidal thoughts, but I was too afraid to follow through on my feelings. The burden of being an unwanted black child was becoming too heavy for me to carry. I wanted the pain to end.

T e n

Life Among the Nuns

Not long after my arrival, I learned the nuns planned a trip for a small group of us. Their order, the Sisters of Good Will, owned a small network of cottages scattered throughout the Northeast. Some of the homes had been purchased, but the Church inherited most of the property from estates of various parishioners. Flourette Hall had been founded with real estate and a sizable donation left by a wealthy member. Rumors spread the church member was related to Guido the Butcher, a notorious crime-family member from Brooklyn, but a mob connection was never proven. The Church nevertheless brushed off the hearsay and put the money to good use.

Right off the bat, I felt uneasy about traveling around with a group of older, often frail nuns and cliquish girls whom I hardly knew. Only girls who held part-time jobs were excused. I thought about seeking employment, even if I had to scrub public toilets, but realized there was not enough time. Running away was another option, but that soon lost its appeal. I heard horror stories about girls who ran away, and the last thing I wanted was to end up on the streets as a teenage prostitute. So, I packed my bag and got ready to go away with the sisters. This time I was not sitting with a group of talkative black women who liked to sit around and dish out the dirt.

Life Among the Nuns

Sister Theophane, a frail nun who looked like she was ready to call it quits, announced Sister Petrina would not be joining us. What a relief! I could not imagine being in close proximity to such a prickly woman, especially because this was supposed to be a vacation.

Hassie arrived earlier than usual to fix us a going-away breakfast. After packing away a meal of buttermilk pancakes with real maple syrup, crisp strips of bacon, and freshly squeezed orange juice, sixteen teenaged girls were ready to go. Flourette Hall operated four station wagons and two large passenger vans, all compliments of a cash-rich car dealer who was related to one of the nuns. I ended up in a van that had Sister Theophane behind the wheel. I trusted her age would not deter her from safe driving. Two other nuns accompanied us. Sisters Eileen and Joan Marie had wrinkled skin, liver spots on their hands, and gray hair. I guessed both women were in their sixties. None of the three nuns wore the traditional black habit, which did not surprise me considering the heat. Instead, they had on loose-fitting, homely gray and white dresses that were several inches below the knee. Each woman's head was covered with a kerchief.

My roommates Grace and Tammy had been assigned to the other van, so I basically kept to myself as we cruised along the New York State Thruway. Similar to the scenery I saw on my trips to Cortland, there were plenty of green trees and rolling hills along the vast stretch of highway. To combat my boredom, I stared aimlessly out the window until I made up a little game—counting the number of buses operated by the two major companies, Trailways and Greyhound. Trailways won. I also gazed at the huge American-made cars as they sped down the highway. Almost everyone, it seemed, drove a monster-sized sedan.

All the color drained from Sister Theophane's face when she glanced in the rear view mirror. I thought the devil was in hot pursuit. A New York State trooper was right behind us. Once the cop got out of his patrol car, the girls traded glances and cracked up. Sister Theophane turned around and gave us such an evil eye that we immediately became silent. Not a peep could be heard. When the red-faced cop saw an old nun and a van full of teenaged girls, he held his head down. Probably to save face, he asked for Sister Theophane's license anyway, but never used his radio to check her credentials. Governor Nelson Rockefeller had recently signed legislation that imposed draconian jail terms against drug dealers as a way to curb New York's insatiable appetite for narcotics. I supposed the cop overreacted and became suspicious when he saw a few black faces in the van. Before pulling away, Sister Theophane took out her rosary beads with trembling hands and said a few prayers.

Our first destination was Skaneateles, a small town at the tip of Lake Skaneateles in central New York. When we arrived, the other van was already there. The nuns and girls quickly separated. I imagine Sister Theophane filled the other nuns in on our encounter with the law. Wisely, none of us girls said anything to each other for fear of reprimand.

I noticed six small cottages. Four girls would share each one and the nuns took residence in another. The last cottage was used only for meals. Without waiting to be assigned a room, I edged closer to Tammy and Grace and asked if I could room with them. Another girl named Claire would be our fourth occupant. From a conversation I had overheard, I knew Claire, a short, skinny girl with dark brown eyes, had come from a dirt-poor family, originally from the hills of Kentucky. She was at the group home because both parents had died in a car accident and none of her relatives could afford an extra mouth to feed. Her father had worked at the gigantic Bethlehem Steel plant in Buffalo but lost his job when the mill closed down the year before. Scores of unskilled workers still reeled from so many plant closings.

The cottage we shared was about the size of a den, with four single beds and very little furniture. Tammy whacked her hand on one mattress and a cloud of dust billowed in the air. We all sneezed and rubbed our eyes, then realized we had to make the best of it. I considered opening the window but opted not to. Without screens to keep out the bugs, I figured we would be eaten alive. As I saw them, the aging log cabins were primitive, even though there was electricity. The summer camp I had attended, where I met Penny, had better accommodations than this place. There were no television sets, no comfortable chairs, and no refrigerators. I was surprised the sisters wanted to spend time under such rustic conditions.

As we got settled, Claire acted standoffish but I had aloof tendencies, too. A little while later, I found out I was the first black person Claire had shared a room with. She did not strike me as a racist, only somewhat ignorant. For instance, she asked me a number of times if she could touch my hair, which I now wore in a big Afro. I complied, but once she asked me if my underarm hair was as tightly curled, I drew the line and told her there would be no more demonstrations.

The weather was delightful. Temperatures were in the low eighties and the skies were bright blue, free from clouds. A light breeze kept us cool. The lake seemed appealing, even though I could not swim. In fact, I did not own a bathing suit. While the girls jumped in, I wandered around the area. Peeking inside a few windows, I was stunned to discover the nuns had a television, two fluffy chairs, cotton throw rugs, a two-burner stove, and a refrigerator. Why should we have to live like Davy Crockett when the sisters enjoyed the comforts of home? But complaints might end up with a scolding if I opened my mouth. The others quickly discovered their away-from-home comfort, but no one said a word.

Each cottage was expected to rotate duties. It was my cottage's turn to prepare dinner on our first night. Without any outdoor experience, I could not master the art of cooking on a barbecue grill. I became flustered trying to start a fire. Tammy, who was more familiar with outdoor cooking, promptly took over. She took me under her wing and demonstrated how to grill hamburgers and hot dogs so that they did not resemble charcoal. Despite the torrid heat, I stood next to Tammy and threw burgers and franks on the grill. As Grace and Claire set dinner tables, the nuns relaxed in lounge chairs and supervised our every move. No wonder Hassie rarely smiled while she was on the job.

Sister Theophane craned her neck and shouted, "Theresa, watch those burgers. I don't like mine too well done."

Sister Joan Marie chimed in. "Don't forget, Theresa. Make me two cheeseburgers. I like mine on the rare side. A little ketchup on my bun, OK hon?"

Not to be left out, Sister Eileen added, "And I like mine sort of medium. Not too well, not too rare."

I flashed a bogus smile at each nun as she called out her order. Deep down, I wanted to coat their burgers with cayenne pepper, and lots of it. Sure, I knew they were older, but they were far from helpless. They seemed to delight in the fact we waited on them hand and foot. Grace had filled each of their glasses with iced tea and Claire had set their table. I thought about placing a tack on each chair, yet never acted out my fantasy.

We passed the time by playing volleyball, hiking around the lake, or munching on snacks. Because the Finger Lakes region was a popular tourist attraction, dozens of people splashed around the water. Without a life vest, I was too afraid to give the water a try. A few male lifeguards with very long hair and tanned bodies were on duty. Nonetheless, I was still uptight.

The nuns mostly kept to themselves, unless it was mealtime. They were blessed with hearty appetites. Whatever cottage had been charged with meal preparation had to fix food to the nuns' liking. A separate group of girls were summoned to clean the nuns' room. Tammy and I were stuck with the chore of washing and waxing the two vans. Every morning and evening, the nuns held a prayer group, but none of us joined them. I thought about attending to pray for relief from the chores, but I changed my mind. I figured the nuns would sense I was insincere, and I did not want the other girls to think I was looking to score brownie points.

Unlike Flourette Hall, where we had a strict ten o'clock lights out, the nuns let us temporarily slide. The relaxed bedtime was not the thrill we had expected. Staying up late lost its appeal out in the middle of nowhere without anything to do. None of us used drugs or alcohol. If we had, there was absolutely no way to get any. My roommates and I hung around until midnight, chatting about current events, such as the recent killings at Kent State, Vietnam, and the movie *Midnight Cowboy*. We packed away bags of potato chips, Cheese Doodles, and popcorn. The nuns had given us pocket money for the trip, and we spent our allowance on snacks. I felt as if these girls were slowly starting to accept me.

The evening before we left, Sister Theophane announced we would be traveling to Vermont to spend some time at the order's property outside of Manchester in the southern part of the state. I was moderately excited to expand my horizons, because I had not traveled outside New York. Sister Theophane also said we would be stopping in Utica, a small city in upstate New York where a Catholic hospital was located. Our plans were to visit the nuns who worked at the hospital. Apparently, the nuns were all members of the Sisters of Good Will.

Life Among the Nuns

To get an early start, we left Lake Skaneateles shortly after sunrise. The lake looked so peaceful, with the huge reddish orange ball creeping above the horizon. Still groggy, we packed ourselves into the vans for the next leg of our journey. I was a bit hungry because we had skipped breakfast, but Sister Theophane promised to stop at a service area so we could all get something to eat. Sister Theophane admitted she needed a cup of coffee, a habit only a few of us had picked up. The drive from the Finger Lakes region to Utica, via the New York State Thruway, took almost three hours, including three stops at rest areas for food, gas, and to use the rest room. Similar to our earlier trip, Sister Theophane drove but she hardly spoke to us. I wondered why Catholic Charities expected her to act as our surrogate parent when she acted like we were strangers.

At one of the rest stops, we parked near a run-down beige Volkswagen van with bright flowers splashed across both side doors. A hand-painted sign with the words "peace and love" hung from the rear window. Heading toward the bathroom, we ran into a few glassy-eyed hippies in tattered blue jeans and tie-dyed T- shirts. One of the long-haired and bearded young men noticed Sister Theophane and staggered toward her. He handed her a flower and attempted to give her the high five. "Yo sister, be cool. Peace and love."

Sister Theophane turned her lobster red face toward us and said, "Girls, keep going. Pray for these people. They need our prayers."

We arrived in downtown Utica at midmorning. St. Mary's Hospital was a red brick building that reminded me of the older industrial structures now abandoned in Buffalo. In single file, we marched behind the three nuns through the busy hospital lobby toward the elevator. I felt weird because we attracted hordes of attention. Maybe the visitors thought we were nuns in training.

Sister Theophane introduced us as her girls rather than as young ladies from Flourette Hall. We gave one another uncertain stares, but held our tongues. She should have introduced us as her servants.

The head of nursing, also a nun, faced Sister Theophane and ignored us. "Would your girls like to visit our patients?"

The patronizing talk was wearing thin, but I knew better than to speak up. Sister Theophane broke out into a hearty grin and said,

"They'd love to." Slowly, she shifted her frame in our direction and said, "Won't you?"

Like we had a choice. Acting like robots, we all nodded in the affirmative. Seconds later, we split into groups. I found myself trailing behind a young nurse wearing the familiar headgear of a nun. The freckled-faced nun guided us through different rooms to greet indigent patients. In addition to being poor, these people also had no family. Now that was something I could relate to.

Most of the patients were frail elderly men and women who looked as if they were one step away from the final curtain. These patients, sick as they were, smiled when we stopped in their rooms to visit. After the third elderly patient started to cry, I felt choked up myself. I never expected our presence would move these patients to tears. Their obvious discomfort temporarily took my mind off my own unhappy life.

The scene inside the last room was mind-boggling. An old woman was in the end stages of lung cancer. Her bone-thin body made her appear as if she had been in a concentration camp. The antiseptic smell permeating the room reminded me of how much I disliked hospitals. The lifelong cigarette smoker had such an addictive habit, she was actually smoking an unfiltered *Camel* through the trachea tube in her neck. I almost gagged. She flicked her wrist in our direction, but I was so revolted I turned my head away. That hideous sight, in addition to my scant memories of Mr. Chester as he struggled with emphysema, kept me from ever lighting up. I rushed into the nearest bathroom, where I got sick to my stomach. That was a sight I will never forget.

Our vacation was largely uneventful. For me, the biggest thrill was crossing over the state line. None of the other girls seemed to share my joy as I stared at the big green sign that said, "Welcome to Vermont." This was a significant step in my sheltered life, but I kept a lid on my feelings. The girls already thought I was offbeat because I wore dowdy clothes and enjoyed looking at houses more than anything else.

One afternoon at our charming, freshly painted lakeside cottage in Vermont, Sister Theophane offered to drive us around to check out the surrounding towns. A few girls, including me, accepted her offer.

Riding around with Sister Theophane was not appealing, but this was the only way I could see Vermont. I was anxious to experience life outside of Buffalo.

Sister Theophane was raised in a small town called Londonderry, Vermont, not far from where we stayed. One of the girls asked, "Why don't you visit your family since we're not far away?"

The nun's voice dropped as she solemnly blessed herself. "They're all with the Lord now."

The terrain in much of upstate New York and Vermont was similar. Both were largely rural but Vermont had fewer main highways, hardly any billboards, and more cows. There were small dairy farms everywhere. Nonetheless, I was thrilled to drive along meandering, one-lane country roads that swooped and turned up and down hills, studying my new surroundings. Thousands of majestic pine trees dotted the lush landscape. I imagined the scenery in winter was breathtaking.

With Sister Theophane guiding us through familiar territory, I was impressed by her vast knowledge. She recited a few salient facts about the state's history, mostly about Ethan Allen and Vermont's role in the Revolutionary War, its strong distaste for development, and how the citizens worked hard to preserve their rustic way of life. She explained how thousands of people made their living from dairy farms. The cow was as popular to Vermont's image as the orange was to Florida—in fact, until recently Vermont had more cows than people. When Sister Theophane spotted a Volkswagen van full of young people, she rolled her eyes around and moaned.

Since we had left Flourette Hall almost two weeks ago, this was the first time Sister Theophane actually seemed relaxed. I enjoyed her company that afternoon. She certainly made our brief tour of the area fun as well as educational.

On the drive back, Sister Theophane reverted to her former self—a sullen, moody woman. Maybe she was irritated she still had to take such an active role in childcare at her advanced age. She probably looked forward to retirement. Instead, she got us.

At summer's end, Sister Petrina banged on my door with such force the noise sounded like a cop looking for a robbery suspect. I was alone at the time. My knees felt shaky even though I had not misbehaved. "Yes, may I help you?"

Sister Petrina said, "Theresa, it's time for school soon. You have to decide which one you want to attend." She handed me a few brochures and walked away.

I sat down on my bed and studied each of them. There were brochures outlining Catholic schools, public schools, and a few private ones. I was surprised, because I had been mistakenly told all the girls were required to attend the nearest Catholic school, St. Cecilia's Academy. Moreover, I was stunned to find out girls were also permitted to attend public school. I thought that was taboo. With absolutely no guidance, I decided to wait until Tammy and Grace came back. Maybe they could recommend a school.

Tammy and Grace attended different high schools, one public the other Catholic. Both girls said they had mixed feelings about their schools and would not go so far as to make an endorsement. To make my choice, I tossed a coin, and came up with Christ the King High School, located a short distance away in a middle-class section of Buffalo. Here I go again. Another school and another set of uniforms.

E l e v e n

Coming of Age
in the Group Home

None of the other girls attended Christ the King. Oh, no—maybe that
was a bad sign of strict teachers, tons of homework, or rough students.
I asked Sister Petrina if I could change my mind. She waved the forms at
me and snapped, "No, the decision is final."

To get to Christ the King, I had to take the bus. Public transportation
in this affluent section of Buffalo was sporadic, presumably because
most people commuted by car or were chauffeured around. On my first
morning of school, I waited for more than twenty minutes until a bus
arrived. I was surprised they allowed us to commute to school on our
own. I was sure the nuns would have seized another opportunity to control our lives, but to my amazement they did not. We were all on our
own getting to school, except for the handicapped girl. A special bus
picked her up every morning. I wondered what the nuns did all day.
Hassie cooked their lunch and Rosario cleaned up the place. Miss Booke,
the secretary, kept the office impeccably neat, handling all the paper-
work and opening and sorting the nuns' mail.

Assuming I was late for my first day, I hustled down the block. But as
soon as I approached the two-story, L-shaped brick building, I slowed

down my pace. At least twenty white girls chatted among each other as they strolled down the well-kept block. They looked as if they were on their way to the mall and not to Catholic school. None of them seemed to notice my chocolate-colored skin as I slid by. Obviously, punctuality was not that important.

About seven hundred girls attended Christ the King. Most were white, with a smattering of blacks, Hispanics, and Asians. In earlier years, Catholic school tuition had been free, but due to escalating costs the Church now charged each student about three hundred fifty dollars a year in tuition. My tuition had been waived.

I met my teachers, only a few of whom were nuns. The Catholic Church had trouble recruiting young women to a lifetime of hard work, celibacy, and no pay. The lifestyle did not appeal to me either. To keep within its budgetary restrictions, the Catholic school system often hired inexperienced teachers, many of whom lacked proper credentials. Catholic school teachers were non-unionized, and both the teachers and the Church benefited from this arrangement. The teachers obtained the necessary training to become licensed, and the school got away with paying them less than public school teachers.

During lunch, I followed the crowd into the small cafeteria. Popular songs such as "Stone Love" by the Supremes and "Gotta Get a Message to You" by the Bee Gees blared from the jukebox. Three nuns looking like CIA agents patrolled the cafeteria, eavesdropping on conversations and otherwise maintaining order.

On the food line, I scrunched my forehead when I saw the selections in front of me. The choices offered were pizza that looked like tomato sauce on cardboard, hamburgers that resembled shoe leather, and tuna salad that could have passed for cat food. Instead, I settled on a cup of chicken broth and plain white bread with butter.

A group of girls beckoned me to join them. As I sat around the lunch table, my eyes were opened to some of the teenage maneuvers widely used at the school. Every girl was required to wear a skirt hemmed at the knee line. Mini skirts were popular, but the nuns viewed them as too risque for teenagers. Defiant girls tried to weasel around the guidelines by rolling up their skirts around the waist. As soon as they reached the school's front door, they lowered their skirts. After school, hemlines went up again.

Coming of Age in the Group Home

To verify hemline compliance, the nuns occasionally surprised us with an impromptu check-up. Anyone suspected of wearing a skirt failing to meet school regulations had to kneel down. If the skirt touched the floor, she was given the OK to get up; if not, she had to serve detention.

Long hair was also a teenage favorite. Most white girls sported shoulder-length hair. The few black girls, including me, also followed the fashion of the times by wearing large Afros similar to Angela Davis. I had to use a hair pick the size of a rake to get through my hair, but I was proud of my Afro. Mrs. Woodson probably would have had a stroke if she had seen me. Large Afros seemed to frighten her.

My initial impression of Christ the King was neither good nor bad, but I felt OK. Maybe the bad news would come later, but I left not worried about coming back. Perhaps the addition of so many lay teachers lightened up the school just a bit.

I looked for a part-time job. My weekly allowance of twenty dollars was stretched for entertainment, field trips, lunch if I did not eat at school, dry cleaning, and toiletries. Eager to earn my own living, I was tired of listening to people gripe about the costs involved in looking after me. Mrs. Woodson had griped about money and so did the nuns. The chronic objections made me feel like I sponged off other people.

So I made a list of every grocery store in the vicinity of Flourette Hall and filled out applications at each one. Within a week or so, I was hired as a cashier at the A & P. I started at the minimum wage, then $1.85 an hour. Because I would not be sixteen until January, I fibbed about my age. I hoped no one would ask me for proper identification, and no one did. I suspect the manager at the A & P trusted me because I wore a Catholic school uniform.

When I received my first paycheck, I was like a little kid who finds a treasured toy underneath the Christmas tree. I held a check for $45.86, to me a princely sum, I did not cash until a month later. Every night, I stared at the check, made out to Theresa Cameron and felt proud of my accomplishments. I finally started to feel as if I would make something of myself.

Realizing I had to cash the check, I went to the nearest bank and opened a savings account. Every week when I got paid, I always put aside twenty-five dollars. Sure, it was not much, but to me it was a down payment on my future. It also was a big step toward my independence. Foster care made sure a child had the bare essentials, but it did nothing to prepare her for independent living or self-reliance. Those were boots I had to fill on my own.

My salary allowed me to buy clothes that were from neither a second-hand store nor a bargain basement. Having spent a lifetime dressed like a ragamuffin, I settled on fewer but better quality outfits. I also made sure the clothes fit me. I had always hated the way Mrs. Woodson bought clothes two to three sizes too large. Because I wore a uniform to school, I saved my clothes for pleasure. With hardly anywhere to go, my good clothes sat in the closet, but at least I knew I had them in case I was ever invited out.

At six o'clock every morning, I rolled out of bed to get into the shower. With so many girls sharing a bathroom, I had to get up at sunrise to take a decent shower or wait on a long line and barely have time to wash or brush my teeth. Haven risen at the crack of dawn at Mrs. Woodson's served me well. I was one of the few girls who rose early without complaint. Except on weekends or holidays, when we usually had pancakes or eggs, every girl was on her own for breakfast during the week. Hassie the housekeeper did all the grocery shopping and rarely asked us for input. Our breakfast choices included a variety of cold cereals, English muffins, frozen waffles, Pop Tarts, and juice or milk. The nuns frowned when girls asked for coffee or tea.

The housekeeper, Rosario, basically did the bulk of the housework, but we chipped in by cleaning our own rooms. The nuns, however, supervised Rosario as she cleaned their quarters. Sometimes, I thought they wasted scarce resources by employing both a full-time housekeeper and a cook. These nuns led charmed lives, far removed from the abject poverty many other people endured. I doubt any of them would have lasted a day working in a downtrodden community.

My days became full. I rarely had time to be depressed because I usually left for school by seven o'clock due to unreliable bus service. Classes started at eight-thirty. If I arrived early, I used the extra time to study. As a rule, I did not get back until almost seven-thirty in the evening, a valid excuse for missing dinner. Hassie left hot plates for all the girls who worked after school. Once I had dinner, I usually stayed up until ten o'clock to finish all my homework.

All the girls were required to do their own laundry. To make life easier for us, there was a fairly modern washer and dryer behind the kitchen. A barely used ironing board and iron rested in a first-floor closet. One evening, Sister Petrina heard me and another girl lament it was one heck of a wait to use the washing machine. She reminded us we were lucky, because Flourette Hall provided the soap powder and the bleach.

As it slipped into late autumn, the weather grew cooler. Fall foliage in splendid colors was scattered over much of the city, a gorgeous sight but a certain sign another dreary winter was around the corner.

Although all of my teachers knew I had a special background, none of them ever revealed my secrets in class. Several offered me special tutoring because I still had trouble understanding a few subjects. Algebra almost sent me to an early grave, but I stuck with it. The extra attention kept me from failing, but I knew I would never major in math or engineering.

I got along with the other students, but I purposely maintained a low profile. I clammed up whenever someone asked me about my family or where I lived. Perhaps they thought I was stuck up for not responding, but I was too ashamed to tell the truth. Most girls had two parents as well as siblings and lived in solidly middle-class areas. I got along with most of the girls, but I kept my distance. That was the safest emotional route to follow.

Whereas I was shy and reserved, some of my classmates were a bit on the wild side. They defied the nuns by cracking jokes in class, smoking cigarettes in the bathroom, and showing off love bites on their necks. One girl, who probably grew up to be a comedian, showed up in class one afternoon in her underwear. The nun gasped and a room full of teenaged girls cracked up so hard most of us were in tears. Grabbing the scantily clad girl by her hair, the nun dragged her out of the room to the principal's office. I guess the principal read the riot act to the practical joker. Secretly, I admired this girl's spunk, knowing I would never have the audacity to be so bold. I had always wanted to let go of myself, but I was firmly surrounded by my own fears, rarely taking such daring risks. For the duration of that school year, I was amused by some of the antics played out before me. Quite a few girls served detention, one was expelled, and numerous parents were called to the office, but the nuns could not seem to break the girls' spirits.

Once, I made slip of the tongue that landed me in trouble. I had been staring out the window at the stormy skies, daydreaming about my precarious future. The steady rainfall must have momentarily lulled me to sleep. All of a sudden, I became startled when the nun called out my name. In a loud voice, she said, "Theresa, Theresa, what is rhythm?"

The nun had lectured the class about human sexuality and her talk blew right over my head. Ignoring my dry mouth, I said the first thing that came to mind. "It's when you keep the beat." The class fell out laughing and the nun glared at me.

The nun admonished the class to keep quiet. She reiterated the details of this method of birth control, the only one approved by the Catholic Church, and asked me to repeat them. I felt embarrassed because I had been caught napping, but the girls seemed quite amused by my faux pas.

For the rest of the lecture, I paid closer attention. I was tickled by the nun's choice of words as she talked about certain parts of the human anatomy. For instance, the nun warned us, "Never let a boy touch you down there." Mrs. Woodson used to issue the same warnings. I once thought I was pregnant when a neighborhood boy, who was probably nine years old, inadvertently ran into me, knocking me over. As we struggled to get up, his left hand brushed against my pubic area.

A smart-mouthed girl flapped her hand in the air and said, "Down where?" She stopped giggling when the nun peered at her with the eyes of an assassin.

As the lecture continued, I had to stifle my smile. The nun said, "Don't touch a boy's thing." I figured out what she meant.

I almost fell off my chair when she said, "Watch out for patent leather shoes. Boys use them to look up your skirts to look at your things." Was this a lecture on sexuality or a comedy class? This nun never cracked a smile as she poured out these ridiculous warnings. Little wonder teenage pregnancy had become more common.

One evening as we sat down at the dinner table, Sister Petrina made her usual somber appearance to lead us in prayer. She obviously did not trust us to pray on our own, so she took charge of mealtime prayers. After she blessed herself and said amen, she reached out and clapped her hands. "Girls, girls, may I have your attention?" Dinner that night was one of our favorite meals, chicken and dumplings. Most of us ignored Sister Petrina and started to dish out the food on our plates. Her pale face turned the color of a red bell pepper. She pounded her fist against the table and yelled, "Girls, I want your attention."

The room was so silent you could hear a pin drop. I was more interested in digging into my plate of dumplings, but nevertheless turned my attention to Sister Petrina. She announced a social worker would visit Flourette Hall every day to provide us with counseling. A few girls looked at me, and we all shrugged. Why now? And did the nuns really expect counseling would make us forget we lived in a group home?

Later, I noticed an envelope with my name on it under my door. I opened it and saw a note from Bridgett McManus, the new social worker. She reminded me social work visits were voluntary, yet she recommended I make an appointment to see her. To keep the peace, I penciled in my name on the sign-up sheet.

I was not thrilled the nuns expected me to talk to a stranger about my personal feelings, especially someone employed by Catholic Charities. They paid for the roof over my head, but they had also never found me a permanent home. On the other hand, I did not hold them culpable for my mother's reckless actions. Nor were they entirely responsible for the deeply rooted institutional racism that permeated much of the child welfare system, a system I believed was stacked against the poor and minorities. Over the years, a number of caseworkers had been paid to keep track of me, yet I could count on one hand the number of visits I had actually received. If I had been maltreated at any of my foster homes, I doubt the abuse would have been uncovered. Caseworkers rarely visited Flourette Hall.

On the afternoon of my appointment I took a seat outside the social worker's office. She used a small room reserved for family conferences that hardly ever happened, but Rosario had been instructed to keep that room neat and tidy at all times.

Miss McManus called me into her office. Her smile was either insincere or the sign of a novice. She instructed me to take a seat. Then, she took out a pen and a pad, scribbled a few notes and said, "So . . ."

"Theresa. That's my name."

"What can you tell me about yourself?"

"I'm black." I knew that remark was flippant, but I resented the whole concept of counseling. I thought it was all a crock.

Miss McManus maintained her composure. "What else?"

"What'd you want me to say? I don't want to be here."

The social worker sighed loudly, so I guess she was exasperated. The other girls mentioned she had recently graduated from social work school and had been unable to secure employment elsewhere. She was also the niece of a retired nun from the Sisters of Good Will. I felt as if I had been handed leftovers instead of something fresh. Even if Miss McManus had bona fide intentions to help, asking me questions like "How do you feel?" was not the way. I had no faith Miss McManus or any other social worker could change the course of my life. She was one more person Catholic Charities threw in my face.

At the end of the unproductive session, Miss McManus asked me to make another appointment. I asked, "What for?" Then, I sensed I hurt the woman's feelings because her eyes became watery. So I agreed to see her again, but only because I felt guilty. By this time in my life, the last person who I would seek out in a time of need was a social worker. These unpleasant experiences most likely caused me to omit social work as a career choice. I felt it was an invasion of privacy to probe strangers with so many personal questions. I did not like it when people asked me questions about my private life, nor did I ask those kinds of questions of the people in my life. While at Mrs. Woodson's, I had most of my intimate conversations with Boomer the dog and Sophie, my imaginary friend.

Thanksgiving was not the traditional holiday celebration found in most American homes. The nuns planned a special dinner for us, but I felt particularly gloomy as the holiday approached. From the look of the mirthless faces surrounding me, I imagined the other girls shared my feelings. Indeed, I had my health, I was not on the streets, I was not caught up in famine like the starving children in Biafra. Their sunken, hollow faces on the nightly news sent chills up my spine, but pushing those frightful images aside, what did any of us wards of the state have to be thankful for?

Hassie spent the week before procuring Thanksgiving fixings, including three extra-large birds, several pounds of sweet potatoes, and a case of cranberry sauce. She was paid overtime to cook a splendid turkey dinner for us.

The hectic schedule of work and school had left me feeling wiped out. The previous week, the nuns had sprung for new bed sheets and the soothing feel of soft, crisp sheets was so inviting I stayed in bed on Thanksgiving morning longer than usual. Around ten o'clock, I showered and changed, then strolled downstairs. I was surprised to find all the nuns were out for the day. They had plans to eat dinner with another group of nuns in a convent belonging to their order. Except for Hassie, we were left without adult supervision, something that rarely happened. I suppose because none of us were mischief-makers, the nuns figured it would be safe to skip out for the day. In reality, I was glad to be free of them for a brief period but I also felt betrayed. They were supposed to be our surrogate parents, yet they abandoned us on a very important family holiday.

About ten girls were also out for the day. Some had made friends at school and had received dinner invitations from their families. A few girls had relatives who asked them to dinner. One girl had volunteered to serve dinner at the Salvation Army. But Tammy, Grace, and most of the others, including me, had nowhere else to go. We diverted our sad feelings by watching the Macy's parade on television. When that got boring, a few of us lumbered into the kitchen to help Hassie with dinner. I think the haggard- looking woman was pleased we offered to help her. In an instant, Hassie delegated kitchen duties, and the next thing we knew a feast fit for a king was ready. Hassie's eyes glowed when we asked her to join us for dinner.

After Hassie had gone home, most of the girls retreated to their rooms. Despite a wave of nippy air, I slipped on my hooded parka and went out for a late afternoon walk. Tammy and Grace asked me to play cards with them, but I felt like being alone. Wandering through the neighborhood, I felt a few people staring at me. Almost all the residents were affluent and white. The only blacks who ventured into this area worked as maids, gardeners, or drivers.

Without realizing it, I must have walked for a few miles. I found myself in the downtown section. Despite my empty feelings, I nonetheless studied the architecture of some of the noted buildings, such as City Hall and St. Paul's Episcopal Cathedral. That kept me occupied for a while, and I moved on. I stared inside store windows recently decorated for Christmas. I smiled as I looked at little figurines of Santa Claus, snowmen, candy canes, and reindeers that filled each window. One window contained miniature trains that circled a nativity scene. These holiday scenes reminded me why Christmas was my least favorite day of the year. It would soon be here, and I braced myself for another bout of depression. As I crossed a main street, I was so caught up in a fantasy where I spent a holiday with my own family that I was almost creamed by a car. It was now after dark, so I pulled up my collar to shield me from the cold and headed back to Flourette Hall. I still had a hard time calling it home, but at least I had someplace to go every day. I was lonely, but grateful for the little piece of stability the group home offered. Although we were all unrelated and from different backgrounds, most of the girls had formed some type of camaraderie. It may not have been a real family, but it was something. It was better than no home at all.

As Christmas drew closer, I closed down more and more. I dreaded another holiday. I hated all the hoopla surrounding Christmas. Television commercial after commercial featured family togetherness. My high school planned a few special events for students and their families. A friend asked me to join her family, but I did not want to feel like a third wheel. I would have preferred to be in a coma for the entire Christmas holiday. Seeing that was not possible, I reached deep inside myself to find some threadbare holiday spirit. I scrounged up enough to make it through one more Christmas.

A week before the big day, one of the sisters took a group of girls to a neighboring tree farm to cut down a fresh pine tree. Sister Petrina, wearing an unusually cheerful look, called everyone to the family room for a night of Christmas carols and decorating. Not to be petulant, I joined the others. One of the nuns served hot chocolate with marshmallows and Oreo cookies. With Bing Crosby singing in the background, we sang Christmas carols and decorated the tree with bargain-basement ornaments and a lopsided star.

On Christmas Eve, the weather was cold and blustery, usual for that time of year. I was sure the nuns would have volunteered to take some of us to midnight Mass, a long-standing Catholic tradition, but lo and behold the sisters tuckered out early. By ten o'clock they were all in bed. A few girls with friends or family members were given permission to stay out late, but the rest of us, including me, retired early.

The next morning, I strolled downstairs to find presents for all of us under the tree. Tammy whispered that Hassie had been given money to shop for us. Opening the two packages meant for me, I found a rayon-blend scarf and a bottle of cheap perfume called Jungle Gardenia. Judging from the other gifts, it seemed that girls with jobs got the short end of the stick. Tammy and Grace, neither of whom worked, received fancier presents such as Elizabeth Arden dusting powder, leather purses, and Walt Disney stuffed animals. I suppose it was the thought that counted. A few days later, I dropped off my gifts at the poor box behind the nearest Catholic Church.

After New Year's Day, Sister Petrina announced a party. The nuns were a rather staid bunch, so I wondered why they were entertaining. Their lifestyle seemed more appropriate for mourning.

The party turned out to be a special Sunday Mass followed by a reunion of former group home residents and their families. On the day of the big gathering, God must have heard Sister Petrina's prayers, because the forecasted snowstorm passed us by. Hassie showed up early to set up. A caterer, related to Sister Petrina, arrived with a large plate of hors d'oeuvres. Hassie brewed a gigantic urn of coffee and made a huge bowl of fruit punch. In addition to the food left by the caterer, she put together an assortment of deviled eggs, pigs in the blanket, and finger sandwiches of ham, turkey, and American cheese. Shortly before noon, someone from the Lynden Bakery arrived with a three- layered chocolate cake topped with flowers made of butter cream. This must have been a special celebration, because even a few of the nuns helped out around the kitchen.

I avoided parties, so when the guests arrived I retreated to my room. Tammy and Grace had asked me to join them for a movie, but I declined, figuring I would spend the time catching up on my homework or getting extra sleep. As I tried to make sense out of World War II for history class, the party in full swing distracted me. Out of curiosity, I stuck my head into the kitchen to see what was happening. Acting like a proud parent, Sister Petrina introduced me to a number of young women, all Flourette Hall alumni. I flashed my usual fake smile, sipped a small cup of punch, and snacked on a few cookies.

One thirty-something woman with a mop of curly brown hair and cheeks as pink as a carnation followed me to the kitchen. Bubbly like Donna Reed, she said, "Hi, I'm Franny. Nice to meet you."

In my usual sullen manner, I said, "I'm Theresa."

Still smiling, she said, "What do you think of the place?"

"It's OK." Why was she so happy?

"I lived here for a few years. The place looks pretty much the same. I guess some things never change."

"How nice." Honestly, I did not care.

Franny read my body language well because she backed away and said, "Nice to meet you. I'm going back to the party. Why don't you join us?"

"No, thanks."

"Come on. It's fun rapping with the nuns."

That was not my idea of fun. "I'll pass."

When she left, I ducked out of the kitchen and went to my room. All in all, I was pleased to see most women seemed relatively normal. A few brought along husbands and children. I assumed they had gone on with their lives, which is exactly what I intended to do.

Late one evening, I found a baby-faced nun sitting alone in the family room. She watched me pass by with inquisitive blue eyes. I turned around when she said, "Hi, I'm Sister Rose."

When I did not respond, she said, "I'll be living here for a while."

I was hungry, tired, and not in the mood to talk to a strange nun. I said, "I'm Theresa," and headed toward the kitchen. From the muffled voices, I could tell a few of the girls were eating dinner and I wanted to join them.

The cheery-faced nun followed me and smiled so much it made me nervous. "If you want to talk or anything, let me know. I'm here for you."

I grabbed a bowl of soup and set my eyes on an empty chair at the table. I heard Sister Rose's voice rise slightly. "Theresa, did you hear me? I want to be there for you."

Coming of Age in the Group Home

Was this woman dense or what? I wanted to get off my aching feet and do something about the hunger pangs inside my stomach. No one seated at the table acknowledged Sister Rose either. They chatted as they stuffed themselves. Ever so slightly, I nodded at the pesky nun then took a seat. Finally, Sister Rose got the message and walked out.

Several days later, there was a knock at our door. Tammy and I both were both cramming for math tests. Grace had fallen asleep. I could tell from the way Tammy slammed her textbook shut she was annoyed. She answered the knock and I was surprised to see Sister Rose. Tammy forced a polite response when she said, "What's up?"

Sister Rose, wearing a larger than usual crucifix around her neck, was like sunshine. "I wanted to check in on my girls. Everyone OK in here?"

Tammy mumbled, "We're studying."

"I'll leave you alone then. Don't forget, girls, I'm here if you want me."

Sister Rose was more irritating than the other nuns who, for the most part, ignored us. I preferred that arrangement. I asked Tammy why Sister Rose was so tenacious. Tammy explained she had recently taken her vows and was supposed to teach freshmen girls in a Catholic school in Rochester starting in January. In the interim, the Church sent her to us. I was still not sure of Sister Rose.

The following Sunday afternoon, the house was surprisingly empty considering how frigid it was outside. Most girls had gone on an ice-skating outing organized by a parish priest. The nuns treated a few girls to a rerun of the *Sound of Music* at the movies, but I had already seen it. I thought about joining the ice-skating group, but knowing I had two left feet, I stayed home and ventured down to the family room to watch basketball instead. Staring at a crucial half-court play that could have tied the game, I was startled when I heard a voice behind me. It was Sister Rose. She asked if she could watch the game with me. My first reaction was to say no, but because this was not my place, I shrugged and said, "Sure, if you want to."

"I thought it would be nice if we could spend some time together."

I was surprised when Sister Rose stayed. I acted like she was not around and focused on the rivalry between the Celtics and the Lakers. When the final buzzer sounded, I shut off the set. I was disappointed because my favorite team, the Lakers, had lost the game.

Walking out of the family room, Sister Rose asked, "Theresa, do you feel like company?"

"Not really," I said.

"Visit with me."

"I was going to rest."

"For a little bit."

"Alright, but not for long, OK?"

Inside her closet-sized room, Sister Rose motioned for me to sit down. She had hardly any furniture so I plopped down on the edge of her bed. Sister Rose sat next to me and plied me with a number of questions about my background. I was surprised, yet simultaneously pleased she expressed so much interest in me. None of the other nuns had asked me about foster care. I was glad to release some of the steam inside me. Maybe Sister Rose would not be such a pain after all.

The mood abruptly changed when I saw Sister Rose inching closer to me in a provocative way. My heart started to pound, and I knew something was wrong. Sister Rose rubbed her hand up and down my thigh and continued to talk. "Doesn't this feel good?"

No, it did not. Frozen with fear, I could not move. True, I appreciated the extra attention she had given me, but her unwanted advances had crossed the line. I kept my eyes glued to the floor, refusing to look at this woman who was violating me. I lacked affection for much of my life, but this physical attention was not what I wanted.

Sister Rose stroked my cheek and said, "This is nice. Real nice. Tell me you like it."

By this time, my hands were shaking so badly I looked like someone who had Parkinson's disease. I prayed for help. I could not stand the lust in her eyes. When I found enough courage, I pushed her hand away and bolted out of the room. Alone in a stairwell, I burst into tears. I felt helpless and did not know what to do. I considered talking to Bridgett the social worker, but I doubted she would believe me. Who else was there? Sister Petrina? No, she would blame me and exonerate Sister Rose. Trapped, I vowed to keep this secret to myself.

I walked to my room to find Tammy and Grace. Smiling, Tammy said, "Hey girl, what's happening?"

I pretended to happy, but I shivered inside. "Not much."

Tammy took a deeper look at me and asked, "What's the matter? You look terrible. Did Sister Petrina get on your case or something?"

"No, I don't feel well. I think I'd better lay down."

Without removing my penny loafers, I jumped into bed. I stayed there for hours, declining my roommates' offer to join them for dinner. Only an urgent call from Mother Nature prodded me to get out of bed. Once the lights were out, I tried desperately to sleep, so I could bury my angry, confused feelings. Instead, I tossed and turned all night, worrying Sister Rose would return.

I got up early the next day, hoping to avoid Sister Rose. She had been at the breakfast table every morning that week and Tammy cursed me for getting up so early. I apologized but could not tell her why I was so upset. On my way out of Flourette Hall, I stopped in the kitchen to grab something cold to drink. Thinking I was alone, I stood by the refrigerator, gulping down orange juice. When I felt a hand rest on my shoulder, I spun around and came face to face with Sister Rose. I dropped my glass, spilling shards across the kitchen floor. The loud noise evidently caught Sister Petrina's attention, because she flew into the kitchen, demanding to know what had happened. When I said I had inadvertently dropped my glass, she frowned then said, "Pick it up. And be careful. These things cost money."

Sister Rose offered to help me, but I wanted no part of her. "Please leave me alone."

In record speed, I swept up the tiny bits of glass, dumped them into the garbage, and rushed out the door. Huddled inside the bus stop, I almost froze. Having left in such a hurry, I had neglected to put on my tights. The tops of my legs felt like slabs of ice by the time a bus arrived.

I avoided Sister Rose, as if she was infested with lice. I stuck close to my roommates, refusing to stay alone in my room. Tammy looked at me cross-eyed a few times, probably wondering why I was acting so skittish, when for months I had tried to be so cool.

On the evenings I worked, I barely touched the leftover dinners Sister Rose had fixed for me. I told her I was not hungry, but somehow I do not think she bought my pack of lies.

Out of desperation one evening, I came down to the kitchen for a snack. Sister Rose greeted me with sensuous eyes. Immediately, I averted my glance, wishing she would leave me alone. Sister Rose brushed up against me. I wanted to scream, but I controlled my tongue. I was so upset I left my plate of cheese and crackers on the table and ran back to my room.

Later, I lay in bed wondering if Sister Rose had molested anyone else. Sister Petrina, who I never saw as a potential ally, proved to be more astute than I could have imagined. She approached me the next day, and I sensed her concern. She asked, "Is anyone bothering you?"

I could feel my eyes widen, but still I maintained my silence. "No sister."

"Are you sure?"

"Yes, ma'am."

Sister Rose kept a low profile. I was thankful she no longer stared at me with lust in her eyes, and I felt relieved not to look over my shoulder all the time. If Sister Rose was in the family room or the kitchen whenever any of us were around, Sister Petrina always marched in and asked her to leave. And then Sister Rose was suddenly gone. I heard she had been transferred to her new parish. The thought of her being surrounded by teenage girls sent chills through my spine, but at least she was not around to torment me.

Twelve

Farewell to Flourette Hall

When I first arrived at the group home, the place seemed to be a surprising collection of well-behaved girls all under one roof. Typical problems among teenagers, such as substance abuse and pregnancy, were noticeably absent at Flourette Hall. Because we were girls who carried extra baggage, I expected there would be at least a few troublemakers on board. The nuns proclaimed Flourette Hall was an example of the power of faith. Prayer, they claimed, kept everyone on the right path. The nuns worked hard to bolster their public image, especially among their more affluent neighbors. From time to time, I overheard well-dressed people make such comments as, "Those girls are such nice girls" or "I wish my daughter was so well-adjusted." More like the real world than the nuns would admit, Flourette Hall had a fair share of inner turmoil. How could it not?

The real truth surfaced when I found out a girl had become pregnant. That caused a major uproar among the nuns. Sister Petrina gave her two choices: get out or go to a Catholic home for unwed mothers in a rural part of Pennsylvania and give the baby up for adoption. The girl got out. A few weeks later, another girl ran away. Someone heard she had joined a cult. Just when I thought the rough seas had calmed down, another tidal wave flared up. A girl was arrested for selling drugs to an undercover police officer. Sister Petrina forced her out, praying while the girl packed her bags.

I expected we would have group meetings to discuss the fate of our housemates. To me, that seemed a sensible way to handle the trouble, because rumors swarmed all over the house. I felt I had a right to know what had happened to these girls. If nothing else, the nuns could have used these negative experiences as examples of how girls could easily go awry. But nothing ever became of our requests for a group meeting. Sister Petrina insisted what these girls had done was none of our business. That was that.

I drove myself to succeed. No matter how drained I was after a full day of classes and checking out groceries at the A & P, I studied for a few hours, even when my roommates tempted me to horse around. Most of the girls at school had families to fall back on. Because I did not, working toward my high school degree became even more crucial. More importantly, at age eighteen, the state no longer supported young people in foster care, whether you were prepared for the outside world or not. My emancipation date was getting closer and I was determined not to plunge from foster care into welfare. I had already spent a lifetime feeling trapped.

Unlike grammar school, where I struggled, I found high school more palatable. My dyslexia forced me to work harder than most other girls, but I held my own. I passed all my classes and stopped believing I was stupid.

The teachers permitted us a bit of freedom at lunch time. I suppose because there were no boys at the school, the sisters felt comfortable allowing us to eat lunch off the premises. Because I scrimped and saved the money I earned at the A & P, I usually ate the cafeteria food. It was generally tasteless, but at least it was affordable.

I broke out of my shell enough to socialize with a small group of white girls. Every now and then, we crashed at someone's house for lunch. Sometimes the parents were home, but mostly they were out. Women had entered the workforce in greater numbers, so many girls had mothers who worked at least a few hours a day, if not full-time.

I was the only black girl among this clique. Racial tensions at Christ the King were minimal. The real problems centered on drug use and pregnancy. Whenever a girl got pregnant, she was mysteriously whisked away from school. Why was I not surprised when the same thing happened at Flourette Hall? The nuns at school refused to acknowledge certain girls even existed. Aware of the big secret, we kept conversation about the bad girls to ourselves. Teenage pregnancy was less of a taboo than it had been, but I was not about to go down that perilous road. I had enough problems as it was.

As a rule, I kept my nose clean, but some of my classmates experimented with drugs. The drugs of choice included marijuana, hashish, speed, mescaline, and acid as well as uppers and downers. A few girls brazenly hawked drugs on school premises. The school turned a blind eye on student drug use, never inviting any outside professionals to talk to us. Furthermore, I knew of a handful of girls who got stoned before school every morning. I do not remember any receiving a reprimand, even when some could barely speak.

One day, a group of us piled into a girl's house at lunchtime. We had stopped at McDonald's for cheeseburgers, fries, and shakes. To everyone's surprise, the girl's mother was home. Evidently, she left work early because of illness. The round-faced woman had teased blonde hair fluffed out to the size of a football helmet. As soon as she took one look at my dark skin, her puffy cheeks became flushed. I surmised she was not a civil rights activist.

The woman glared at her daughter with steely eyes and made a demanding motion with her index finger to follow her to the kitchen. The rest of us sat there, not knowing what to do or say. I felt on the spot. A few minutes later, the girl returned. She tried to act nonchalant, but I knew what was up. An oppressive silence hung over the room as we slowly ate our lunch. One small-minded act of bigotry robbed me of a pleasurable experience.

Over time, my popularity among these girls slowly started to wane. Word buzzed around school that others had been similarly scolded for bringing me into their house. I felt like a knife had ripped through my heart. Was my dark skin that intimidating to people?

Instead of being honest with me, the girls shut me out like I was a thief. I imagine they probably felt guilty because I was a well-respected student. I was no longer invited to join them for lunch, but the residual effects of these incidents failed to end there. I became more of a social misfit and developed even greater trouble forming attachments to other people. I was fed up with racism, but I was equally fed up with my life. How much more could I tolerate?

Despite strained relationships with my classmates, one white girl named Amy broke with tradition and remained my friend. I suppose Amy took quite a bit of flack for this, but she was a stubborn, defiant girl. Nobody was going to push her around. Once, I heard Amy broke a girl's nose because she called her brother a wimp. She said her parents were cool. They were older hippie types who now worked as college professors.

I was invited to Amy's house for the evening. I had confided in Amy a little bit about my past. That I was an a ward of the state seemed to have no effect on her all. I was glad because Amy honestly seemed to enjoy my company.

When I arrived that evening, Amy introduced me to her parents. After a brief yet pleasant introduction, Amy said she had a documentary tape about changing family dynamics she wanted me to see. Because her father taught English, Amy had access to a film projector. We filled up a bowl with popcorn and retreated to her room.

In the tape, a black boy, perhaps ten years old, was sent to summer camp by his single mother. At the end of the boy's two-week stay, the mother failed to return. The little boy, however, was never told the truth. The main camp counselor, not knowing what to do, let him remain, without explaining why his vacation had been extended.

Over time, the camp counselor became attached to the young boy. When summer ended and it became evident the boy had been abandoned, the counselor applied to become his foster parent. The counselor, an unmarried white woman, had a long-time, live-in boyfriend but they had no plans for marriage. Of course, she worried this would cause the state to reject her as a foster parent. Amazingly, the state did not object, and neither did the little boy. He lived with the couple for almost a year. The couple then tried to adopt him, because the boy's mother had never been found.

The boy, although reserved, was very intelligent. He followed the rules and never acted out. During food shopping trips, the boy expressed pleasure his input was considered when planning for meals.

The boy had also developed a good rapport with young children, but he had trouble relating to kids his own age. Nonetheless, adoption proceedings went smoothly.

Several months later, the boy asked for a new more expensive toy, a request his new family turned down. He surged with anger and shouted, "I hate you." His outburst caught the adoptive parents off guard. They realized the boy felt a certain amount of trust otherwise he never would have felt safe enough to express his hurt feelings.

As the film ended, I was gripped by a wave of cold bitterness. Momentarily immobilized by rage, I had a brief taste of what I had missed. I was so mad I could have rammed my fist through a plate glass window and screamed until my throat was raw. I never felt secure enough with anyone to express my deepest feelings—good, bad, or indifferent. Slightly more than sixteen years old, I had lived with more families than I could remember, feeling left out of each one. I always had to be accommodating, even when I did not want to. In home after home, I felt like an outsider, a stranger, in a place the caseworkers expected me to feel comfortable. The little girl and now the teenaged Theresa was aloof. Sometimes, I felt so lost I worried I would never find myself anywhere. What should have been a childhood of fun had been snatched away. I continuously did and said what I thought people wanted me to do or say. I learned how to anticipate other people's needs, never finding my own. I was a robot with no mind of my own.

When the film credits appeared on the screen, I broke down and wept, something I rarely did in public. With the floodgates finally unlatched, the tears poured down in buckets to the point where I became inconsolable. Until then, I always kept a tight lid on my feelings. I felt ashamed someone had seen me bawl my eyes out. For the first time, I felt the pain stab through me, leaving my heart throbbing with anguish. Amy hugged me and said, "I'm your friend." She said this several times while I cried.

"I'm sorry."

"Don't be."

I said, "But I never do this in public."

"I'm not just anyone. I'm your friend."

"I wish I hadn't done this."

"Why? Are you ashamed?"

"Yes."

"I can't tell you how to feel, but I'm trying to understand. If you don't let anyone in, no one can do anything for you."

"I know."

I left, feeling simultaneously relieved and mortified. What would Amy think of me when she saw me in school? That I was a wimp, or what? By the time I got home, I already decided not to give her a chance at being my friend.

I became accustomed to group living, more or less. I learned how to coexist with the girls. Not unexpectedly, we had our bad days. A brawl almost erupted around the washing machine when one girl accused another one of stealing her designer jeans. Two girls once fought over a misplaced tube of lipstick. Despite a few minor imbroglios, we basically we got along. Dealing with the insensitive nuns was rarely a problem for me anymore. Sister Rose was gone and I kept to myself, doing what was expected of me.

I continued to work at the grocery store. More people bought groceries with food stamps, and not all of them were black. As more factories closed down or relocated to the South, many people were left in the lurch. Growing poverty now stained Buffalo's once solid blue-collar image. One afternoon, I checked out groceries for a white woman with two small children, one of whom appeared to have Down's syndrome. The haggard-looking woman burst into tears when I said her food stamps were not enough to cover her bill. Another afternoon, I had to tell a middle-aged black man that he could not buy dog food with food stamps. When he pleaded, "My dog has to eat, too," I overlooked this minor infraction. I felt sorry so many people were on the edge.

My savings account had grown to more than five hundred dollars, and I was very proud of my accomplishment. I had no idea what would happen when I turned eighteen, my separation date with Catholic Charities. By then, I hoped to be finishing high school and preparing to go off to college, but nothing in my life had been certain. Consequently, I worked a few extra hours each week and stuffed the money in my bank account—just in case. I did not want to end up on the streets, a frequent fate for girls who ran away from Flourette Hall.

Although not very outgoing, I went to a dance at my high school. Boys from a neighboring Catholic school had been invited, so the purity patrol was out in full force. Whenever a couple danced too closely, especially during a slow dance, one of the nuns pried them apart and preached a lecture about the dangers of lust. I danced with a skinny white guy who looked like Eddie Haskell from *Leave it to Beaver,* but otherwise I spent the night making small talk with Amy and some of the girls and getting into the Motown sound.

During the semester, the girls who had given me the cold shoulder spoke to me once in a while, but none of us ever made an effort to revive our friendships. I continued to eat lunch with Amy and some of her friends. A few times, I joined Amy's family for dinner, but again I was afraid to get too close so I kept Amy at arm's length. Over time, I think she sensed what was up because she eventually stopped asking me to visit her at home.

I thought about college. On my own, I browsed through dozens of brochures at the school guidance office. I felt excited about continuing my education. Perhaps this was a bit sooner than most students explored options for college, but I felt it was my only choice to avoid the road to nowhere. I never sought assistance from the guidance counselor because I doubted she took my aspirations seriously. Gains had been made for blacks and other minorities, but black students were rarely viewed as college material. We were not encouraged to take calculus or advanced English composition like other college-bound students. I liked my job at the grocery store, but I did not want to spend a lifetime at the checkout line. Not that a cashier is a dishonorable job, but I wanted a career. I started out my life as a nobody, but I wanted to end up as a somebody. I now believed I could climb and I wanted to see how far I could go.

And so life went on. Days turned into weeks. Weeks transformed into months. I had been at the group home for more than a year and a half. Thinking I had finally settled into an acceptable routine, the walls came tumbling down around me again. It was late March and winter was about to take a hike for another year. I no longer had to bundle up like an Inuit, and I looked forward to a brief respite from the cold. Over the summer, I planned to work additional hours at the A & P.

Sister Petrina made a surprise announcement one evening at dinner that sent a biting chill through my body. She said, "The Church has decided to close Flourette Hall."

I felt a melon-sized lump in my throat as I looked around the room. The other girls had dazed looks on their faces.

"But why?" I asked, shaking. "How could the Church do that to us?" According to our housekeeper and cook, the bishop and his entourage of priests lived in a luxurious eighteen-room house in a fashionable section of Buffalo. They employed a full-time staff of five that included a housekeeper, administrative assistant, cook, gardener, and driver.

Sister Petrina's voice sagged as she said, "Girls, I'm sorry. The bishop made his decision. When school is out in June, Flourette Hall will close. There's not enough money." The grim-faced nun turned around and walked away, leaving us alone to fret about our futures.

While doing her laundry one day the previous week, Tammy had mentioned she had overheard Sisters Petrina and Theophane talking inside the kitchen.

I asked, "What'd they say?"

Tammy said, "The bishop wasn't happy because the newspaper ran a story about Jeanine who got arrested for selling drugs. I heard he was worried about the Church's unsullied image. It didn't help when Monica got pregnant. He claimed Flourette Hall was attracting the wrong element."

I said, "But I thought there was an endowment to run Flourette Hall? Didn't somebody die and leave lots of money?"

"Most of the money is gone. I heard Sister Petrina say they spent most of it. The money they get from the state to look after us isn't enough to keep this place going." Tammy looked at me with a long, cool stare. "That's what I heard them say."

A group of us sat around the table and mulled over our future. What would become of us? I could hardly believe this was happening again. Although I tried to remain calm, I broke out into a cold sweat. Hassie had baked four deep-dish apple pies for dessert, but no one had an appetite. In single file, we dragged ourselves upstairs, surrounded by a suffocating silence. My roommates and I made feeble attempts to study, but with gloomy faces we glanced at one another and went to bed early. For the first time in my life, I felt like having a good, stiff drink.

I tried to sleep but tossed and turned instead. Huddled underneath the covers, I could feel a few tears slowly drip down my cheeks. I thought about my small savings account, but I was still a teenager without a high school diploma and no marketable skills. With those credentials, I knew my future was as bleak as the growing population of displaced factory workers. Suddenly, I started to shiver all over, as if my body was racked with fever. Tammy and Grace must have heard the noise, because they sat on the edge of my bed and said, "We're scared, too."

I sat up and wiped my sniffles with the tissue Tammy handed me. Not only saddened, I was also in a state of total disbelief. "I can't believe all the money is gone."

Tammy said, "Me neither, but it must be. I sure as hell don't want to start all over again, but I guess I'll have to. We all have to."

"I feel crappy, too," Grace added, "I'm not crazy about this place, but it's all I've known for the last five years."

I sat up and said, "Maybe we can see the bishop."

Tammy made a sarcastic sucking sound as she slammed her fist against the bed. "And do what? Wash his new Lincoln Continental?"

I was not going to bow down without a fight. "Maybe if a group of us show up and protest in front of his house, he'll reconsider."

In contrast to my usual docile personality, the bad news sent new life through me. I organized a group to express our opposition to the closure. Some of the girls recruited a few of their friends, and we set a date for our protest. None of us were sophisticated when it came to public demonstrations, and we did not realize we needed a permit. But that did not deter us.

Three days later, we skipped school and gathered in front of the bishop's residence. Holding onto our hand-made placards, we marched up and down the street. In unison, we shouted, "Save our home. Save our home." My hands were shaking, but I held up my head high. I saw this as an important battle, one that, if lost, could have grave implications for the other girls and me.

Needless to say, we attracted some but not much attention. We were much quieter than some of the rowdy mill workers who used to picket at the steel plants. Except for a few passing cars, the streets were basically empty. The only people who saw us were the mostly black cooks, housekeepers, and gardeners who passed us by on their way to work in the neighborhood.

The bishop was at home, but he sent one of his older priests as an emissary to deal with us. I could see bulging veins in the priest's thick neck as he warned us to disperse. The priest was adamant, almost hostile. "I warned you girls to stop this foolishness. Now you'll be in trouble. Wait and see."

Undaunted by his threats, we kept up our spirited march. A little while later, two police cars showed up. A tall, leathery- skinned officer approached, sneering at us as if we were causing a major riot. He waved his nightstick at us and said, "I got a call you're disturbing the peace."

I protested, "But officer, we want to see the bishop. He wants to close our group home. We don't mean any trouble."

The cop was unmoved by our plight. "No permit, no march." He placed his hands on his hips and said, "You got one?"

I said, "No sir, we don't."

The cops herded all ten of us into their patrol cars. We never got the chance to plead our case before the bishop. The police drove us back to Flourette Hall. That in itself caused a major scene. When Sister Petrina opened the front door and noticed the revolving beacons, she probably assumed we were intoxicated or something. I could tell we were in for it.

The second we passed through the front gate, Sister Petrina ran out and snarled at us like an angry dog. "Get in here now."

It really did not matter to us our actions had ticked off Sister Petrina. We felt we acted appropriately. To the nuns, Flourette Hall was probably a plum assignment with extra benefits. To us, it was our lifeblood, the only thing we knew as home. The nuns would be reassigned to other parishes or go into retirement, where they would be taken care of. The same could not be said about us.

Once inside, Sister Petrina ranted and raved so much I thought she needed a sedative. She had not become this angry when someone got pregnant or stayed out late. "You girls made me look bad in front of the bishop. The bishop of all people."

I volunteered to act as spokesperson. "We protested because we need this place. None of us has anywhere else to go. Maybe you can't understand how we feel, but we're all scared."

Still fuming, Sister Petrina waved an index finger at me. "We'll make other arrangements."

Along with my housemates, we turned and slowly walked away. It seemed a moot point to continue. Like the great Wizard of Oz, the Church had spoken. Flourette Hall would close in another two months.

Our next few days were as depressing as the late winter weather. Not only did we have to worry about our immediate future we had to contend with a lot of in-fighting. Sister Petrina still stewed about our protest, harping on everything we did. If there was a single dirty glass left in the sink, she had a fit. If one of us came home even two minutes later than expected, she grilled her like a detective working on a hard-to-solve case. I wanted to call her Atilla the Nun but I kept a lid on my mouth. For the first time, she referred to me and the other black girls as "you people." And the sister of mercy was good at back-stabbing. She spread rumors to the other girls we were only out to save ourselves. That was a blatant lie, because our goal was to save Flourette Hall for all of us. Tension became so thick around the house I could have easily been crushed by it.

My teachers at Christ the King had been forewarned about the closing and that I might have to transfer schools in the next academic year. I studied as much as I could, but my concentration level was almost nonexistent. Having this rug pulled out from under me fortified me with the belief I should never get too attached to anyone or anything. Not even the Catholic Church could provide me with security.

Sister Petrina called Tammy, Grace, and me into her rarely used office. I felt like I was sitting with the director of a funeral home. She instructed us to take seats and explained, "Girls, I have some news about your living arrangements."

I could hardly wait for the news. With every ounce of courtesy I could muster, I asked, "Are we going together?"

"Do any of you remember Franny?"

We looked at one another and shook our heads we did not.

"She was here in January. I introduced some of you to her. Anyway, she read in the papers Flourette Hall was closing down and approached me with a very generous offer."

I asked, "Did she donate money to keep us open?"

Sister Petrina said, "No, not that, but she offered to have some of you live with her and her family."

The offer surprised me. "But she seems so young. Doesn't she have children of her own?"

Sister Petrina frowned at my question, but she remained composed. She explained Franny Candelaria was in her thirties, married, and had three young children. Franny had been approved as a foster parent, most likely because we were all older, two of us were black, and all of us were labeled as hard to place. I felt as if I was being left in her hands not because it was the best choice, but because it was expedient and convenient.

And so my immediate future was set. But set for how long? Only God knew the answer to that. I hoped I was on His good side.

I was suspicious about making this next move. I thought black children were only supposed to live with black families. Moreover, I did not know Franny or her family. Then again, I had no previous knowledge about any of my other foster families. With no other prospects, I packed my bags. Ready or not, I was about to walk away from Flourette Hall for the last time.

Thirteen

Around and Around I Went

What little I owned could have fit inside my usual moving-day luggage—a couple of shopping bags. Besides my clothing, I only had a few school supplies. Like the other girls at the group home, I attached very little sentimental value to the items I owned. They were possessions that served some useful purpose in my life. The only things of value that could not be taken from me were my thoughts.

As a parting gift on our last day, the nuns slapped carfare in our hands. I was surprised when I noticed we each held onto a twenty-dollar bill. The nuns bowed their heads and prayed quietly as we walked out the front door. I felt like I was on an emotional carousel ride and wanted the insanity to stop. As for their prayers, I wanted to say "Why bother?" but I assumed praying somehow made them feel better. Perhaps if I had prayed harder and more regularly, I would have found a home. For me, prayer was now of little use as I headed out to live with yet another set of strangers. At this late stage, I was sick of the up-and-down routine that dictated the lives of foster children. All I could think about was my eighteenth birthday, now only a shade over two years away. I surmise that, due to my hard-to place status, Catholic Charities stopped trying to place me in permanent homes. Adoption no longer entered my mind.

Around and Around I Went

The weather was seasonably warm but without the awful heat and humidity. To save money, we rode the bus instead of hailing a cab. After a forty-minute bus ride that took us from one of the more affluent sections of Buffalo to a decidedly working-class neighborhood, our stop finally arrived. With gloomy faces, Tammy, Grace and I got off the bus and dragged ourselves toward our next temporary refuge.

Walking in awkward silence, I noticed Grace and I were the only black faces around. Although this was the early 1970s, racial segregation was still a way of life in Buffalo, as it was in most American cities. Enforcement of the few antidiscrimination laws was weak.

When a black family found a realtor willing to show them homes in white neighborhoods, for sale signs usually shot up soon after they arrived. I remember that happening when Mrs. Woodson bought a new house in a white neighborhood. The mass exodus fueled by fear and bigotry transformed white neighborhoods into predominantly black ones in just a few years. Only the elderly who could not afford to move, the enlightened who believed in equality, and interracial families who did not fit in either world remained. I had the impression white people viewed blacks as degenerate invaders ready to cause harm to a respectable neighborhood. This was not true. Black people wanted their children to have a better life. They only moved to white neighborhoods to take advantage of better-managed school systems and to live under decent conditions. To achieve equality blacks often had to endure hatred in the form of nasty taunts and despicable acts of violence. The city neglected us as well. Burned-out street lights were not replaced on a regular basis. Street repairs were often neglected. Trash removal was sporadic. Perhaps my feelings were extreme, but I hoped no one would burn a cross on Franny's lawn because she had invited Grace and me to live with her family.

I looked up at number 231 and said, "Well ladies, I think this is it."

Tammy said, "I wish I could show some enthusiasm."

The house was a faded light blue, two-story wooden structure with tiny flecks of paint falling off the exterior. A two-car garage rested behind the house. The property, although small, was kept up, but the house was not like the regal structures surrounding Flourette Hall. People in this area worked hard for a living, often at minimum-wage jobs in the service industry, because better-paying factory jobs were scarce.

Tammy said, "What do you think it'll be like?"

I shrugged. "Let's not look for miracles. A roof over our heads will do."

We exchanged anxious glances, then opened the front gate. Walking up five wide steps, we found ourselves on a clean but rickety front porch. I took the lead and rang the bell. Within seconds, a tall woman, wearing tight shorts and a sleeveless V-neck top that revealed a generous amount of cleavage, answered. She flashed a silly grin and giggled. "Hi girls, come on in. I've been expecting you."

As we entered, a little boy who was about four years old appeared. He slid behind his mother, looked at us like we were aliens, and asked, "Mommy, who is them?"

Franny tried to act cool. She brushed a tuft of long, wavy dark hair from her face. Nudging her son closer to us, she said, "Paulie, this is Theresa, Tammy, and Grace. They're going to be staying with us. Remember?"

Clad in faded plaid shorts and a Buffalo Bills T-shirt, Paulie sucked his thumb. When Franny yanked his hand from his mouth, the boy kept staring at Grace and me. I guessed this was his first encounter with people of color.

Franny shoved a piece of gum in her mouth and said, "Let me show you to your rooms."

The three of us followed Franny and her son up a flight of uncarpeted stairs. I sensed Paulie's persistent staring must have made Franny uncomfortable. When we reached the second level, she looked at us, smacked the gum, and said, "Wait a minute. I got to put him in for a nap."

A door slammed. Franny and her son disappeared. Not knowing what else to do, we stood outside the boy's room and waited. My eyes darted around and noticed there were only three other bedrooms on this floor. Because I had been told in advance Franny and her husband, Joe, had three children, I wondered where we would all sleep.

Franny returned, and she explained the living arrangements. Her two older children, fifteen-year-old Tony and twelve-year-old Maria, slept in separate rooms downstairs. Paulie had his own room next to the master bedroom she shared with her husband. She rested her hands on her rounded hips. "Two of you will have to share a room. Do you want to talk about it and let me know?"

I looked at Tammy, then at Grace. "Probably a good idea. Give us a few minutes."

Once we were alone, we arrived at a decision quickly. Tammy and Grace agreed to share the larger room while I planned to take the smaller one. When we informed Franny about our choice, she chomped on the gum, tilted her hips to the side, and said, "Whatever you girls want. I want you to feel comfortable here."

Franny, whose real name was Francesca, was an Italian-American woman originally from the Greenpoint section of Brooklyn. She had been sent upstate to Flourette Hall when her parents split up. Franny's mother had a nervous breakdown and was sent to Creedmoor, a public asylum in New York City. Franny's father, a chronic alcoholic, moved to Rhode Island with another woman. None of Franny's relatives were willing to take in a teenager known to have a wild side. Franny said her relatives blamed her for the mother's breakdown. She admitted she used to stay out past her curfew, dated older boys, and stole clothing from the Manhattan department store where she worked. Franny said she was happy as a mother and homemaker. Joe was a fireman, and due to the nature of his job, he often slept at the firehouse.

Regardless of Franny's past, she seemed as if she had cleaned up her act. Motherhood must have done the trick. What prompted her decision to take in three teenaged foster girls no longer mattered. It seemed as if I had a place to stay, at least for a while.

Because the store was located some distance from this neighborhood, I reluctantly resigned from the A & P. I figured travel back and forth would be too much of a burden, especially in winter when Buffalo temperatures often hovered near zero. The store manager and I got along well, so he promised to give me a good recommendation.

The day after I settled into Franny's home, I checked the Yellow Pages for grocery stores in the area. After applying to all three of them, I was hired to work at Grand Union, another chain of grocery stores in the Northeast. The store was short-handed, so they welcomed my offer to work full-time until school started. Besides my desire to build up my bank account, I also wanted to keep a low profile. Franny seemed like a decent person, but she had a lot of nervous energy, reflected by her constant gum chewing and nail biting.

Tammy and Grace quickly followed suit, landing part-time jobs within days. Tammy found work as a cashier at a downtown sporting goods store and Grace was hired to work the grill at a fast food outlet, not far from the house.

Franny knocked on my door late one afternoon. She looked at me sheepishly and asked, "Do you like the furniture? Joe and I picked it out at Sears the week before you girls came."

Honestly, the single bed was as comfortable as any I had slept on. The wood veneer desk looked tacky and the corduroy armchair was not very comfortable, but I did not want to hurt Franny's feelings, I said, "It's all fine."

Again, chewing gum, Franny said, "Let me know if you need something."

"OK."

I thought Franny wanted to sit down and talk, but I was not in the mood. Maybe she wanted to get to know me, but I never expected much out of this deal. Franny's family was not mine, and I wanted to keep a solid distance between us. To me, this was only a place to stay. I had no feelings about Franny and her family one way or another.

Franny nodded, turned around, then came back in. "You know, you and the girls can eat dinner with us."

Sensing I should make some efforts to be cordial, I said, "What time do you eat?"

"Food goes on the table at five o'clock. When Joe is at the firehouse, I like to make sure the kids eat early."

I agreed to join Franny and the kids for dinner. Tammy and Grace were not home, presumably at work. I neglected to ask Franny what was on the menu. What did it matter? I was going through the motions to be polite. As long as she did not serve mystery meat or oatmeal, I assumed I could get through the meal.

Easing into a chair at the dining room table, I found Franny's rambunctious kids already seated. They were engaged in a loud shouting match over who ate the last of the Oreo cookies. Little Paulie staunchly defended himself against his older brother, Tony. He claimed their sister must have gobbled up the sweet treats, leaving only a box filled with crumbs inside the kitchen cabinet. The kids were in such a frenzy they barely paid attention to me as I took a seat.

Franny bounded into the dining room, holding a potholder in one hand. She smacked Tony on the back of the head and yelled, "Shut up and stop picking on your little brother. Wait till your father gets home. He won't be too happy when I tell him you kids were fighting over cookies. He might put an end to snacks."

Tony protested. "But Ma."

"But Ma nothing. I said shut up. You deaf, or what?" Franny pointed at me and said, "Show some manners. Otherwise, Theresa won't want to eat with us."

She was right. I preferred not to stay for dinner, but I assumed that, if I ducked out, Franny would be offended. The confusion was too much for me to handle. Instead, I flashed one of my phony smiles and unfolded my napkin.

Franny stood next to me and said, "I hope you don't think we're a bunch of loonies or something."

I handed her a stiff nod. "No, not at all." I thought they were loud and obnoxious.

From the interactions I had just witnessed, I wondered if this was an authentic family experience. For years, I had eaten dinner with foster families where personal melodramas were rarely played out. Mrs. Woodson would never have tolerated such bickering. The nuns at Flourette Hall frowned upon vocal disagreements. Television characters provided no help either. Imagine seeing a battle like this on any of the popular family programs, especially *Family Affair, Father Knows Best*, or *That Girl*. In an odd way, I felt relieved to learn real families were not as ideal as I made them out to be.

After Franny served a dinner of baked ziti with meatballs, a green salad, and Italian bread, she returned to the kitchen, saying she forgot the salad dressing. Seconds later, all hell broke loose. The boys still roiled about the Oreo cookies. Paulie dug his hand into the salad bowl and hurled a chunk of tomato at Tony. In turn, Tony grabbed the loaf of Italian bread and smacked his little brother on the head.

Paulie ran around the table and started to pound his little fists on Tony's back. As Maria attempted to separate the two boys, Franny walked in. She slammed the bottle of salad dressing on the table, took one look at the two boys, and shouted, "Stop it right now. Look at you kids. I can't turn my back on you for one minute." She threw her arms in the air and said, "That's it. I've had it with the nonsense. No cookies for any of you."

Paulie protested. "But Ma."

Franny yelled, "Sit down and shut up, I said."

If this was what family life was like, then perhaps living my life as an orphan was not all that bad. During dinner, no one spoke. The only sound was food being chewed. After I took my last bite, I excused myself and retreated to my room. I had paid my dues. Now, I wanted to be alone to think about where the rocky road I traveled on might lead me.

I came home from work one day to find a set of new curtains hanging in my room. The grocery store had been busy all day, and I was beat. Taking off my shoes and socks, I responded to a knock at my door. It was Franny. She was all smiles. "Can I come in?"

"OK."

"Do you like the new curtains? I had them on back order."

The lime green, ruffled nylon curtains dappled with tiny red roses were not in my taste. I would have preferred something plain; these curtains were too gaudy. Ignoring my aching feet, I pointed to the window. I pretended to be satisfied. "I'm sure they're fine. I haven't had a minute to myself since I left the house this morning."

Franny's bright eyes dimmed a bit. She whipped her head to the side as if I had insulted her and said, "I was trying to make it nice for you."

I sensed she was on the defense. To diffuse her anger, I tried to mollify her. "Franny, the curtains are nice. Really, they are. I'm exhausted. I hope you understand."

The last thing I wanted was to engage in a verbal banter about curtains I did not like. As calmly as possible, I said, "I know you're trying. But I need a few minutes to rest. I'll see you later."

Franny asked, "You coming to dinner with us?"

"Not tonight. Grace, Tammy, and I are going out. With all of us working, we haven't seen much of each other."

I also felt upset Franny never asked the other girls or me about our culinary preferences. Because she received money to care for us, I thought she would have consulted us about meals. I assumed my lactose intolerance was never explained to Franny because she served a lot of meals with dairy products. Moreover, I had lost my taste for meat. Mrs. Woodson used to feed us meat two to three times a day, and now I preferred a vegetarian diet.

Franny lowered her head. "You can eat with us if you change your mind. You be careful not to get hurt by these girls."

"Thanks for the advice, but we've lived together for a while. They're good people."

I sensed Franny was envious. Even though she had not discussed too much of her personal life with me, it was apparent she had married and had children at a fairly young age.

Suddenly, I remembered an earlier conversation I had overheard on the day I met Franny during the reunion at Flourette Hall. Franny had been talking to one of the nuns about her plans for college. She mentioned wanting to study nursing at Buffalo State University. Lots of women deferred careers to raise a family, so I assumed Franny's role as a mother and housewife was the one she wanted. I thought she was on edge all the time because she had three rowdy kids, an indifferent husband who rarely took part in child-rearing, and a stack of unpaid bills. That would have been enough to give me gray hair.

I wondered if I should have included Franny in our dinner plans. No, I reminded myself, she may be my legal guardian, but I have a right to my own life. I motioned toward the door. "It was nice talking to you, but I have to rest now."

From the sulking look on Franny's face, I gathered she was pissed off. Moments later, I heard her plod down the stairs with such force she sounded like a soldier in combat boots, not a woman wearing thongs. I had doubts Franny was the happy homemaker she appeared to be, but I was not in a position to bail her out of an unfulfilling life. I had my own fish to fry, and they were big fish.

In the midst of a dinner of egg rolls, fried rice, and chow mein that night, Tammy, Grace, and I talked about our jobs. None of us particularly enjoyed the drudgery and low wages associated with retail employment.

A few of the girls in my class made wads of cash selling drugs, but I steered clear of illicit narcotics. I could not imagine drug peddling could improve my life. The only sure end I saw it leading to was a life behind bars or an early grave.

Grace said, "I feel so greasy after I leave work. Even when I take a shower, I still feel like I'm not clean. Girl, I can't fry hamburgers forever."

"I know what you mean," Tammy added, "some of those people in the sporting goods store get on my nerves. They come in with flashy clothes and expensive jewelry, then demand to know what's on sale. Cheap bastards."

I agreed. I worked my buns off for slightly more than minimum wage of $1.95 per hour. My coworkers were pleasant and the manager was fair, but the customers sometimes irked me. I wondered if it was related to race. Every so often, I noticed that white customers helped white check-out girls pack the groceries they had just purchased. When on my line, these same people refused to lift a finger to help me, even when their kids were screaming and the lines snaked down the aisles.

I said, "A lot of people have no choice but to work in these jobs. I admire them for putting up with the indignities. Not me. I hope I can get paid to think, and not obey orders."

Tammy and Grace nodded agreement. Both girls were about to start their senior year of high school. I was a year behind, but I kept my mind focused on higher education. Foster care may not have found me a home, but over the years it instilled necessary survival skills—not the kind needed to endure a month in the woods, but ways to cope with reality. Because I could not rely on a trust fund or hefty inheritance to keep me afloat, I knew I would have to do it alone. I needed to find a way of shedding my fears. At the age of eighteen, I would be officially on my own. I had to be ready. It was either that or crumble.

After dinner, we strolled along the mostly quiet streets. Because it was late August, many of Franny's neighbors milled about their front yards. I felt crude stares bearing down on me as we passed by certain houses. Grace must have felt the glares as well, and Tammy had to be in a coma not to notice. Tammy said nothing, but I am confident she felt the tension. It seemed doubtful all of Franny's neighbors were thrilled at the sight of two black girls, but at least they did not hurl nasty names at us. Their icy stares said enough.

I was allowed to continue my education at Christ the King, even though I no longer lived in that parish. At least that was one less adjustment I had to make. It was a thirty-five minute bus ride away, much further than the Catholic school nearest to Franny. I planned to use the extra commuting time to study. Buffalo was not always scenic, which made it easy to avoid looking out the window. Besides, the sight of so many closed factories, boarded-up stores, and homes for sale made me depressed. I attached no fond memories to Buffalo, but I hoped this proud and gritty city would not cave in and die.

To achieve my goal of self-sufficiency, I took every lesson seriously. Some of my classmates goofed off by cutting classes, not handing in assignments, or cracking jokes in class. One of them once called me a brown nose, but I was not insulted. I was on a mission no one could interrupt. A college education was my ticket out of nowhere.

A few of my teachers noticed my constant efforts to succeed. Miss Morse, my history teacher, asked me to stay after class one day. When all of the students cleared out of the room, she approached me with a lot of tact and respect. "I admire you for sticking with high school the way you have. I had a student like you who dropped out. If there is any way I can help you, please let me know."

Still reserved, I smiled slightly. "Thank you for asking."

Miss Morse, a slender woman probably in her early forties, gently rested her hand on my shoulder and said, "Don't forget to come to me."

When she must have sensed I was unwilling to divulge more information, she picked up a few folders and said, "Remember what I said. And keep up the good work."

On the bus to my job, I mulled over the conversation with Miss Morse, one of the few teachers who showed faith in me. Her brief outpouring of support would carry me a long way.

I pulled better grades in my junior year of high school than in my first two years. Trigonometry almost did me in, however, and I sweated through it by hitting the books until midnight. I learned to survive on less sleep.

I even became popular among some of the girls. In October, when each homeroom was asked to elect a class president, a group of girls nominated me and I won the election. Thrilled with this honor, I finally felt like I would be somebody.

The biggest disappointment I faced was not attending social events planned for families. In late October, the school had planned a mother-daughter night. I thought about asking Franny, but I figured her white complexion would let everyone know I had no family.

I figured out Franny was a deeply troubled woman. Whenever her husband Joe was at home, which was not very often, they bickered constantly. Franny complained about the high cost of living, her ill-behaved children, and Joe's parents. Joe claimed Franny whined too much, especially when it came to his mother. Evidently, there was bad blood between Joe's parents and Franny. On days when they were all in the house at the same time, I either hid inside my room or sought refuge in the public library.

Once in a while, I felt brave enough to walk through the neighborhood. I wanted to check out the houses because I was still fascinated by housing design. But when some of the white neighbors saw me staring at their split-level, wood-frame homes, they hurried inside. I was afraid they would call the police, so whenever I felt like taking a walk, I hopped on a bus and walked the downtown streets. I felt safer that way.

As time passed, I sensed Franny resented our independent lifestyles. The three of us came and went on our own, a routine we picked up at Flourette Hall. I felt comfortable not having someone harp on me all the time. I had grown into a responsible young woman who did not have to be needled to study, help around the house, or do my laundry. We each carried a full load of classes at school and held part-time jobs. By the time we arrived home, we had either eaten on our own or skipped dinner altogether. Now and then, I fixed myself a peanut butter and jelly sandwich or heated up a can of vegetable soup. We spent most of our spare time with the books. None of us confided in Franny, and it dawned on me one day Franny probably felt shut out of our lives. I appreciated her willingness to open her home to me, but I did not feel obligated to blend in with her family. They were decent people, yet highly dysfunctional. I had always wanted my own family, but not with the Candelarias.

One evening, the girls and I had dinner at a fast-food restaurant. We discussed some of Franny's erratic behavior. Tammy said, "I don't know what she wants from me."

Grace added, "I keep my room clean and do my own wash."

"Whenever I eat with them," I said, "I usually stay to help with the dishes."

Tammmy said, "Franny seems so needy."

I said, "I'd like to tell her to leave me alone, but I don't want to hurt her feelings."

Grace agreed. "If we say something, she might kick us out. Then what do we do?"

"We stay out of her way," I replied, "that's what. Sometimes, I think she confuses us with her own kids."

Grace said, "I'll be so glad when June rolls around. Then I'm out of here."

"That's not until next year," Tammy said. "We should try and chill out until then. Make her think we're happy."

The minute we breezed through the front door, I noticed Franny in the living room. She aimed her head toward the living room clock and said, "Where have you girls been?"

I was confused. Until now, Franny had refrained from comments about our time schedules, which none of us had ever abused anyway. Not once had we arrived home at a very late hour, intoxicated, or with shady characters. I asked, "What're you talking about?"

Franny blew a bubble and fidgeted in her seat. "None of you girls asked me if it was OK to go out."

There was no way was I going to seek her permission to eat at a fast-food restaurant with my friends. In a tight voice, I told her what was on my mind. "Franny, we're old enough to look after ourselves. I realize you're our guardian but check the time." I pointed to my watch. "It's only eight o'clock."

Franny pursed her lips. She stood up and pointed her finger at me. "Don't get snippy with me, young lady. I'll call your caseworker." So who could she call? I had not met with any caseworker since moving into Flourette Hall. To my knowledge, neither had Tammy or Grace.

Here it comes, I thought. Tammy, Grace, and I exchanged tentative glances. Silently, I counted to ten and said, "Franny, let's call it a night. It seems like we all need to cool down a bit. We'll talk again tomorrow."

Franny still behaved like someone who sizzled with anger. "Did you hear what I said?"

The three of us walked upstairs and ducked inside our rooms. I sat on the edge of my bed, waiting for Franny to knock on my door. Half an hour later, she had not arrived, so I got out my books and devoted the rest of the evening to homework. I could not let her foolish behavior stand between my studies and me. I surmised she had a fight with someone, probably her husband, kids, or in-laws. Maybe she was lonely and wanted someone to talk to.

On my way out the next morning, Franny seemed to have done a complete turn around. She smiled at me as if she was in a terrific mood. "Have a nice day. See you later."

I shielded myself from the family's personal problems, which seemed to ebb and flow like ocean tides. From inside my room, I often heard yelling. On those occasions, I kept the door shut until there was calm. Franny needed an ally, but I believed she had unrealistic expectations of me. I had trouble keeping up with my own life.

I focused my thoughts on my education and my job, spending most of my time alone. My social life was practically nonexistent, so I rarely spent time with other teenagers, except for occasional dinners with Tammy and Grace. I was disappointed, but no longer angry the normal life of a teenager continued to elude me. Once in a while, I felt sorry for myself, but I soon realized pity would only drive me further into a hole.

Tension between Franny and Joe continued to rise. I hated being around them because they disagreed on almost everything. The children continued to act out. Tony started to hang around with some local street urchins, causing Franny's blood pressure to rise. Franny wanted her son to steer clear of trouble, but, on this particular day, I sensed she had gone overboard. Tony wanted to attend a high school football game, and Franny refused to give him permission. Perhaps I was out of line, but I defended the boy. Franny was obviously upset. She snapped, "This isn't your problem."

Around and Around I Went

I approached her with the tact of a seasoned diplomat. "I know it's not, but I thought you could reconsider. He wants to go to a football game."

The look on Tony's face showed gratitude. With the politeness of an altar boy, he said, "Ma, I'll be good. The other kids are going. Can I?"

Franny spun around in a huff. "All right, just go. But I'm warning you, mister. If you don't come home on time, this is it. I won't put up with you hanging out on the streets."

Tony returned home on time, but I thought Franny did not appreciate my intervention. After that, she picked on me for the least little infractions. I sensed she dumped her anger on me, but, still I did my best to stay clear of her. She seemed like a volcano, ready to blow up at any minute.

Thanksgiving rolled around, and Franny treated this holiday with the usual American fanfare. I saw it as just another day. I would have preferred to spend the day either walking around downtown or holed up in my room. Assuming Franny would not understand my need for privacy, I joined her in the kitchen that morning. The room was loaded with food in various stages of preparation. I stood next to the stove and asked, "Is there anything I can do?"

A disgruntled look soured her face. She reminded me of an overworked waitress at a crowded diner. "Help? God knows these lazy children of mine won't help. My no-good husband is still in bed. Jesus, they must all think this is a hotel or something."

I wanted to help Franny with meal preparation, but I was not there to serve as her personal therapist. That was a role I was ill-prepared to fulfill. I let the snide comments about her husband and children slide off my back. "Should I peel potatoes? Or stuff the bird?"

Franny glanced at me as if I had two heads. "What bird? We're having roast beef."

I said, "That's fine, but what can I do to help with dinner?"

"Cut up the potatoes, then put them on the stove. Maybe later you can wash the dishes already in the sink. I got a lot more to do."

I spent the next two hours in the kitchen washing pots and pans, taking out dishes, and keeping an eye on the stove. Around noon, Franny announced it was time to eat. A bit early, I thought, but I joined the others in the dining room.

A bright plastic tablecloth with figures of scrawny turkeys covered the table. Inexpensive, orange, green, and brown candles along with a cardboard cutout of an unhappy looking pilgrim rested in the center. Each setting contained a yellow paper plate, plastic silverware, and orange paper napkins.

Once seated, Franny led us in a prayer of thanksgiving and then we all dug in. Tammy handed me the bowl of lumpy mashed potatoes soaked in butter. I passed on the potatoes and settled for a slice of roast beef, a small spoonful of salty green beans, and a slice of Italian bread. Franny noticed my slim pickings. "Theresa, you eat like a bird." She handed me the bowl of mashed potatoes and said, "Here, take some and eat."

What could I do except grin and bear it? I wished the family had a dog so I could dispose of my meal. I ate as much as I could, then feigned satisfaction by holding my hand over my stomach. "I'm stuffed. I can't eat another bite."

After dinner, Joe and the kids dashed off to the living room, where they all plopped onto the sofa to watch football. Tammy, Grace, and I helped clean up. Franny, as usual, bitterly complained about her husband and kids. Looking like someone about to vomit, she mentioned her in-laws would be stopping by for dessert later in the day. I was surprised she did not ice the chocolate cake she baked with laxative frosting. When we had finished, I put on my coat and took a long walk, hoping to miss the fireworks when the in-laws arrived. Perhaps the cold air would help to restore some of my sanity.

A week before Christmas, Franny decorated the house for the holidays. Her supply of Christmas decorations was as unfashionable as the ones she displayed for Thanksgiving, but I suppose it was the thought that counted. Two days before the big day, on a cold, blustery evening after I walked in from work, Franny asked me to join her family for Christmas at their in-laws. I declined her offer without explanation, mostly because I did not want to be surrounded by discord. I wanted to be alone. As long as I could remember, Christmas was one of those holidays that always made me sad.

Franny acted as if I had slapped her across the face. Maybe I expected too much from her, but I wished she could understand I was not all peachy because it was Christmas time. As I was about to head up to my room, Franny dug her nails into my shoulder and yanked me off the stairs.

Turning around rapidly, I could see her cheeks redden. She balled up her fist and snarled, "I'm sick of you always shutting us out. I make this a home for you and look what you do. Always trying to do good for you and what do I get? Smacked in the face by your stupid independence."

Completely caught by surprise, I could feel my mouth drop open. I watched Franny's eyes as they filled with rage. All of a sudden, she thrust her taut body against mine and pushed me. "You're an impossible bitch."

My heart pounded so fast I could hardly speak. I stood back and jabbed my finger in her direction. As much as humanly possible, I controlled my anger, but inside I was on fire. "Don't you ever, ever, hit me again or call me anything other than my given name. Tell me you understand what I've said. I know you're not stupid."

Franny used her flattened palm and shoved me again. She glared at me with angry eyes. "I should've known better than to help you people. You'll end up like your mother. A nobody."

That was a call to war. My entire body shook with rage. Suddenly, my mouth became dry like dust. Indeed, I spent my life believing my mother probably never amounted to much. I was painfully aware I was most likely the product of a one-night encounter. I did not need Franny or anyone else to remind me of it. I would always be haunted by what my mother did.

Franny slapped me. As sweat poured down my face, I lost it. Defending myself, I could feel my steam level about to explode. "Don't you ever say anything about my mother. Not to me and not ever again."

What happened next was a blur, but Franny and I were engaged in a raucous fistfight. We created lots of noise, because Joe ran downstairs and yanked me off of his wife. I noticed her kids stood off to the side with blank looks on their faces. Tammy and Grace were speechless.

Franny yelled as if she was mortally wounded. "I can't believe you did this to me." She grabbed my arm and yanked me toward the door. "Get the hell out of my house." In a jiffy, she unlocked the front door, opened it, and forced me outside.

Blood still boiling, I raced outside, oblivious to the bitter cold. I only had on a pair of blue jeans and a thin sweatshirt. Beyond that, I was also totally stunned. How could this have happened? And over something so trivial? Reality set in when I realized it was below freezing, strong winds whipped across the city from Lake Erie, and it was pitch dark outside. I had never been so frightened or humiliated in my life. I had no place to go and no one to turn to. I thought about calling Catholic Charities, but due to the late hour, I doubted I would have connected with anyone. I had no money, nor did I know if I was assigned a caseworker. Desperate to get out of the cold, I ran around the corner. As I rambled down empty streets, I spotted an unlocked car. Double-checking to make sure the coast was clear, I jumped in. To my good fortune, if you can call anything on a night like that beneficial, there was also a beat up old blanket inside the back of the car. It had a musty smell and was covered with dog hair, but I draped it around myself, because by that time, I was still perspiring but very cold. I risked arrest by taking refuge in someone's car, but who cared? I consoled myself by realizing jail had to be warmer than the car. Staring at the moonlit skies, I could feel a few tears slowly slide down my cheeks. I searched the glove compartment, hoping to find a handgun. On that cold, lonely night, I wanted to die.

I must have fallen asleep, because I awoke when the sun started to rise. My bones ached from the bitter cold and my mouth felt like the polluted water in Lake Erie. Once I composed myself and got out of the car, I thought about hiding out to wait for Tammy or Grace, but I figured Franny might see me and feed the girls a pack of lies about what really happened.

Luckily, I had my bus pass in my back pocket so I sprinted toward the bus stop on the next corner. Boarding the bus, the driver looked at me as if I was a demented street person. I held my head down and showed him my pass. I took an empty seat, ignoring the curious stares of the other passengers. I was glad to be out of the cold. Even though the schools in Buffalo were closed for the holidays, I got off the bus in front of my school. With a shaky hand, I knocked on the door to the next-door convent. I explained what had happened and the nuns invited me in, no questions asked. Here we go again, I said to myself. Another move, another upheaval, and I had not yet reached my seventeenth birthday.

Staying Afloat

Not long after I settled into a spare room in the convent, one of the nuns arrived with a mug of hot cocoa, a Macintosh apple, and a seeded roll with butter. I welcomed the thoughtful gesture. Even though I was now in a safer environment, I was also grungy and tired, having slept in my clothes all night. I desperately wanted to take a bath, but I was too afraid to ask the nuns to borrow some clothes. And if I had, what would I have worn? A used nun dress?

Sister Claudine, the mother superior and also principal of my school, knocked on my door. Her gentle smile immediately made me feel at ease. Taking a seat at the small wooden desk, Sister Claudine sat up stiffly and said, "I spoke to Franny a little while ago. She said you misunderstood her and that she never expected you to take her literally."

I chewed on my lip, then took a second or two to gather my thoughts. "Sister, I don't think it matters if she told you the whole story. She threw me out. If she was so concerned, she could've checked the neighborhood looking for me. How far did she think I'd get on a cold, dark night without a coat or money? I slept in someone's parked car right around the corner."

Sister Claudine sat and stared at me, without saying a word. "You're not going to make me leave, are you?"

Sister Claudine looked exasperated, as if she did not know how to handle this kind of emotional turmoil. "I must say I was taken aback by this Franny's snippy tone. But she did offer to pick you up, if that's what you'd like."

Was she off her rocker? I had no intention of returning to Franny's house. Of course, Franny may have cooled down by now, but I was fed up with her moodiness. She was no more suited to take in foster children, especially teenagers, than she was able to handle her own problems. I wondered if she had volunteered to become a foster parent to three adolescent girls because she needed the money.

"Sister, I don't mean to impose on you, but don't make me go back there."

Sister Claudine stood up and wrapped her arms in front of her chest. In spite of an imposing look, she had a sweet voice. "No my child. For now, you can stay here. But you realize, of course, that some other arrangements will have to be made."

"Yes sister, I understand." Watching her walk out, I said, "Sister, thanks a lot. I'll never forget you for this."

The next day, I borrowed a dowdy-looking coat and took a bus to the bank. I reported my savings passbook had been stolen and immediately had it replaced. I withdrew eighty-five dollars and hit the downtown section to pick up a winter coat, some new clothes, and an extra pair of shoes. I stopped in Woolworth's and bought some new school supplies. Riding home, I considered asking one of the nuns to ask Tammy or Grace to pack up my possessions, but I ditched that idea. All I owned were a few sets of clothes, a small collection of tattered paperbacks, and my school uniforms. I never held onto any mementos. As far as I was concerned, I had little worth remembering.

On Christmas Eve morning, Sister Claudine stopped by my room. Despite a wave of bitter cold that gripped the city, she glowed like the summer sun. I wondered why she was so cheerful. She took a seat on the edge of my bed and said, "I have good news. I made a few calls this morning and your history teacher, Miss Morse, has agreed to have you stay with her and her family for a while."

For a change, this was one move I looked forward to. I liked this teacher and saw this relocation in my best interests. "Really?"

"Yes, my dear. Pack your things and I'll drive you over there."

"Sister, I'm ready." I pointed toward my recently acquired clothes, still inside a shopping bag. "All I have is in that bag."

"Of course. Let's get going."

On the ride to Miss Morse's house in Orchard Park, a well-to-do suburb of Buffalo, Sister Claudine filled me in on Miss Morse's family situation. She lived in a large house with her elderly mother. About a year earlier, Miss Morse's father had passed away after a tough battle with pancreatic cancer. Her mother, approaching seventy-five years, had become increasingly dependent on Miss Morse. Although in fairly good health for a woman her age, she stayed home most of the time, refusing to socialize at the local senior citizen center, church, or anywhere else. Miss Morse cared for her mother, catering to almost all of her needs.

The neighborhood reminded me of the community that surrounded Flourette Hall. All of the stately, two- and three- story homes were constructed out of brick and rested on one-acre lots that were well cared for. Most were enclosed by sturdy iron gates. Although it was winter and there was a lot of snow on the ground, the streets appeared to lack pock marks. Just about everyone had a two-car garage, and I noticed quite a few fancy Cadillacs parked in driveways.

Once Miss Morse welcomed us to her home, Sister Claudine thanked the teacher for her willingness to act on such short notice. A few minutes later, she wished us a happy holiday and took off. Miss Morse said, "Why don't we go into the kitchen? I'd like you to meet Mom." She introduced me to her gray-haired mother, who politely nodded and extended her badly wrinkled hand. That she did not get up from the table led me to believe she was arthritic.

Miss Morse guided me through the exquisite house until we reached the family room. Sitting on an elegant velour sofa in front of a crackling fireplace, Miss Morse said, "We should get you settled in your room. Then we'll have something to eat."

As we walked along the shiny, hardwood floors, I was afraid my scruffy old shoes would make smudge marks, so I quietly removed them and stuffed them into my shopping bag. When we reached the second floor, I saw at least four other bedrooms. I wondered why Miss Morse and her mother held onto such a spacious house. The cost to heat the place alone must have been enormous.

A bad dream had finally come to an end. I also felt weird being amid such affluence. At school, Miss Morse wore simple yet tasteful clothing. She drove a used but well-kept Ford station wagon, not a sign that she came from such a wealthy family.

Christmas was filled with loads of holiday spirit. Without my knowledge, Miss Morse had done some last minute shopping. She knocked on my door and invited me to join her and her family for midnight Mass. I felt blown away from the confusion of the past two days, but I gladly agreed to go. It seemed as if I had something to be thankful for.

The next morning, Miss Morse wished me a Merry Christmas and told me to look underneath the Christmas tree. When I saw a few gift-wrapped packages with my name on them, I felt choked up, yet I smothered the tears welling up in my eyes. I was flabbergasted. Stammering for a second or two, I finally blurted out, "I don't know what to say."

Miss Morse smiled and aimed her hand at the tree. "Don't say anything. Open your gifts and enjoy them."

I opened the boxes to see a new pair of leather gloves, thick thermal underwear, and a pair of flannel pajamas. I was speechless but grateful. Miss Morse tapped me on the back and offered me a mug of hot apple cider. I followed her into the kitchen and joined her for breakfast. Perhaps I read too much into her kind gestures, but Miss Morse became my hero. Once we finished breakfast, I took a much-needed hot bath. I must have fallen asleep because, when I rolled over, it was after three o'clock.

Arriving downstairs, I discovered seven of Miss Morse's relatives seated at a table fit for a king. All of them made me feel at home. For the first time in my life, I felt surrounded by genuine warmth. I wanted those feelings to last forever.

Two weeks passed, and it was time to return to school. The nuns quietly arranged to have my school uniforms and books replaced. For much of my life, I resented Catholic Charities. I always believed the agency never went out of its way to find me a permanent home. Maybe it had to do with race, social class, or a system that could not handle unwanted children. Despite my sour feelings about the Church, I now felt as if these nuns had rescued me from a sinking ship.

Staying Afloat

Living with Miss Morse turned out to be a good situation. I ate healthy meals, slept soundly at night, and kept up with my studies. Of course, I continued to work after school. No matter what happened, I had come a long way thus far and refused to fall apart.

Miss Morse helped me with my homework, corrected my mistakes, and overall showed more interest in me than anyone ever had. Once in a while, we sat around the table and talked. I flourished while under the same roof as her. Maybe my day had come.

When I finally came down to earth, I opened my eyes and smelled the roses. Since I had arrived, Miss Morse's elderly mother became more withdrawn and spoke very little to me. I noticed she took her meals in another room, stopped watching television when I was in the family room, and otherwise behaved like a hermit. At first, I wanted to believe she was a cranky old lady who had become antisocial. In reality, however, she was jealous her daughter had invited me to live in their home. Race may have played a part in her attitude toward me, but I think she was an old frightened woman dead set in her ways. She did not adjust well to change, and this time the change involved me.

Late one afternoon, Miss Morse rapped lightly on my door. She came in and I could tell something was up. I had to strain to hear when she said, "Theresa, don't you think you'd be happier living . . . living . . . with your own kind?"

What the heck was this? My own kind? All of a sudden, my mouth became dry. I saw Miss Morse flinch as I got to the point. "Are you saying I can't stay here anymore?"

Miss Morse's bright green eyes darkened with shame. She could not make eye contact with me. "Yes, I'm afraid so. My mother doesn't think it's right you live with us."

I was too hurt to understand. Sure, I recognized Miss Morse was probably not strong enough to stand up to a domineering old mother. Even if she had, the old lady would probably have made life difficult for both of us. Reluctantly, I accepted the bad news. "What'll happen to me?"

"I spoke to your caseworker. Catholic Charities has found a black family for you to live with."

Great, just what I wanted. Another move orchestrated by a caseworker who I did not know, with another family I knew nothing about. I was angry I had to relocate yet again, simply because Miss Morse's elderly mother was jealous. I was disgusted with a system that stubbornly clung to the notion I could only be happy with another black family. Through the grapevine at school, I heard one of the nuns had a sister who offered to take me in, but she was turned down because she was white. I was only sixteen and the only thing I wanted was the chance to stay put for a while. It no longer mattered with whom I lived or what color skin the family had. I wanted a place of my own, but no matter how much I prayed, my dream was continually deferred.

F i f t e e n

Just Another Stop
Along the Way

During my last class the next day, a voice came through the static on the loudspeaker, ordering me to appear in Sister Claudine's office at once. Whenever a girl was summoned to the principal's office, she was in trouble. My classmates stared at me with wide eyes, probably wondering if I had misbehaved. I picked up my books and walked out of class, holding my head down. I assumed I was about to meet my caseworker or my new foster family.

With teeth chattering and knees shaky, I walked toward Sister Claudine's office. Along the way, I ran into Miss Morse, who said hello. Hurt, I barely acknowledged her. I picked up my pace to pass by.

Sister Claudine's door was open, and there was a white woman seated in a chair next to her desk. I assumed she was my caseworker. Without her usual smile, Sister Claudine motioned for me to come in. I took a seat and dutifully waited. By this time, I had heard the caseworkers' spiels many times before. I could recite them by heart.

Sister Claudine sat behind her perfectly neat desk. She politely made the necessary introductions. "This is Miss Powers, your caseworker from Catholic Charities. She's here to take you to your new home."

Miss Powers had such a baby face I gathered she was fresh out of school. She removed a folder from her barely used vinyl briefcase, opened it, and glanced at me. "I want to talk to you about the Frasier family. You'll be living with them now. Mr. Frasier is . . ."

Normally polite, I was not in the mood to listen to all the glowing qualities of the foster family who Catholic Charities had picked out for me. I considered asking Miss Powers if I could have the money Catholic Charities received from New York State to care for me. I figured that, between the monthly stipend and the money I earned from my job, I could afford my own place to live. But I doubted Catholic Charities would take me up on my offer. Technically, I was still a minor.

I said with much indifference, "You don't have to go through all that."

Miss Powers sat motionless for a second. A few unintelligible words stumbled out of her mouth. She peered at Sister Claudine, then at me. Standing up, she arched an eyebrow, and said, "If that's how you want it. Then let's go. The Frasiers are waiting."

In the caseworker's car, I bit my nails as I thought about the many forced moves I had made. By the early 1970s, changes from the civil rights movement started to filter through the United States. More schools, government agencies, and businesses had adopted affirmative action and other antidiscrimination policies. Admittedly, they were often hard to enforce but at least they had become the law in many places. I thought it was odd that social service agencies almost always refused to permit black children to live with white families when white-owned businesses were legally banned from discriminating against minorities. The policy may have served the interests of the adults who enforced it, but it often deprived black children the chance to find stability. I had no trouble identifying with my racial background. I was a black teenager fed up with the nomadic existence known as foster care.

When we started to pass through neighborhoods that looked kind of shabby, I figured we were close to the Frasiers' East Side home. The caseworker stopped the car in front of a two-story wood-frame house. A huge crack split the sidewalk. When the caseworker turned to face me, I took away her opportunity to speak. I grabbed my shopping bag and jumped out of the car.

Angry and frightened, I felt sweat on my hands and face, even though it was below freezing outside. I was not ready to go through this again. As the caseworker went to ring the doorbell, I almost grabbed her hand and begged her not to do so. Seconds later, a middle-aged black couple appeared at the door. They acted so gracious I felt small for already rejecting them.

Mr. Frasier had expressive dark eyes, skin the color of nutmeg, and a warm thoughtful smile. He said, "You must be Theresa. Please come in. Welcome to our home."

I remained silent, but followed the caseworker inside. Every muscle in my body felt tight. I did not want to be there. Could I go through this again?

Mrs. Frasier, a light-skinned, delicate woman with finely chiseled features, had an angelic look on her face. She seemed like such a good, decent person, yet I wanted no part of her.

The Frasier's spacious living room was filled with inexpensive yet well-maintained furniture. We all sat, but I still held onto my icy feelings. I stared at a framed portrait of the Dr. King, wishing I was dead, too. Perhaps they sensed my discomfort, because I sat there as stiff as a board. Had they taken in foster children before? In fact, I was unaware if they had children of their own. I refused to let the caseworker tell me anything about the family. They were the enemy, my captors.

Mr. Frasier continued to be charming. He sat down close to me. "Theresa, my wife and I want you to be comfortable here in our home."

I nodded, unsure if my frown was visible, and said nothing. I held onto my shopping bag with such force it made my fingers hurt. But then I started to feel bad because the Frasiers had shown me a lot of consideration and I could barely say hello. I hoped they understood, but I was too upset to explain my shattered feelings.

Tenderly, Mrs. Frasier explained I would have my own room upstairs, next to the two rooms used by their children. The Frasiers had a ten-year-old son named Mike and a twelve-year-old daughter named Christine. Both Mr. and Mrs. Frasier held full-time jobs. He was an assistant manager in the payroll department at the Erie County Medical Center, and his wife taught English in a public high school.

The caseworker took off after a few minutes without leaving me her phone number or a visitation schedule. Mrs. Frasier said, "Why don't we go upstairs? I fixed up a room for you."

Forcing myself to show come civility, I decided to speak a little. "OK."

As I followed Mrs. Frasier up a short flight of stairs, I glanced around their home. The hardwood floors held a sheen and the walls were painted pastel colors. Inside the living room window rested at least half a dozen green houseplants, all of which looked as if they were thriving.

Mrs. Frasier stopped in front of a door and knocked. A young, mahogany-colored boy appeared. He extended his hand and said, "Hi, I'm Mike."

I returned the gesture. "Hi, I'm Theresa. Nice to meet you." I did not have the heart to snub him.

Mrs. Frasier moved on and rapped on another door. This time, an energetic, slender young girl answered. Clad in workout gear, she wore her tightly-curled hair in braids and had beautiful unblemished skin the amber color of honey. When she opened her mouth to speak, I noticed sparkling white teeth. "Hi, I'm Christine. Welcome."

I thought she might invite me into her room because we were reasonably close in age, but she did not. I had no desire to share my life with her. With all the disruptions in my life, I vowed never to be close to anyone I lived with. The attachment could be ended, just like that and for no good reason.

Mrs. Frasier accompanied me to a small but cozy bedroom. She seemed so proud of herself when she pointed toward the window and said, "We picked out new curtains for you the other day."

Although I never doubted Mrs. Frasier's sincerity, did she honestly believe new curtains would make a notable difference in my life? I guessed she used this to break the ice. Or perhaps she felt as antsy as I did. Taking in a stranger must have been frightening for the Frasiers.

I made myself smile and showed a mild amount of appreciation. "That's nice. Thank you."

Mrs. Frasier said, "We'd like you to join us for dinner when you can. We generally eat around six o'clock. Let me know if there's anything special I can fix for you."

Maybe this place won't be so bad, I thought. The minute Mrs. Frasier left me alone, I closed the door and slumped over on the bed. I stretched out and stared idly at the off-white, stucco ceiling, wondering how long this arrangement would last. The Frasiers appeared to be a closely knit family, the kind of people who I wished I had grown up around. I was besieged with bitterness that my life had been so difficult. But how could I hold a grudge against people because they were thoughtful and caring? I trusted my presence would not throw off the family chemistry. To make this living situation work, I knew I had to be more amenable and somehow find a way to relax my tightly bound feelings.

Around six o'clock, Mrs. Frasier knocked on my door. As soon as I opened it, she asked, "Join us for dinner? It's not anything fancy. Just broiled chicken breasts and rice."

I felt trapped. If I declined, I might be seen as obstinate. If I accepted, would they think I wanted to be part of their family? The rumbling noises in my stomach reminded me I was famished. "Tonight I can. But tomorrow I have to work until seven o'clock." I had to set limits. No way was I going to let down my guard around these people, even though they had not mistreated me in any way.

The dignified atmosphere at the dinner table was the opposite from the frenzy at Franny's house. Franny's kids bickered back and forth, threw things at one another, and spoke with food stuffed in their mouths. Franny tried to maintain order, but it always seemed as if she lost the battle. But there was a sense of calm at the Frasiers. Both parents spoke to their children as if they were adults. There was absolutely no yelling or name calling. The children displayed perfect manners. Current news topics, such as the continuing war in Southeast Asia, equality for minorities, and plant closings, were commonplace at dinner. For a change, I felt relaxed at mealtime. Although I sat down at the table with an attitude, I left with warm feelings. The food was tasty as well. I never bothered to ask who cooked, but I enjoyed every bite.

For the next two weeks, I rose early. Realizing the Frasiers probably had an established morning routine, I wanted to keep out of their way. I hated feeling like a fifth wheel. By the time they got out of bed, I had already showered and changed into my school clothes. Breakfast was more casual than dinner, and their pantry had plenty of cold cereal and muffins, all of which I was welcome to eat. Every morning, Mr. Frasier brewed a pot of fresh coffee. I loved the fragrant smell of coffee, but I never acquired a taste for it. Once both children headed out for the school bus, Mr. and Mrs. Frasier sat down at the kitchen table and shared a cup of coffee. I sensed their closeness and gradually admired their relationship.

Despite their warmth, however, I still did not feel at ease around the Frasiers. Mind you, they behaved like impeccable hosts, yet I had the unmistakable feeling I was a guest. I hoped the Frasiers would offer to adopt me but, alas, no such luck. I wondered if someone at Catholic Charities had strong-armed them into taking me. I knew foster homes for teenagers were hard to come by. Group homes, while still around, had become less of an option because social welfare advocates lobbied against their use. Why? I felt Flourette Hall had filled an important gap in my life.

I continued to work four afternoons a week, usually from three to seven o'clock. By the time I arrived home, I was exhausted, but my day was far from over. The next few hours were spent hitting the books.

The school had planned a social for students and their fathers. As usual, I felt left out. I must have inadvertently dropped the flyer describing the event on the stairs. I was in my room one night, cramming for a history exam, when someone knocked on my door. It was Mr. Frasier, holding onto the flyer. He flashed a quick smile, then asked if he could come in. I wanted to say no but I acted cordial. "Sure, have a seat."

Mr. Frasier held the flyer out and said, "I found this on the stairwell. I'd like to go with you, if it's OK."

I had forgotten about the event. I was overwhelmed by his hospitality, yet felt heaviness in my chest. I could only stare at him.

Mr. Frasier slowly approached me and gently rested his arm on my shoulder. "Think about it and let me know. I'll understand whatever you decide."

I dropped my head down and could barely force the words out. In truth, I had no desire to go, but if I said no, Mr. Frasier would think I was antisocial. Reluctantly, I agreed, but my heart was not in it.

Every student who planned to attend the father-daughter social had to notify the principal's office. The school always maintained a list of who attended each event. To divvy up the annual recreation budget, Sister Claudine used these rosters to determine which events were the most popular. On the morning when I stopped by Sister Claudine's office to sign up, I felt a sense of dread instead of enthusiasm. This would be the first time anyone ever accompanied me to a school activity intended for students and their families. Throughout my school career, I had inured myself to rejection by always discarding notices for special events. I pretended each affair was a bust no matter how fondly the girls talked about it.

I waited behind another girl to talk to Sister Claudine's assistant, a crotchety old nun who also kept the attendance records. As soon as my turn arrived, I said, "I'd like to sign up for the father-daughter social."

The aging nun's mouth dropped open so wide I could see all her silver fillings. She tilted her head to one side and said, "Did I hear right?"

"Yes ma'am. I'm bringing my foster father."

Walking out of Sister Claudine's office, I decided not to feel slighted. For the past two and a half years, my name had never appeared on any of these lists. I supposed the old nun was truly surprised, and I hoped she meant no harm.

Because the affair had been planned for a Saturday evening, I asked the store manager for the afternoon off. It was late afternoon and I sat inside my bedroom, wondering what I would wear. My wardrobe essentially consisted of three school uniforms, a few pairs of slacks, assorted tops, and two skirts. Until now, I never had the occasion to impress anyone. I rarely socialized, and I did not go out on dates with boys. Due to the extreme cold, I picked out my only pair of dress slacks along with a thick sweater.

Around six o'clock I heard a few noises outside my door, so I presumed it was Mr. Frasier. I shoved a pick through my long Afro one more time, then grabbed my parka with a jittery hand. I could hardly believe I was going to a family social at school.

Mr. Frasier had on a navy blue wool suit, plain white shirt, and a striped tie. He looked dashing. His wife and children walked us to the front door. I trusted they were not jealous. I appreciated their father's efforts to fill in, but truthfully I would have preferred to stay in my room. There was no turning back, so I tried to act smooth.

On the short ride to the school, I fumbled trying to find the right words to say. Mr. Frasier kept his eyes glued to the slick roads because it had snowed another two to three inches the day before. Driving in Buffalo was often treacherous in the winter.

Pulling into an empty space in the school parking lot, Mr. Frasier said, "I'm glad I can do this with you."

I had to show appreciation, so I replied, "Thank you."

The students had decorated the cafeteria with streams of brightly colored crepe paper, plastic flowers, and handmade signs celebrating fathers and daughters. The decorations looked inexpensive and flimsy, but on a limited budget not much else was available. Sister Claudine welcomed everyone as they entered the school. I thought she would have made a superb emcee for a hit game show. The moment she spotted me standing next to Mr. Frasier, she lit up like a ray of sunshine. She pushed pass two or three people and extended her hand to Mr. Frasier. "Good evening. I'm the principal here. I'm glad to see you could make it."

Mr. Frasier smiled carefully. "Me, too."

Politely, I greeted Sister Claudine. I had a hard time not returning her smile because she was so cheery. Sometimes, I thought she could make a cadaver crack a smile. All the attention, however, made me feel uncomfortable, so I guided Mr. Frasier to an empty table. I felt so out of place as I watched other girls introduce their fathers to friends and teachers. For a moment, I considered introducing Mr. Frasier but at the last second I got cold feet. Instead, I sat at the table and played with a stack of paper napkins.

Our table filled up with some of my classmates and their fathers. One girl whose dad had passed away brought her uncle. I knew of one girl not in attendance because her father had run off with another woman. I had no idea if I was the only girl who showed up with a foster father.

Shortly afterward, pop music roared over the jukebox. Sister Claudine, who served as mistress of ceremonies, grabbed the microphone and urged everyone to get up and dance. She wiggled her hips a little. Mr. Frasier asked me to join him on the dance floor, and I said yes. As I looked at Mr. Frasier simultaneously snap his fingers and boogie, I realized I probably danced awkwardly like him. I also had two left feet, refuting the widely held belief all blacks had rhythm. Certainly, Mr. Frasier and I did not.

Just Another Stop Along the Way

I sweated through the rest of the evening, waiting for time to pass so I could ask Mr. Frasier to leave. Fortunately, Mr. Frasier hit it off with another girl's father so I did not have to entertain him. They were both employed in the same field and exchanged boring stories about payroll departments and withholding taxes. I watched as some of my classmates glided across the floor, dancing the night away. Others sat at tables and gossiped. I flashed my fake smile whenever someone stopped by to say hello. Quite often, I was eager to be as socially connected as these girls seemed to be, but I believed I would spend the rest of my life buried in a shell.

Around ten o'clock Mr. Frasier yawned, then asked, "Do you mind if we go home? It's getting late and I'm a little tired."

Within seconds, I had my coat on. I think Mr. Frasier was surprised I got ready so quickly. About twenty minutes later, I was safely inside my room, hoping I would not have to attend one of these functions again.

On my way through the foyer one day, I was surprised to hear Mr. Frasier call out my name. Arriving late from work, I expected to find the downstairs quiet. Mr. Frasier was seated in the family room next to his wife. The minute he saw my face in front of him, he gestured for me to take a seat. I wondered what they wanted from me. Since my arrival, I had followed my usual routine of school and work. I kept my room clean and often helped out around the house. Was I in trouble or about to get a pink slip?

Mr. Frasier cleared his throat, then got to the point. "Theresa, I made a phone call today I thought you'd like to know about."

I felt jittery. Maybe they had decided to adopt me after all. I unbuttoned my coat and took off my gloves. "What's this all about?"

Mr. Frasier said, "I called Mrs. Woodson. We spoke for a while. She said basically the two of you got along. In fact, she said she missed you. I was surprised to hear one of your teachers instigated all the trouble that led to your leaving."

This news made me feel as if I had been rammed by a Mack truck. I viewed the telephone call to Mrs. Woodson as an act of betrayal. I held my anger, but deep down I felt like exploding. "How come?"

Mrs. Frasier took the lead and promptly defended her husband's actions. "We wanted to find out more about you. That's all."

"Why didn't you ask? I would've told you. What is it you want to know?"

I sensed both Mr. and Mrs. Frasier were on the defense. They traded nervous glances and she said, "Don't be so upset. We didn't mean any harm. I wanted to know why you're so private."

"That's how I am. I'm sorry if my shyness offends you. I thought Catholic Charities had told you about me." I tried not to be on the defensive. "Why didn't you call Mrs. Woodson before I got here?"

Mr. Frasier said, "Hey, wait a minute. We didn't do this to cause trouble or hurt your feelings. Try and understand how we feel."

My knees started to feel rubbery. I knew I was either about to cry or start yelling. The conversation appeared to go nowhere so I said, "Goodnight."

I spun around so quickly I tripped over my own feet. Straightening myself, I held up my head and slowly walked up the stairs. I wanted to run, but I refused to let them see me upset. Inside my room, I ripped off my coat and hurled it against the floor. My cheeks felt like they were on fire. Whatever trust I had placed in the Frasiers was immediately wiped out by the call to Mrs. Woodson. For most of my life, other people controlled whom I lived with, how long I stayed, and even what I ate. I believed the Frasiers would be different. Although they may have had a legitimate motive to contact Mrs. Woodson, I felt they could have handled it differently. Taking in foster children, especially adolescents, was risky. In fact, adolescents are still hard to place. If the Frasiers were not prepared to take that chance, I believe they should have declined the request from Catholic Charities. The call to Mrs. Woodson made me feel as if I was a criminal.

My feelings toward the Frasiers immediately plunged. I ate dinner out of the house, left the house earlier than usual every morning, and avoided all of them. Soon afterward, I heard Peter, Paul, and Mary's song "Leaving on a Jet Plane" on the radio at the grocery store. Right then and there, I toyed with the idea of running away. I woke up one morning after tossing and turning all night. Perhaps I had overreacted or I had legitimate reasons to feel cheated, but I shoved my clothes into a small knapsack and walked out after sunrise. I rode the bus downtown and had a cup of hot chocolate and a muffin on Main Street. Shortly after nine o'clock when the bank opened, I emptied out my savings account. I hailed a taxi to the airport. By the time I arrived at the departure gate, I had decided to buy a one-way ticket to San Francisco, hoping to find a better life in the Golden State.

Alone in California

The medium-sized airport seemed abuzz with a life of its own. Arrival and departure times blared over the loudspeaker. Travelers loaded down with luggage and small children dashed through corridors to catch flights. Smartly dressed pilots and flight attendants toted small suitcases as they crisscrossed the terminal.

This was my first time in an airport, let alone on an airplane. Not surprisingly, I felt lost among the crowds. I imagined all those travelers had a destination: family or friends, home, or business. I longed to have such a connection, but I knew no one would be in San Francisco to greet me as I walked off the plane.

With a wallet was stuffed with cash, I marched up to the American Airlines counter. I held my head down and asked about one-way fares to San Francisco. I had no plans to return to Buffalo.

The clerk, a young black woman in a spiffy dark blue uniform, finished plugging some data into her computer terminal. She looked up at me as if I was an ordinary customer. "When are you thinking about traveling? Our economy fare will save you a bundle if you buy your ticket seven days in advance. Want me to book it for you?"

I appreciated the young woman was trying to save me money, but I cut her off. Perhaps she sensed I was a run-away and was trying to change my mind. "I want to go right away."

The clerk gave me a curious stare. "I see. I didn't realize you were in such a hurry."

"Please give me a ticket to San Francisco."

"We have a flight that leaves in an hour. It costs one hundred five dollars. You have that kind of money?"

I pulled out my wallet and showed the woman a small wad of twenty-dollar bills. "I can pay for my ticket."

Soon, I boarded a huge DC-10 jet, still clutching my small knapsack. I was mesmerized by the immense size of the plane. I had some knowledge of physics, yet I was amazed something so large could actually lift off the ground and fly. By the time I took my window seat in the plane's midsection, I suspected the nun who kept attendance had marked me down as absent. She must have been thrown for a loop because I always arrived for school early. She probably called the Frasiers to check up on me. I wondered if they would miss me. I had kept my plans secret, so I doubted anyone had an inkling about what I was up to. On the cab ride to the airport, I had second thoughts about fleeing, but once we pulled up in front of the departure terminal, I decided it was now or never. I saw my life as heading in a downward spiral and I had to act, even if my choices was less than judicious.

As the jumbo jet roared down the runway, I could not stop my teeth from chattering, almost as if I walked through the middle of a Buffalo blizzard without a coat on. I was nervous about flying, but I was also worried about survival in San Francisco. I had heard horror stories at Flourette Hall from girls who had run away. Some had resorted to prostitution. Others barely survived on the streets or in fleabag hotels. These very real possibilities alternately terrified and sickened me.

Because I had several hundred dollars in my wallet, my immediate plan was to locate cheap housing, then look for a job. I was ambitious, hard working, and responsible, but at my age, how could I see through the holes in my plan? Little did I know decent housing in California was expensive and good-paying jobs for unskilled teenagers were extremely scarce. I had been lured to California by the promise of a better life, similar to dreams pursued by the Joad family in the *Grapes of Wrath*. But the Joads showed up as a family, and I was all alone.

Alone in California

I sat next to a businessman on his way home to Marin County, an affluent suburb north of San Francisco. The man with the blue pin-striped suit and neatly slicked-back hair attempted a few times to strike up a conversation with me. He talked so fondly about his wife and kids I felt sad. I wished a handsome man in a suit talked about me like that.

A stewardess served lunch, but all I could do was stare at the sandwich. My stomach in turmoil, I also had a throbbing sensation in my head. The man asked if I was sick. I nodded I was not, then pretended to sleep. I felt bad for snubbing him, but I was petrified I would soon be alone in a big city.

After the plane landed, the fatherly businessman again asked me if I was sick. I had this wild notion about asking him for help, but I assumed he would not want to be bothered with me. I waved good-bye and took off.

I found a phone booth and shut the door. I pored through the San Francisco Yellow Pages to look for an inexpensive hotel. I had to conserve my cash, not knowing how long it would be until I landed a job. Assuming hotel chains like Holiday Inn or Howard Johnson would be too expensive, I called a placed named the Bel- Aire located on Van Nuys Street. The clerk said they rented rooms by the day, week, or month. When I asked how much it cost for one day, he said, "Ten-fifty."

"Please give me a room for one night." I figured I would check out the place for one night. If it was not too seedy, I would stay a little longer.

He gave me bus directions, and I hung up. As I walked outside, I was greeted by a delightfully sunny afternoon. Unlike Buffalo, the weather was cool but not frigid. A light breeze blowing in from the bay caressed my face. Knowing I looked out of place, I ripped off my parka and carried it underneath my arm. I flagged down an approaching city bus and hopped on board. As the bus cruised along the city streets, I was attracted to this bustling yet beautiful place. It seemed so much more alive than Buffalo. I thought I would like living in San Francisco after all. The view of the Golden Gate Bridge was simply more stunning than anything I had ever seen in upstate New York.

Whatever glimmering thoughts I had about the city quickly dimmed when the neighborhood texture started to change. Instead of impeccably neat three-story homes on quaint, tree-lined streets, the bus cruised among dilapidated buildings on filthy streets. There were no tourists or trolley cars in sight. The driver called out, "Hey lady, we passed Market Street. The Bel- Aire is up ahead. You should get off."

Slowly, I dragged myself off the bus, not happy about my choice of hotels. Derelicts dressed in tattered clothes wandered along the streets, some with open bottles of cheap booze in their hands. Others looked dazed, as if life was too much for them to bear.

My mouth dropped open as soon as I saw the Bel-Aire. The building was in dire need of a coat of paint. It appeared to slant a little. If an earthquake struck, it would probably topple over in an instant. Passing through the dank lobby, I was sickened by the smell of stale cigarette smoke. I wondered how many people called this filthy rat's nest home. I was sorry it was all I could afford.

Around early evening, hunger pangs gnawed at my stomach. Too frightened to venture outside, I found a Milky Way candy bar stashed in my pocket. I nibbled on a piece of chocolate and sat by the grimy window, staring outdoors. A small group of men congregated out front and did a brisk business with passersby. Every time a police cruiser passed by, the men scattered. I doubted they were selling Avon products.

I started to panic. My heart pounded so fast I thought it would pop out of my chest. Thoughts about my uncertain life in San Francisco raced through my head with dizzying speed. On impulse, I reached for my stash of Darvon hidden inside my knapsack. For years, I had experienced severe menstrual cramps and a doctor had prescribed Darvon for the pain. Suicide had lurked inside my mind for years, so I made sure I saved enough painkillers. On impulse, I gulped down all the pills, about twenty-five of them. When death did not come right away, I became scared. I staggered down the hallway until I reached the phone booth and placed a collect call to Miss Morse, the only person who I felt I could turn to. She accepted the charges and asked me what was wrong. I told her what I had done.

"Where are you? People have been looking for you all day long. We're worried."

Like a drunk, I could hear the slur in my voice. "I . . . I . . . I'm in San Francisco."

Miss Morse clobbered me with questions. "Where? What's the address? Who are you with? What does the building look like?"

Ready to collapse, I tried to grab onto the wall to hold myself up. My limp hands felt like they weighed a ton. All of a sudden, I felt extremely cold and clammy, so I dropped the phone, dragged myself back to my room, and sprawled across the bed. Staring at the ceiling, I felt like I was on a merry-go-round, spinning around and around. I wanted it to be over. What happened next was a blur. Two days later, I came to in a hospital.

When I opened my eyes, the bright glare from the overhead lights made me squint. The environment was totally alien, but judging from the intravenous tubes connected to my arm, I surmised I was in the hospital. Opening my lips to speak, my mouth felt as dry as cotton. I tried to move around, but I found my hands secured by restraints. Also, I was tied to the bed. Little did I know I was in the adolescent psychiatric ward of a large public hospital. A young nurse with a cheerful face walked in. She checked the intravenous bottle and took my vital signs. "How are you feeling? Better, I hope."

"Where am I? What day is it?"

"You're in the hospital and it's Friday. Can you remember what happened?"

"No, nothing."

The nurse with the sensitive smile pulled up a chair. "You took an overdose. When the police brought you in here, we pumped your stomach." She rested her hand on top of mine and said, "Darling, why'd you want to kill yourself for? Young thing like you."

"Damn," I thought. Feeling angry my suicide attempt failed, I jerked my head the other way. I tried to shut out the kindness emanating from this gentle woman.

The nurse looked at me and said, "I'm glad you're still with us. We got word from the police someone named Miss Morse called up about you."

"Please, may I have some water?"

The nurse grabbed a small pitcher and handed me a cup of water. "Honey, I know you must be having a hard time, but swallowing pills isn't going to solve your problems."

"I live with a foster family. That's why I'm upset."

"Where do they live? Around here?"

The complete message about my identity must have gotten mixed up along the way. It did not sound as if the nurse knew I came from New York.

"No. Buffalo, New York."

The nurse's eyes widened so much it appeared as if she had stuck her finger inside a socket. "Oh, Lordy. You've come a long way."

"Can you take off the restraints?"

"I can't do that, but I'll call the doctor in a second. He'll have to sign your chart, saying you're no longer a danger to yourself, before these things can be removed."

Then, I thought about my money. "What happened to my things?"

The nurse pointed to my knapsack, nestled in between my bed and the small nightstand. I started to panic. "What about my money?"

The nurse unzipped the bag and searched through my belongings. The money was gone. "I'm sorry, but there's no money."

"But there has to be." Someone had helped themselves to my life savings. I imagined the sleazy looking hotel clerk had taken it. Why complain about it, though? I knew I had no recourse.

A little while later, the nurse came back with a young man with curly red hair and freckles who I presumed was the doctor. The man in the white jacket said, "Hi, I'm Dr. Ward. I hear you want to get out of the restraints."

I wanted to beg for my freedom, but that would have been out of character. In this stressful situation, I refused to show emotion. "I won't try anything, I promise. I don't like being tied up."

"Are you sure? We don't want you to try anything foolish."

"Yes sir, I understand."

The doctor gave the nurse an uncertain glance, then removed the restraints. He looked at me with a shy grin. "I hear you're from New York. Why'd you come all the way out here?"

"To get away."

"Know anyone in San Francisco we can call?"

"No."

The nurse squeezed her thin body between my bed and the doctor. She asked, "What about your foster family in Buffalo? Can you give us their name and number?"

I rattled off the Frasiers' address and phone number, wondering how they would respond to the news I was in a psych ward in San Francisco.

From the puzzled look on the nurse's face, I guessed I presented them with a real headache. I had not intended to cause trouble for anyone. My decision to run away may have been rash, but I was about at my wits end. Finding out the Frasiers had contacted Mrs. Woodson threw me over the edge. I hated being second-guessed.

The doctor and nurse walked out together, leaving me alone. Oddly enough, I wanted to talk to someone, but the other bed was unoccupied. The antiseptic smell was overpowering. Staring at the ugly pea-green walls, I noticed flecks of paint peeling off. When I spied a cockroach scurrying across the faded tiled floor, I was reminded I was in a public institution. Amenities such as a television set were lacking. When an attendant served lunch, I glanced at the wilted green salad and moldy white bread sandwich and lost my appetite.

I stared at the water-stained ceiling, wondering what would happen next. My mouth still felt dry. The part of my arm where the needle had been injected was tender and sore. On top of all that, I felt grungy, knowing I had not bathed in several days. I wanted to take a shower, change into fresh clothes, and brush my teeth. Instead, I got a visit from the hospital social worker.

The woman with a twangy voice barged into my room as I drifted off to sleep. She sat down next to me and snapped open her pad, like she was about to conduct a criminal investigation. Already, I decided not to like her because she reminded me of the caseworkers from Catholic Charities. From her abrupt entry into my room, I guessed she was probably in a hurry, too.

"What did you expect would happen here?"

I sensed she was irked because my presence in another state confounded my discharge plans. Sensing this woman would not understand why I ran away, I looked down and said, "No reason, in particular."

The social worker scribbled notes on a pad. Tugging at her collar as if she was too warm, she frowned as she looked at me. "The Frasiers don't want you back. I'm still waiting to hear from Catholic Charities to see how they want to handle this."

"What about Miss Morse? Can she take me?"

"Miss Morse? The Frasiers never mentioned her. Who is she?" Evidently, the message the nurse received from the San Francisco police about me did not mention Miss Morse's name.

"A teacher. She let me live with her for a while."

The social worker's hands shot apart so quickly I already knew what she would say. "We can only release you to the Frasiers. If this Morse lady wants to take custody, she'll have to arrange it through Catholic Charities. As soon as the doctor clears you medically, you'll go to Stryker House."

"What's that?"

"A detention center for juveniles."

Because the system often could not place black teens in foster care, many ended up in detention for lack of space elsewhere. I guess I was fortunate this was my first time.

Understandably, most of my memories about this time have faded, so I am not entirely clear about what happened. I recall spending a few miserable days in the hospital under constant watch. Even though a doctor certified I was no longer a danger to myself, the hospital staff remained cautious. I hated the intrusions, especially when I used the bathroom. A staff member had to be with me at all times. I had no intention of trying to take my life by eating a bar of soap.

I received a visit from a psychiatry resident who evaluated me for medication. Did this young man honestly believe a few happy pills would significantly impact my life? I cooperated with the doctor in training, sensing I was already in hot water for running away and crossing state lines. Every time he grilled me about my family background or medical history, I repeated, "No, I don't know who they are. There is no way to know what kind of medical conditions I may have inherited." This went on for at least ten minutes. Was this guy dense, or what?

As I became more aware over the next day or so, I noticed other residents attended a variety of group therapy sessions. I wondered why I was left out. When the young nurse who I took a liking to walked in, I asked, "Why don't I go to the groups?" True, I was not eager to open up about personal matters in front of strangers, but I wanted to know why I had been singled out. This time, race did not seem to be an issue because about half the young girls on the ward were black.

The nurse sat down. I doubt she knew what to say. "Because . . . because . . . they're working out their feelings about going home to their families. We didn't think this was the right group for you. The people from Stryker House are coming for you in the morning."

I felt like the world had come crashing down on me. I thought about asking for a sleeping pill, but changed my mind. If at all possible, I wanted to avoid medication. As it was, the doctors had recommended I take antidepressants, but I refused. Because I was a ward of another state, they let the matter drop. It could have mushroomed into a delicate and costly legal battle that, in all likelihood, they wanted to avoid. When I thought about the detention center, I felt a surge of fear shoot through my body. I started to shiver. Sweat poured down my face and neck as I curled myself into a fetal position, feeling crushed my suicide attempt had failed.

Early the next morning, as the staff changed shifts, I was wide awake. I washed up and put on clean clothes. By the time a caseworker from Stryker House showed up, I was ready to go. Mr. West, a middle-aged black man with hair graying at the temples, a slight paunch, and an easy smile, escorted me to the nurse's station, where he picked up a large manila envelope that contained my chart. On our way out, Mr. West rested his strong hand on my shoulder. "The state doesn't know what else to do. You'll have to stay in Stryker until we can work out arrangements with the people in New York. I'm sorry, child."

On the drive through stop-and-go traffic, we made small talk about San Francisco. The man came from a housing project in Oakland and wanted to help young people stay out of trouble. He looked at me and said, "I hope you'll avoid gangs. Nothing but trouble. I've seen it over and over again."

The idea of joining a gang had never entered my mind. "Yes sir, I hear you. I won't do anything like that."

For the rest of the drive, the man delivered a stern lecture about the dangers of drugs, the drawbacks to teen pregnancy, and the risk of serving jail time if I hung around with the wrong crowd. I appreciated his sincerity, but when he pulled into the parking lot of the detention center, my eyes almost popped out. Thick iron gates surrounded Stryker House and a guard who reminded me of Frankenstein was posted at the entry. I felt like a criminal instead of a lonely, lost girl. I tried to swallow, but couldn't.

The man gently guided me toward the entrance. I felt warmed by his fatherly approach. "Try not to be so afraid. I'll help look after you. I don't expect you'll be here that long."

"Thank you, sir."

Terrified, I refused to show emotion. I would have to get through this trying period, no matter how hard I had to work at it. If I had come this far, I could push myself a little further. Maybe there was a pot of gold waiting for me over the rainbow.

Certainly nothing I had seen on television or in the movies could have prepared me for the harsh reality of a detention center. It was a jail for minors. The place felt as cold as ice and looked like a decaying relic from earlier times. Like the public hospital I had been released from, the detention center was ominous and in dire need of a make-over. Teenagers were kept apart from the more hard-core criminals in the state's network of prisons. I had heard lots of gossip about the infamous California prison system from reading about Angela Davis and the Black Panthers, who at one time had a huge following in the Bay Area. Now on the other side, I felt panic-stricken that I had ended up in jail, but I acted as if it was no big deal.

Mr. West had me placed in solitary confinement for my own protection. Some of the other girls had been convicted of more serious offenses, such as armed robbery, assault, and attempted murder. I felt sad when Mr. West had to leave. My safety net disappeared.

For the next week, I sat alone in a tiny corroded cell about the size of a walk-in closet. I felt as though the walls were closing in on me. Only a toilet that did not always flush, a small leaky sink, and a bed as hard as cement filled the space. Guards served my meals, which usually consisted of processed food either too salty or too bland. Every so often, Mr. West, my guardian angel, brought me newspapers or magazines, but otherwise I had nothing to occupy my mind. Twice a day a guard unlocked my cell and accompanied me outside for some fresh air and a bit of exercise. All the other girls glared at me, probably wondering why I received special treatment usually reserved for notorious criminals.

Mr. West entered my cell one day. "Somebody from Catholic Charities will be here tomorrow. You're going back to New York."

"Do you know where I'll be going?"

"No, but the caseworker will fill you in." Mr. West extended his cal-lused hand. "I wish we had met under better circumstances. Don't get caught up in drugs and gangs like these girls in here. Most of them are in big trouble and they're not eighteen years old. I know your life is hard, but hold on, my child. Just hold on. We black folks have been doing that for years. I'm off tomorrow, so I won't see you any more." Mr. West reached out and tenderly hugged me. "Good luck, honey. I'll say a prayer for you."

"Thank you, sir. I appreciate what you did for me."

As Mrs. Kendall, the salt-and-pepper-haired caseworker from Catholic Charities, led me out of Stryker Hall, I let out a huge sigh of relief. I hoped I would never again see the inside of a detention center. The short time I spent behind bars convinced me I should always play by the rules. Confinement in a crummy jail cell was not how I wanted to spend the rest of my life.

On the cab ride to the airport, I felt sad in a way to leave San Francisco. The Golden Gate Bridge was the most beautiful structure I had ever seen. I had not been introduced to the scenic, more romantic side of the city, but I'd seen enough, to convince me this was a place where I someday wanted to live. More than anything, I wanted a home with a view of the Golden Gate bridge.

I expected the flight back to Buffalo would be filled with more drudg-ery, sharing a seat next to a caseworker who would probably act like she was sitting on a bed of nails. Instead, I was pleasantly surprised. Mrs. Kendall showed genuine interest in me. She had recently started to work for Catholic Charities after serving as a child abuse investigator for the state. Mrs. Kendall asked me relevant questions such as whether I planned to finish high school, and what my plans were for college. For a change, I felt treated as an equal.

When the subject of my immediate future came up, Mrs. Kendall avoided looking at me and said, "That's the not-so-good part. Mr. Frasier was very hurt by what you did. I think his wife seemed to under-stand. I tried to explain how you've been through a lot, hoping they'd be more tolerant. I'm sorry this didn't work out."

"So, where will I go?"

"To a group home in Peekskill."

"But I go to school in Buffalo. You mean I have to start another school?"

The sparkle in the Mrs. Kendall's blue eyes dimmed. She said, "Yes, I'm afraid so. We couldn't find any place for you in Buffalo. I made lots of calls, but right now, there's nothing."

Back in New York

Once the plane landed in LaGuardia Airport, I felt frightened at the idea of living in New York City. Much of my life had been sheltered. Buffalo, a medium-sized city, cannot compare to a giant metropolis. Life upstate was not without problems, but it was much calmer. I pointed to the skyscrapers visible from the window and asked, "What're we doing here?"

"You're going to Nicholas Hall. It's in Peekskill, about an hour or so from the city, depending on traffic. Supposedly, we'll have a cab service pick us up. I'll be with you as far as Peekskill."

Nicholas Hall, operated by Catholic Charities, was on the outskirts of a small town outside of New York City. The home was a network of tiny cottages along with one four-story red brick building that served as the center of operations. It was winter and the temperatures were still nippy. A blanket of fresh snow covered the ground. Instead of an armed guard at the entrance, there was a middle-aged man in a security uniform along with a fierce looking German shepherd.

Mrs. Kendall accompanied me to the front office, where I met the nun in charge. She was an older woman, probably in her late fifties, with shoulder-length gray hair tied back in a bun. The pear shaped, brown-eyed woman wore a plain blue dress and a pair of black loafers. Taking a seat at her desk, she gripped the large cross hanging from her neck and said, "Hi, I'm Sister Mary. I hear you'll be with us for a while."

"Yes, ma'am."

Sister Mary thumbed through my file and looked up to at the caseworker. She quickly signed one of the papers and handed it to the woman. She said, "You may go now. Have a safe trip back to Buffalo. Drive carefully and may the Lord be with you." The nun blessed herself and nodded at Mrs. Kendall.

The caseworker gently squeezed my shoulder. "Good luck, honey. It was nice meeting you."

Sister Mary explained the rules. Six girls lived in each cottage. I was assigned to cottage number 5, supervised by a nun named Sister Clara. I grimaced at the thought of sharing space with five other girls I did not know. The nun with wrinkled skin continued to recite a litany of regulations. "Everyone gets up by six-thirty. No exceptions unless you're sick. Once you're up, proceed to the shower in your cottage, but be orderly and ladylike at all times. Make sure you wash quickly. Other girls will be waiting. After you're dressed, breakfast is served in the main house. Chores begin right after breakfast."

Nicholas Hall used a ranking system to instill discipline and structure into the lives of teenage miscreants. To step up the ladder, points had to be earned. The only way to earn points was to comply with all the rules. Slip-ups meant a loss of points. If a girl wanted to go home, she had to acquire a certain number of points. All new residents, including me, started at the bottom.

I was perplexed by the system and failed to see how it applied to me. After all, the court system had not sent me to Nicholas Hall. The other residents were girls who carried the labels "truant" or "delinquent."

I voiced my disapproval. "But, Sister, I haven't done anything wrong."

"You're right, my dear. I hadn't thought about it that way. For now, you'll have to go along with the rules. If you don't, the other girls will raise a stink. As long as you're here, I'd like you to comply. Let me see if I can work something else out."

Sister Mary pushed her chair away from her huge wooden desk and stood up. She motioned for me to follow her. I walked to the cottage with wobbly legs. Losing my privacy made me crazy. No matter what happened to me during the day, I had always been able to seek refuge at night. How would I, a shy, reserved girl, survive in a strange place like this? Thoughts about running away raced through my mind, but because all of my money was gone, I doubted I would try again, and I had no desire to end up on the streets.

As Sister Mary introduced me to my new housemates, I quickly nodded at the girls, hoping the introductory phase would be over soon. Most looked at me and shrugged indifferently. I hated having to go through the whole routine all over again: meet new people, learn new rules, and adjust to new living arrangements. At this point in my life, I should have received an award for my long-standing role as a foster child, but nonetheless, I felt awkward. I was also scared, because all these girls had been in some kind of trouble. I had more in common with the girls at Flourette Hall. We were there because we had nowhere else to go.

Sister Mary guided me to a bunk bed in a place as stark as an army barracks. "This is your bed. You'll sleep on top. That's the rule for newcomers. Put your things inside the small foot locker. Don't forget. Dinner is at five o'clock. Be prompt or you lose points."

Now alone among the girls, I almost passed out. My heart skipped at an out-of-control rate. I could feel everyone's eyes focus on me. I hated feeling on display. Not knowing what to say, I slowly unpacked my things, purposely taking my time. I did not want to face the girls.

One tall, skinny black girl took the lead and approached me. "Yo, I'm Robin." She looked around at the other girls and said, "Come on, y'all. Say hello. Show the girl you have manners."

The other girls introduced themselves. Each one explained why she had been sent to Nicholas Hall. One was a chronic truant, one got caught shoplifting for the seventh time, one gave her mother a bloodied nose, one hawked drugs in high school, and the other had troubles getting along at home. Four of the girls, all of whom were black, came from New York City. The only white girl was from Syracuse.

I found out about one hundred fifty girls lived at Nicholas Hall. The census changed often, with some girls receiving a discharge while others were admitted. Stays averaged from several months to several years. Courts throughout the state used Nicholas Hall as one option to deal with out-of-control teenagers. Reform school, as detention centers were also called, was common in the early 1970s. If you got sent to reform school, you were seen as a loser or a tough girl.

Smoking was permitted, but only if you had enough points. Even then, you could only smoke outdoors. Drug and alcohol use were strictly prohibited, but a few girls had marijuana mailed to them. They usually smoked it outdoors and were never caught. Oddly enough, the nuns placed more restrictions on gum chewing than on smoking. Gum chewing was banned at all times, and getting caught warranted stiff punishment.

Once we left our cottages in the morning, each was locked until dinner was over. Only the nuns held the keys. If you needed something, such as a sanitary napkin, that was too bad.

A recreation room with a television and radio was available, but only girls with points could use it. Because there was only one television set and one radio for so many, arguments often erupted. The black girls liked the Motown sound, but the white girls disagreed constantly about music. One time, two hot-tempered girls got into a bout of hair pulling. One clamored for rock and roll groups such as the Rolling Stones and the Grateful Dead, while the other preferred the folk sounds of Joni Mitchell and Simon and Garfunkel. The nuns broke up the fight and switched the channel to soft music, the kind you heard while waiting in a dentist's office.

Strolling around the grounds for fresh air or exercise was not permitted unless you had earned points. Hardly a soul used the outdoors for exercise, mostly because winters were too cold, but some girls went outdoors to smoke.

Every so often, the nuns organized recreation nights. We went bowling a few times, saw a few G-rated movies, and once went to an dude ranch to ride horses. Watching the nuns ride horses gave us a good laugh. Every time we went out as a group, however, I felt ashamed. We received quite a few stares. Peekskill did not have a large minority population and I assumed people knew we were from Nicholas Hall. Through the grapevine, I heard the residents viewed us as the bad black girls from New York City. I wondered what they thought of the white girls.

A couple of times, we had in-house recreation. One Saturday, we spent the day involved in relay races. Cottages competed against another. For a change, we all let down our guard and had a lot of fun.

Another evening, we had a sing along. One of the nuns strummed her guitar and we joined her by belting out some popular folk tunes, including "If I Had a Hammer." Most girls preferred rock and roll music to folk songs, but we had a good time.

Almost all residents had street savvy. They greeted each other with, "What's happening?" Every so often, they exchanged the high five. The black girls viewed proper English as "too white" and the white girls saw it as a sign of someone who was a smart ass. Quite a few bragged about their sexual exploits, claiming they did it in such weird places like a public bathroom or on top of a desk in an empty classroom. One girl claimed to have had multiple sex partners at once. Around them, I felt like a country bumpkin.

For the next eight months, Nicholas Hall served as my home. The meals were typical institutional food—tasteless, salty, and nonnutritious. I went months without eating fresh fruit or vegetables. Juice was rarely served. Instead, we drank either store-brand soda or cheap juice drinks made from corn syrup and flavored with some kind of fruit. Fresh milk was available, but mostly they served the powdered stuff.

Chores consisted of scrubbing the bathrooms, which were fairly dirty because so many girls used them. Long hair on whites and atlas sized Afros on blacks were still popular, so the sinks were frequently clogged with hair. At one time, I enjoyed taking long luxurious baths. I let go of this habit at Nicholas Hall for two reasons. First, each girl was allotted no more than ten minutes in the bathroom and, second, the tubs were almost always grimy. I could barely stand to shower in them. Taking a bath would have to wait.

Besides cleaning the bathrooms, we had to mop the floors, dust the windowsills, and change our linens once a week. A washer and dryer were available in the main house. Each girl was responsible for her own laundry, but to get detergent, points were needed. Unlike Flourette Hall, we did not have to clean or cook for the nuns. They did it themselves or hired someone to do the job.

After meals, every girl participated in clean-up by putting away leftovers; washing, drying, or putting away the dishes; or hauling out the garbage. Three meals were served every day and girls were not permitted to skip meals, unless they were sick and had Sister Mary's approval.

Back in New York

Mealtime was a very solemn affair. Grace was said before each meal. Not participating in grace was cause to lose points. Cracking jokes at dinner also led to point loss. One of the nuns always supervised meals and, not surprisingly, the girls mostly ate in silence.

Girls at Nicholas Hall were allowed to send and receive mail. Depending on who was in charge of mail, certain nuns read our letters. Amazingly, no one ever got caught receiving drugs in the mail. A pay phone was available, but because most of the girls lived far from Peekskill, it was rarely used. When it was, a nun usually eavesdropped on the conversation. Any shred of privacy at Nicholas Hall was hard to find.

Classroom education was provided, but the program was far from rigorous. We were taught the basics, so bright girls were never challenged. Instruction was little more than a series of boring lectures where questions were not encouraged. With the exception of one or two faculty, most displayed little enthusiasm in the classroom. I had my doubts all of them were competent, because teaching at a reform school could not have been high on teachers' lists. It seemed most teachers were afraid of the girls. Students in those days did not carry weapons, but some of the girls wore mean, nasty looks that could frighten most people.

Jack Ortman, a young black teacher who wore wire-rimmed glasses, paid special attention to me. He asked me to stay after class a few times to see if I had understood the lesson. One day, Mr. Ortman said, "I know you don't belong in this place, but don't let your studies fall down. You have a future ahead of you. I'm not sure how many of these girls will straighten themselves out. But you, you're different. Whatever little bit of hope you have, make sure you cling to it. Don't forget."

That sage piece of encouragement went a long, long way. Finally, I started to believe in myself again, because I was not sure anyone else would. At least once a week, Mr. Ortman spoke to me before or after class to see how I was doing. It was like I had a spark in my eyes only he could see.

Because of my reserve, I rarely gravitated toward any of the cliques. Mostly, I kept to myself. A few of the girls branded me as a traitor for doing my homework or reading. Behind my back, they made crude jokes. Several nuns also got into the act. I expected to be the butt of jokes from the girls, but not from the nuns. I was nervous most of the time, so I occasionally stammered. Whenever I stuttered in front of certain sisters, they imitated me behind my back, then cracked up.

Family visits were encouraged, but not many girls had families who could make the long trip to Peekskill. With the nuns' permission, I visited Miss Morse just once, via the Trailways bus, because Peekskill was more than a six-hour trip from Buffalo. I enjoyed my visit, but our relationship was strained. I felt uncomfortable around her, and I imagined she did as well. We barely moved beyond superficial chatter.

I missed my old high school, where I had established some foothold. I knew many of the students and teachers and was familiar with the routine. Lunch hour at Christ the King was sometimes entertaining, depending on who jumped on top of the jukebox and broke out in a dance. I also missed my job, and I longed for the independence I once enjoyed. A regular paycheck also enabled me to buy my own clothes. Now, I was forced to wear state-issued clothes, most of which were either second-hand or cheaply made.

The nuns offered us another way to earn points as well as extra money. The local Catholic Church hired us out to clean people's homes. I volunteered for one of these assignments, seeing it as a means to get away from the stifling atmosphere at Nicholas Hall. Most girls used this work to make money for cigarettes or long distance telephone calls to boyfriends.

On my first day at the job, I was introduced to a stern-faced woman whose name was Mrs. Meenan. She appeared to be in a hurry and whisked me into the house so quickly I almost fell over the doorjamb. As she instructed me on the most efficient way to clean her house, I noticed three young boys dashing through the rooms, playing tag. Mrs. Meenan screamed at the boys to stop running, but they ignored her.

I started by dusting and polishing the living room furniture. The furniture was grimy and sticky. When I thought I had given a nice shine to the coffee and end tables, Mrs. Meenan came over and ran her fingertips across the furniture. She waved her index finger, which contained a trace amount of dust, in my face and said, "You haven't finished yet, have you?"

I gave her a phony grin. "I guess not."

A little while later, I hauled out the vacuum and ran it across the aging carpeted floors. I took more time than usual to make sure the floors met with Mrs. Meenan's approval. After I turned off the vacuum, she paraded over and said, "Look over there. I see some dust. Can you run the machine a little more?"

It was a good thing I was patient.

As soon as I finished cleaning the living room, her three little terrors ransacked the place. It hardly looked as if it had been cleaned at all. I thought about asking the boys to behave, but I changed my mind. Hey, I did my job.

I scrubbed the bathroom fixtures until the smell of Lysol cleaner made me nauseated. I thought the room looked spic and span until Mrs. Meenan entered and pointed to the wall. "I see a spot you missed. Go over there and wipe up, will you?"

On my way out, I had a pounding sensation in my head. Working under the watchful eye of Mrs. Meenan left me feeling sick. I felt sicker when she handed me ten dollars for five hours of back-breaking work.

I agreed to return two more times, but after the last visit, I called it quits. To make only a small amount of money meant I had to endure Mrs. Meenan hovering over my back, whining about the tiniest smudge mark I missed, and listening to three bratty kids scream and yell. It was not worth it anymore.

Another way to score points, but not earn money, was to volunteer for a recreational assignment at a one of the few orphanages Catholic Charities still ran. When foster care placements were unavailable, the orphanage became home to maltreated children, most of whom were in the two- to five-year-old range. The particular children changed often but, on average, there were at least twenty-five children in residence. Finding homes, even temporary ones, for children with severe emotional problems was always a daunting task. Although child welfare advocates frowned on orphanages, where else where these children supposed to go?

On my first day, I met a group of youngsters with unusual behavioral traits. In spite of bright-colored walls covered with popular cartoon characters and an ample supply of stuffed animals, dolls, and games, the toys and the cheerful surroundings failed to produce even faint smiles. Blank stares dampened their tiny faces. There was no display of the typical rambunctious behavior I expected of children this age. Such a sad scene was shocking as well as disturbing. Who or what robbed them of their playfulness?

The nun in charge hastily gave me some background information. Every child had been physically and/or mentally maltreated, some in rather gruesome fashion. A knot burned in my stomach as I listened to horrific tales about child abuse. I was sickened to learn about an alcoholic father who burned his three- year-old son with a scalding hot iron. Another little girl, with sky blue eyes and silky blonde hair, had a drug-addicted mother who exchanged her child for sex with strangers so she could buy acid. The sight of a sweet-faced young boy with whip marks all over his arms and neck made my eyes watery. What made their parents inflict such brutal, torturous injuries? My own life had been filled with more emotional anguish than I could often bear, but I had never been physically victimized, except for the unwanted sexual advances by Sister Rose at Flourette Hall. I doubted anyone, including me, could comprehend the depth of the pain that haunted these children. The nuns seemed to do the best they could but, in retrospect, I was sure they lacked the necessary expertise to treat the complex psychological maladies associated with childhood physical and sexual abuse. But the orphanage, although far from ideal, was the only safe haven these children had.

The nun politely excused herself, leaving me on my own. Nervously, I called the children into the play area. Within seconds, they complied, showing the obedience of robots. None caused a fuss. Not even a personal visit from Bugs Bunny would have helped. As a way to ease my introduction to these lost souls, I picked up a few toys to initiate play but the children showed no interest. Running out of options, I talked to them in a calm, peaceful voice. When I tried to cuddle next to a young boy, he recoiled in panic as if I was a monster. I felt so woefully unprepared. I thought by dealing with their pain I would let go of some of mine.

As hard as it was, I spent a few hours each week at the orphanage. I had the children form a group while I read fairy tales or picture books to them. At every available chance, I smiled, even though smiling never came easy to me. They needed to be showered with as much love and concern as possible. When they tired of story time, I asked who wanted to play games, but the little boy whose father had scalded him continued to show fear. Always aloof but never too far away, he watched us but never spoke or participated in playtime.

I learned quickly these children were not very fussy. It did not matter to them if I pronounced some words incorrectly or if I stammered once in a while. The fact I had dyslexia, lived in a detention center, and had no permanent home was of no consequence either. My regularity enabled a few children to start trusting me. From my weekly visits, these children slowly thrived on the personal attention I showered on them. The nuns, although thoughtful and considerate, lacked sufficient time to spend with each child. The children and the nuns who cared for them showed me compassion, patience, and courage. I felt proud I had the chance to share myself with such badly maltreated children.

Ever so slowly, my housemates and some of the other girls at Nicholas Hall started to accept me, shyness and all. One day, a new resident attempted to bully me and she caught hell. From then on, the new girl stayed out of my way. I had always despised the term "brown nose." Snide comments about my proper use of language were no longer muttered behind my back. I refused to call this hellhole a home, but at least the camaraderie had improved.

One of the more serene sisters had been assigned to mail duty for a while. She was so passive I think terrorists could have slipped pipe bombs into Nicholas Hall through the mail without her knowledge. Sometime that week, one of my housemates received a package from her younger sister with some essentials, namely hair oil, deodorant, and a few joints. I went for a walk around the courtyard. The weather was decent, so I brought my homework outside. As I sat on a bench preoccupied by a chapter about World War I, a few of my housemates passed in front of me. They gave me the high five as they breezed by. Instead of reading, I watched the girls as they lit up. My nose twitched from the unmistakable pungent aroma, and I wandered over to their table. "Hey, can I try some?"

One girl had sucked in an incredible amount of smoke. She looked at the others and they all cracked up. When the laughter died down, one of them said, "No way. Stay cool and don't get into this."

Another girl said, "If you ain't into drugs, then don't start now."

The white girl from Syracuse said, "Don't get messed up like us."

My curiosity was at its height. "Come on, once."

In unison, the girls yelled, "No."

"But . . ."

A black girl said, "Get your ass out of here and stay away from drugs."

A trickle-up effect was soon evident. The nuns who had also made fun of me cleaned up their act as well. I continued to stammer from time to time, but the nuns did not mocked my anxiety anymore, and I stopped wishing their hair would fall out.

Just as I was getting into a rhythm at Nicholas Hall, Sister Mary unexpectedly called me into her office one afternoon. She seemed like a decent woman but was as bland as white bread. She held out her palm and motioned for me to take a seat. "We all know you don't belong here. This is a place for girls in trouble. It's taken a while, but I've made arrangements for you to live in a group home in Buffalo. We think you'll be happier there."

"So, I'm free to leave?"

"Yes, my child. You'll leave tomorrow. We bought a train ticket for you to get to Buffalo. Someone will drive you to the train station. A caseworker from the new home will meet you once you get there."

"What about school?"

"School?" The nun reacted with such surprise she seemed as if I had asked her for permission to enter the convent.

"Where will I go?"

"I don't know yet."

I told my housemates I would be leaving. They reacted with disappointment, expressing sadness and envy I would soon be gone. I was surprised when they displayed so much emotion.

The next morning was dreary. The skies appeared as if they would open up at any minute. My spirits felt dampened by the menacing clouds spread across the sky. During the long train ride, a lot filled my mind. What should I do? Take a chance and try to live on my own or stay in Buffalo at another group home? I longed for a calm voice to listen to my woes and help me sort out my life. Whenever I slipped into a flash of pity, I wasted no time switching gears. Immediately, I focused on the abused children I had met. If they could get through another day, then certainly I could, too.

Sheets of rain pelted the moving train, exacerbating my apprehension about another move. This would be at least my tenth upheaval, and the rain made me feel more pain. By the time the train pulled into the dimly lit depot in Buffalo, my legs felt so weak I could hardly stand. As I walked off the train and into the bleak uncrowded waiting area, a tall slender white woman with soft blue eyes that radiated a sense of calm walked up to me. I felt at ease around the woman with the tender smile. She led me to one of many empty seats and said, "You must be Theresa. Hi, I'm Miss O'Rourke. With the home. I'm a house parent."

I cracked a small smile. "Thank you for coming,"

Miss O'Rourke aimed her hand at the train sitting in the station and said, "I guess we should be going. Do you have any luggage or anything?"

I squirmed in my seat like I was sitting on a pine cone. "No luggage, but wait, I have to tell you something."

Miss O'Rourke brushed a tuft of long blonde hair away from her face and said, "We can talk once we get there. I've set aside time for you. Let's wait. This place doesn't have any privacy."

"I can't go."

"I know this must be terribly disruptive for you."

"No, I'm serious. I'm planning to get a job and find my own place."

"I realize you're upset, but dropping out of high school would be a terrible mistake. You'd end up in low-wage jobs. I've seen other young people make that choice and end up regretting it." Miss O'Rourke spoke with such a calm voice I felt a tad more at ease. I nonetheless was still leery about living in another group home.

"If I go with you, how long can I stay?"

"Until you finish high school."

"I'm already eighteen. Will they kick me out?"

Miss O'Rourke's attitude shifted to a more serious tone. "Not unless you drop out of high school."

With few exceptions, once foster children reached the age of eighteen, they were cut off from the system. Those who remained in high school were exempted from this strict rule. I was glad for the temporary reprieve but very anxious about leaving foster care. For all my life I had depended on the system for every aspect of my care. Catholic Charities clothed me, fed me, educated me, and decided where I lived, for how long, and with whom. The idea of being on my own alternately appealed to me and frightened me to death. Education was my best choice.

On our way to the parking lot, Miss O'Rourke tried to shield us from the rain with her umbrella. The storm was so strong we got soaked anyway. Because it was already June, I was surprised by the gloomy weather.

We discussed the group home, a place called The Good Samaritan Home for Young Girls. I would have a private room for the time being because a girl had returned to live with her family. There was no particular timetable for new arrivals, so in the meantime I would have a respite from the past few months of sharing quarters. What a relief, at least for now.

Miss O'Rourke looked at me with a serious stare. "We need to get you enrolled in high school. It's important you finish."

"Can I go back to Christ the King?"

"I suppose you could, but it's clear across town. I was thinking about Our Lady of Mercy High School. It's not too far from here. I've already talked to the principal and she's ready for you to start in the fall."

"What about tuition?"

Miss O'Rourke let out a worrisome sigh. "That's going to be a problem. This school is Catholic, but it's independent of the archdiocese. It's a good school, though. Almost all the girls who graduate get accepted to college." She fiddled with a paper clip for a few seconds. "But you'll have to pay for tuition."

"How can I do that?"

"I'll help you pay for it. I've asked them to consider you for financial aid, but they won't make any promises."

Good Samaritan, a two-story brick building, was actually a private home in an upper-middle class neighborhood. It had only twelve girls. I found out the number was intentionally kept low to conform to city zoning regulations and to appease the neighbors. Local residents feared and resented group homes in their neighborhoods, even when they housed disabled children.

From the make-up of the small staff, it was evident times were changing. Four of the five workers were lay people. Only one nun was involved in the daily operations. The home had the usual assortment of Catholic embellishments—photos of Jesus and crucifixes scattered throughout. Otherwise, the inside of the place was actually quite bland. The furniture was unadorned, the kind bought in bargain stores. All the curtains were beige and no houseplants were to be found. Regular meals were served twice a day, except on holidays and weekends. The institutional flavor of the food had not changed much. Of course, we had to recite grace before every meal. Residents had a fair amount of freedom to come and go, but there was a curfew of nine o'clock. We could stay up until eleven, an often-overlooked rule. Curfew, however, was strictly enforced.

The day after I had settled in, I pounded the pavement looking for a job. If I had to fork over money for tuition, I did not have time to spare. Because so many factories had closed down, there was more competition for retail jobs. After a week or so, I landed a part-time job as a cashier in Wegman's, another chain of grocery stores upstate. School did not start for a couple months, so I spent the rest of the summer working full-time. Besides saving money for school, I was desperate to buy a few new outfits. I despised the shoddy clothes I had been wearing.

In September, classes for my final year resumed. I met with the grim-faced principal, a nun by the name of Sister Regina, who informed me financial aid was unavailable. I had applied too late and all of the scholarship money had been promised to other girls. I could pay my tuition of seven hundred dollars on a monthly basis. From the furtive look on the elderly woman's face, I surmised she did not think I would follow through, but I had a job and a promise from Miss O'Rourke to help.

Although I had misgivings about adjusting to a new school, knowing this was my last year relieved my anxiety. Because I had to pay for tuition, I planned to work every day after school and on Saturday. I trusted Miss O'Rourke's advice that this school had an excellent reputation. I could have gone to another Catholic school and paid much less.

On my first day of class, I was relieved to discover there were other new students. A few girls had transferred there from out of state. Of course, making new friends was never easy for me, and breaking through the tightly bound cliques at Our Lady of Mercy was next to impossible. At the behest of Miss O'Rourke, I threw myself into schoolwork, knowing that college was around the corner. During an earlier conversation in which I expressed a tepid interest in college, she came down hard on me, insisting I keep going. "If you don't try, then how will you know you won't succeed?"

For much of my academic career, I had not been a brilliant student. I failed first grade and had grades that were just so- so. If Miss O'Rourke was right, I would have to compete against a lot of talented students. I wondered if my grades would ever be good enough to get me into college, but I vowed to give it a try. Miss O'Rourke was right. What did I have to lose?

Exacerbating my quandary about college and how I would make it on my own, I remained depressed. Every day I woke up feeling covered by a heavy blanket of gloom. I was unable to shed the sadness. The world around me seemed eternally dark, yet if I did not press forward, I was certain to be swallowed up by my own misery.

No matter how hard I would have to push, I listened to Miss O'Rourke's advice. A college degree was the only way to save myself, and that dream was within my grasp. For years, I clung to the degradation associated with my out-of-wedlock birth. I still felt harmed by something that was not my fault. By the early 1970s, single parenthood, especially among teens, was becoming more common. Society seemed to go with the flow, yet I never let go of the shame.

The workers at Good Samaritan tried to make the place as home-like as possible, but I felt empty. I would be nineteen in a matter of months and Miss O'Rourke checked in with me a few times a week to make sure I was doing alright. I appreciated her guidance and sincerity. I still had my own room, but I knew that, at any time, arrangements could change because the schedule for new arrivals was unpredictable.

On the way to Wegman's, I ran into Tammy, the young woman whom I met at Flourette Hall and lived with at Franny's for a while. A long time had passed since I had last seen Tammy and I barely recognized her. She wore make-up, had on a fancy dress, and seemed all grown up. Tammy grinned from ear to ear and said, "I can't believe it's you!"

I smiled a bit and in my usually subdued manner said, "Hi. It's been a long time, hasn't it?"

"It sure has."

I asked, "What have you been doing?"

"I'm in my second year of college. And I also work downtown at a law firm after school. That's why I look like this." Tammy's eyes lit up as she said, "And guess what? I've got my own place."

"Where?"

"Not far from campus. Hey, you want to crash with me? I've got a spare room. My roommate moved out. I've been looking for someone else, you know, to share the bills. So, how about it?"

"I have to think about it. Give me your number and I'll call you."

Tammy passed me a slip of paper. "Don't take too long. I've had a few offers for the room. I won't make any choices until I hear from you."

I weighed my options. I could stay at Good Samaritan until I finished high school, but I was unhappy there. If I took Tammy's offer, I would have a place to stay until late August, when I expected to enroll in college somewhere.

When I approached Miss O'Rourke's office, the door was slightly ajar. I knocked and asked, "May I come in?"

"Sure, take a seat. I always have time for you." Miss O'Rourke must have noticed my jittery hands and said, "Anything wrong?"

My voice cracked as I blurted out, "I'm leaving."

"I figured you would. Do you mind if I ask where you're going?"

"I met this woman I knew from Flourette Hall. She's at the university and has her own place off-campus. She has an extra room, so I figured I'd go."

"I wish you well, but please, please, keep up with your homework. I'll help you fill out college applications. Remember, I'll be there for you, and I'm still going to help you pay for your high school tuition."

I hesitated. She had to know I essentially trusted no one. "Are you sure? You don't have to, you know."

"A promise is a promise."

As I headed out the door, she said, "Check in with me regularly."

"OK, I'll stay in touch."

In mid-September, I packed my things and moved into Tammy's apartment. The extra room was about the size of a bathroom, but I figured I would have to make do. I had much more on my mind, namely finishing high school and applying for colleges. Unlike our room at Flourette Hall, Tammy's place was in disarray. Dirty dishes clogged the sink. The floors looked like they were rarely swept. Huge chunks of paint hung precariously from the ceiling. Although I did not see any pesky little creatures, I imagined, over time, I would either see mice or roaches.

Like clockwork, I went to school every day and did my homework. I still struggled with math, but I managed to get by. I increased my hours at Wegman's. The busy schedule wore me out, but failure at this point was not an option. I kept plugging away, even on days when I could barely roll over.

I kept my word and called Miss O'Rourke on a regular basis. Although I would never admit my fears to anyone, including her, I needed a shoulder to rest on. Miss O'Rourke believed in me. Her encouragement kept me going on days when I felt like chucking it all.

Tammy and I got along, but we were never more than roommates. We had a mutual respect for one another, but I had my doubts we would ever be good friends. She left me alone and I steered clear of her, too. Every so often, we shared meals, usually pizza or hamburgers. Mostly I grabbed a sandwich during my dinner break at Wegman's. I developed the bad habit of skipping breakfast, but I normally ate lunch at school. The inexpensive meals were not the most appealing yet they kept me from starving.

Out of necessity, I grasped money management fairly well for a nineteen-year-old. By the time I paid for food, rent, clothing, and tuition, I had nothing extra for my savings account. Having to work every day left me with no time to get involved in after-school activities. Not that I was a very social person, but I enjoyed the semester when I played on the basketball team.

As cold temperatures settled across the area, I had to give Tammy additional money each month for the oil bill because heat was not included with the rent. Due to our tight budgets, we had to use the heat sparingly—and I mean sparingly. To make matters worse, valuable heat escaped through cracks in the windows. The apartment often felt like a refrigerator. I scrimped for a few weeks and saved enough to buy myself an electric blanket, a well-earned reward.

When I first started to live with Tammy, I honestly thought she was serious about school. She had occasionally mentioned a desire to break into publishing. I wondered why she did not live on campus, because dorm rates were cheaper than private apartments, but we rarely discussed anything personal. I was secluded in my own world, so I paid little attention to what went on in her life. Once I opened my eyes, however, I realized Tammy was more of a party person than a diligent student working toward a career. A lot of nights she stayed out late. Due to my naivete, I assumed it was work related. I was wrong. Tammy indeed worked after school, but she also caroused in the local bars with dozens of other students until all hours. I was in bed by the time she arrived home and I normally left before she got up. With this schedule, I never knew she had been bringing home young men to spend the night with her. A few times Tammy and I crossed paths in the kitchen during the morning. She had huge bags under her eyes, but I assumed she was tired like me from working and going to school. It took a few weeks, but it finally dawned on me she was suffering from hangovers.

A result of Tammy's reckless lifestyle showed up when November's rent came due. Tammy had gone on a drinking spree, spending all her money on late-night parties. To avoid eviction, I shelled out all the rent. I fed the school a sob story about why I could not pay tuition that month. The assistant principal seemed to accept my little white lie, but Sister Regina, the principal, raised such hell I was surprised a woman of the cloth could be so snippy. At least five times the following week, Sister Regina needled me about my tuition payment. She acted more like a professional bill collector than a high school principal. To make ends meet, I asked Miss O'Rourke to lend me some money. I expected to hear a lecture about the chances I took by moving in with Tammy, but she asked no questions. I promised to pay her back as soon as I could. I reminded Tammy she owed me money and to repay it as quickly as possible. I trusted she got the message.

Still bristling that Sister Regina treated me like a financial delinquent, I sought a mild form of revenge. I took the forty dollars Miss O'Rourke had lent me and had it converted into eighty rolls of pennies. Lugging the heavy bag into school, I dropped by Sister Regina's office to pay tuition. She gave me such a dirty look I could almost feel her annoyance with me. When I asked for a receipt, she waved me away without saying a word.

Now over this financial hump, Tammy could not come up with her share of the utility bill. Phone service had already been disconnected. Not wanting to freeze, I used my food money to cover the utility bill. I was in a snit. Tammy's heedless behavior affected me, too. I even ate dinner a few times at the Salvation Army soup kitchen.

One night, I approached her and said, "You're sticking me with your share of the bills."

She acted like it was no big deal. "You're jealous."

"Of what?"

"I see it in your eyes."

I abhorred her behavior. She was the one, not me, who woke up in the morning with hangovers next to strange men.

"I can't keep paying all the bills."

Somehow, Tammy came up with the money for December's rent and heating bill. I trusted she finally got the message about responsible behavior. I found out differently when the landlord showed up waving Tammy's bounced check in his hand. Steaming, he demanded to be paid in full on the spot. I told him what happened and he threatened to begin eviction proceedings.

Instead of using the cash I gave her to settle our obligations, Tammy had splurged on new clothes, make-up, and records. She had a new beau and wanted to impress the guy. For me, that was the last straw.

Tammy asked, "What're we going to do?"

"I don't know."

"We could get thrown out."

"Yeah, it might happen."

"What then?"

I said, "Why didn't you think about that when you were spending the money?

I had become friendly with a black girl at school named Lena Wilson. We ate lunch together a few times. Our casual relationship centered mostly on school, and although I liked her, we did not share much in common. I think we gravitated toward one another because there was only a handful of black students at the school. Over chicken soup one day, Lena must have noticed my shaky hand. She asked, "Girl, what's up? You look terrible."

"I've got money problems."

"Like what?"

"My roommate stiffed me for the rent again. We're probably going to get evicted and I have no place to go."

"I can't imagine being on my own in high school. What a bummer."

Not wanting to get into personal details, I made light of my dilemma. "I'll get by. I've been through much worse."

Lena said, "I'll ask my folks for the money."

"No thanks. I don't know when I can pay them back."

"Wait, I have a better idea."

"What? Play the lottery?"

"Come live with us. We have a spare room."

"Are you sure?"

"I'll ask my parents when I get home."

The offer sounded too good to be true. "Sounds good. If it's OK with them, I'd like to move in. Soon."

And so it was set. I made plans to move in with the Wilsons shortly before Christmas in 1972.

It Finally Came to an End

The Wilsons lived in Allentown, one of the few racially diverse middle-class sections of Buffalo. A successful attorney, Lena's father had his own practice. Her mother worked part-time as a doctor's receptionist. Besides Lena, who was seventeen, the Wilsons had eight-year-old twin daughters. I felt at home with the Wilsons as soon as I walked through the front door. They were fairly dark-skinned so I doubted color would become a problem. They also lived in a comfortable, stylish home in a safe section of town. Their hospitality was inviting, and I did not feel like a guest.

Because my arrival coincided with the holidays, the Wilsons home was festively decorated with a nativity scene in the living room, tasteful ornaments on the fresh pine tree, and a fancy wreath on the front door. Colorfully wrapped packages in assorted sizes and shapes rested underneath the graceful-looking Christmas tree.

On Christmas Eve, I assumed we would be going to midnight Mass, but the subject never came up. After a delicious meal of broiled flounder, rice pilaf, and a tossed green salad, we retired to the family room where we sat around and talked. The Wilsons had a large, extended family, but most of them lived in Virginia. Mr. Wilson attended law school at the State University of New York at Buffalo, where he met Mrs.

Wilson. Originally, the couple planned to return to Virginia because of their close family ties. Upon graduation, however, he was offered the chance to take over the law practice of a retiring attorney. Despite gains made by blacks in many areas of employment, Mr. Wilson questioned whether he would find such an opportunity in the South.

The Wilsons were not devout Catholics. Like other blacks, they converted so they could send their children to Catholic school, where they believed the educational system imposed stricter discipline and higher standards than the public schools. Both expressed genuine interest in seeing me through high school. Maybe I would see the promised land after all.

On Christmas morning, Mrs. Wilson left a present for me under the tree. I was delighted with the black leather wallet with twenty-five dollars hidden inside, along with a date book and a pair of fleece-lined gloves, but more importantly, I appreciated her thoughtfulness. I also enjoyed watching the twin girls rip open their presents. At their age, they no longer believed in Santa Claus, but their enthusiasm toward the Christmas holiday was infectious. They were also nice young girls who respected my need for privacy.

The holiday season with the Wilsons was quiet but extremely pleasant. Several distant cousins who lived in upstate New York dropped by to visit. A number of friends also paid social calls. The Wilson's circle of friends and acquaintances impressed me. One day, I hoped I would be fortunate enough to have the same.

I checked in with Miss O'Rourke right after Christmas, and we had lunch. I gave her an update on my living conditions. She seemed pleased I lived with a family who had a good reputation. She asked, "Are you keeping up with your classes?"

"Yes, I am."

"Let me know when the other kids start to fill out college applications. I'll help you complete yours."

"Are you sure you don't mind?"

I could feel a ray of sunshine in Miss O'Rourke's voice as she replied, "No, not at all. I said I'd get you through this and I will."

"I appreciate your help."

"You have to keep up your end of the bargain."

It Finally Came to an End

At the time I moved in with the Wilsons, school was on holiday recess. To take advantage of the extra time, I worked overtime at the grocery store. The Wilsons did not charge me for rent, but I felt obligated to contribute to the food bill and utilities. Also, I still had a few more months of tuition to pay.

Mother Nature was unkind that year. Snowstorms arrived one after another. Steady waves of subzero temperatures made me consider college in some place like Hawaii. A few times, Mr. Wilson offered to give me a lift on his way to the office, but the grocery store was in the opposite direction, so I declined. I did not want to impose on him any more than I already had. Bundled up with a parka, my new gloves, and thermal underwear, I braved the cold weather and rode the bus to and from work.

The Wilsons generally had dinner before I got back, but Mrs. Wilson always saved me a plate of leftovers. Most evenings, she sipped a cup of tea while I ate dinner. In the beginning, I was apprehensive about viewing her as a maternal figure. The unsteady nature of foster care reminded me Mrs. Wilson, too, could be torn from me at any time. We generally talked about current events, namely Richard Nixon's second term, the continuing war in Vietnam and the steady decline of the Black Panther party.

Mrs. Wilson met her husband when she was a sociology student at the university. Once they were married, she dropped out to help him through law school. Once Lena was off at college and the twins were older, she had plans to get her own degree. In the interim, she worked twenty-five hours a week, so she could be home with the children after school. I respected this woman for her commitment to her husband and to her family. And I was thankful I was now a small part of her life.

Once school resumed, I followed the same routine. Lena and I rode the bus together every morning. After school, I headed to Wegman's and usually worked until seven o'clock. Back at the Wilsons, I ate dinner and then hit the books. Every so often, I took a break and sprawled out on my bed, thinking about my past, present, and future. Life as a foster child made me different from the average young person my age. In a lot of ways, I lacked spontaneity and a sense of adventure. I felt overly cautious for a teenager. I could never "hang loose," a popular phrase of the 1970s. If at all possible, I tried to nail down all the loose ends on my life.

Days became weeks. Spring loomed ahead. At the end of another long, harsh winter, life in Buffalo became more light-hearted. One morning, on our way to school, Lena seemed more subdued than usual. She looked at me with resentment brewing in her dark eyes and said, "I wish my mother would get off my back about a job. All she talks about is how you work after school. Theresa this, Theresa that."

I had been in a fog, worrying about an upcoming trigonometry test. Math still made my life miserable. Lena's remark unexpectedly shocked me into reality. I jerked my head around to face her. "But Lena, I have to work. I'm on my own now."

"I'm sorry. I know." She clenched her fist and said, "I'm sick of her comparing me to you. It gets old after a while. My mother talks about you like you're a saint."

"I'm sorry your mother is doing that. I hope you'll tell her why I work so many hours. It's about survival. You have a family to fall back on. I don't. I think it's unfair for her to compare the two of us."

Lena sat there speechless. I hoped she understood what I had said.

Mrs. Wilson devoted a lot of her energy toward her children, especially the twins. She diligently supervised every aspect of her children's homework. After school, she accompanied the twins to Girl Scouts and dance lessons. In spite of her obligations, she had dinner on the table by five-thirty.

No matter how busy Mrs. Wilson was, she always found time for me. She stopped in the kitchen if I ate alone. She, too, talked about college, saying how important it was for young people, especially blacks, to get a degree. As time passed, I felt we shared a special relationship. As much as I was loath to admit it, I had become more dependent on her than on Lena. I neglected to see how my presence tipped the family balance.

Mr. Wilson's law practice consumed much of his time, but when he was home, he spent time with his children. Because Lena was a senior, he often talked to her about plans for college. He wanted her to attend an historically black university in the South. He was a graduate of

Morehouse College in Atlanta. Lena had other intentions, not all of which won accolades from her parents. She wanted to move to New York City and take up acting. Her parents, in particular her father, were dead set against it.

As time passed by, I became rattled by the tension. Lena and her parents were constantly at odds over her desire to pursue an acting career. They believed she would end up on skid row if she followed that road. I understood she had dreams of her own and wanted to pursue what was in her heart. Understandably, her parents only wanted the best for her. Both parents had come from poor families who used education as a way to rise above poverty. In this case, the best for Lena may not necessarily have been admission to college, but perhaps a chance to throw herself into acting. Lena realized she might fail, but she wanted to find out for herself. That seemed like a reasonable proposition.

The twins avoided the fracas by spending time in their room. Being eight, I was not sure how much they could understand about the rift taking place in their family.

Gradually, my relationship with Lena deteriorated. I assumed it was connected to the dispute with her parents about college versus acting. She started to leave earlier than usual for school, so we stopped riding the bus together. I had grown used to her company, so I felt a little lost at first. At school, she no longer asked me to join her for lunch. She found a new crowd to hang around with, tough girls who I doubted would meet with her parents' approval. Assuming she was going through a hard time, I brushed aside my hurt feelings. I continued to study and to go to work every day. I had come this far and I refused to allow Lena's petulance to get in my way.

I should have picked up on Lena's jealousy earlier, but I did not. Juggling a part-time job along with classes kept my eyes focused in one direction. There was also a part of me who soaked up the attention Mrs. Wilson was giving me. I was like a thirsty plant that had finally been watered and put in the sun. I liked sharing her mother. I never intended to take her away.

Miss O'Rourke, as promised, helped me with the college application process. Reading all the applications gave me a headache. There were dozens of schools I could apply to, but, at Miss O'Rourke's suggestion, I limited my choices to a few. My grades had improved from mostly Cs to As and Bs, so I was no longer ashamed to submit them to an admissions officer. She watched over me as I completed different forms. I was surprised college admissions offices wanted to know so much about me. Besides all the questions, every college wanted an essay along with the application. The process took much more time than I expected. Despite my hours of dreaming, I had a difficult time describing myself and what I wanted to do in the future.

The applications required a fee, and Miss O'Rourke wrote a check for each one. I thanked her again and again for her kindness, and vowed someday I would repay her.

Miss O'Rourke insisted, "Don't repay me. But when you can, help someone else in need." Throughout my life, I have tried to keep that commitment I made so many years ago.

An unexpected downturn in business saw Mr. Wilson arrive home from work by four o'clock. Because bus service was slower in the evenings, I usually did not arrive at the Wilsons' until around eight o'clock. One night, as I waltzed through the front door, Mr. Wilson called out my name. He was seated in the living room. He motioned for me to sit down and asked, "Want me to pick you up from work?"

"What'd you mean?"

"I have more time on my hands these days. I don't mind giving you a lift. I used to work in a grocery store, too, when I was in college, so I know what you're going through."

"No thanks. I study when I'm on the bus."

"Are you sure?"

"Yes, I've been taking the bus for years."

The real reason I turned down his offer was because of Lena. I was afraid that, if she learned her father had started to pick me up from work, her envy would fester. Traveling the bus after rush hour was a pain. I wanted to jump at the chance for a ride, but I did not want to cause more disruption in the family.

My relationship with Lena had now grown as cold as ice. She barely acknowledged me at home and rarely at school. I questioned whether she had made the right social choices. What little I knew of her parents made me realize they probably would not approve of Lena's new friends. These girls were headed for trouble.

After a busy tour of duty at Wegman's one day, I came back feeling wiped out. I considered going to sleep instead of studying. With lead feet, I carried myself through the front door. I had picked up a sandwich at Wegman's because the Wilsons had plans to attend a parent-teacher night at the twins' school.

Lena and three of her new friends sat in the living room, watching television. I was surprised to see the friends, wondering if they had met her parents. I glanced over and waved. In unison, all four girls spun their heads in the opposite direction so quickly it's a wonder they did not get whiplash. I got the message and kept walking. On my way up the stairs, I heard one of them snicker about the mismatched clothes I had on.

Inside the safety of my room, I felt teary eyed. The comment was rude and uncalled for. I assumed our friendship had cooled down because of the difficulties Lena had trying to convince her parents she was serious about acting. Once I calmed down a bit, I slid out my clothes and rested on my bed. Staring out the window at the starry skies, the full brunt of Lena's jealousy hit me. I had never intended to come between mother and daughter, but I guess I had.

The next day at school, I cautiously approached Lena at noon and asked her to join me for lunch. She looked at me with a smirk on her face. "I can't."

"But I'd like to talk to you."

"I'm busy."

"Just for a minute."

"No."

"Will you reconsider?"

Lena finally agreed. We took seats at an empty table, near a window. "Why are you mad at me?"

"What'd you mean?"

"You know what I'm talking about."

"Then tell me."

I said, "You're mad because I get along with your mom."

"I didn't say that."

"I like her very much, but I don't want to lose your friendship either. Let's try and work things out."

"Why should I? She thinks you walk on water."

"I didn't ask for this."

"I'm sorry I ever asked you to live with us."

"If you want, I'll leave."

Lena sighed, sitting up stiffly. "No, don't leave. I'd feel bad knowing you have no place to go. Just stay away from my mother."

After that, I avoided at spending time with Mrs. Wilson. I had cherished the time we shared and the advice she gave. Against my resistance, Mrs. Wilson had become a mother figure to me. I think she felt satisfaction from providing me with guidance and stability. I should have asked to talk with Lena and her mother, but I thought that would be too intrusive. I felt sad, knowing I would have to keep my distance.

Perhaps Mrs. Wilson saw me as a more diligent student than her daughter. College did not seem in Lena's future, no matter how much her parents wanted it to be. Lena was often combative about her demands to pursue acting. Quite a few times, I heard loud exchanges emanating from the living room followed by slamming doors. The once-tranquil environment became saturated with discord. I regretted that, through no fault of my own, yet another opportunity to blend in with a family had slipped through my fingers.

To keep the peace, I stayed in my room whenever I was home. I no longer joined the family for meals or other social affairs. Lena kept a low profile as well. I imagined her parents noticed we rarely spoke to each other, but no one discussed the chill in our relationship.

I came in from work one cool, crisp April evening. When I got to my room and saw a letter addressed to me from the admissions office at Boston College, I dropped by book bag and started sweating all over. This was it. With hands that shook like someone holding ice cubes, I grabbed the envelope but I could not open it. Finally, I sat down and counted to ten. I tried again and this time opened the envelope. Goosebumps popped up all over my arms when I read the words, "We are pleased to announce you have been accepted to Boston College on a full scholarship."

Buffalo held lots of unpleasant memories for me. Part of me was glad I had a place to go to, far away from upstate New York. Admittedly, moving to a big city terrified me, but I was determined to make things work. Besides, Boston College was the only place I had to go.

Tension at the Wilsons was at an all-time high and I could not wait to move on. Lena and I barely spoke any more. Her mother was in a snit because Lena had not applied to college. After graduation, Lena had plans to move out on her own. Mrs. Wilson must have noticed the changing atmosphere at home, but she said nothing.

As high-school graduation neared, so did talk about the senior prom. That became the focus of lunch room gabfests every day. Girls bragged about their dates, the cost of their dresses, and how late their parents said they could stay out that night. When asked if I had plans to attend, I hung my head down and said, "No, I don't have a date."

Upon hearing that, one of my classmates known for her social skills, threw down her sandwich. Her eyes sparkled as she moved closer to me. "Girl, don't say that. I know this guy Jimmy. He needs a date, too. I'll set it up."

"No, that's OK. I don't mind not going."

"Of course you're going to the prom. Everyone's going to be there. You have to come. This'll be our last celebration together before graduation."

"But . . ."

"But nothing. I'll take care of things. This is right up my alley."

I had to scramble to buy a dress. Even though I worked part-time, money was still scarce. I could not afford to splurge on a stylish gown like Lena had. Her father's business had improved, enabling her to avoid shopping for bargain basement specials. Her date was also from a well-to-do family. The young man had made plans to pick her up in a limo. My date said he would pick me up in his father's 1965 Ford station wagon.

On the day of the prom, Mrs. Wilson spent all afternoon helping Lena and me fix our hair for the big soiree. Lena was surprisingly gracious about sharing her mother. I suspect she was accommodating because she knew I would be leaving in a short time. I thought she might poke fun at me when she saw my not-so-classy dress, but she never made any snide remarks. In some ways, I was jealous, because Lena always seemed to fit right in with the crowd. At school, she was a popular student. Not me. I always felt like an outcast, no matter how hard I tried.

It Finally Came to an End

All during the prom, I felt awkward, even though I sat at a table with four classmates. Most girls had fancy gowns, wore jewelry, and had smiles on their faces. They danced, they talked, and they laughed. My date, a skinny eighteen-year-old with smooth copper-colored skin, was about to enlist in the Army. He looked sharp in his light blue tuxedo. Like many young men at the time, he wore his hair in a large Afro. He was not, however, interested in what I had to say. For the most part, I talked about college and my plans to move to Boston. I could tell his mind was far away and I soon found out why. He had only one thing on his mind. He repeatedly asked me about sex. When I told him no, a twisted smile cropped up on his baby face. "You're kidding."

"No, I'm not."

His dark eyes got wider as he exclaimed, "What'd you think all these people are going to do tonight? Go out and have coffee and donuts?"

"I'm not them."

"But . . ."

"I said I'd go to the prom, not go to bed with you."

For the rest of the evening, he sat at the table and sulked. I felt so dreadfully uncomfortable, I was sorry I came.

With no one to join me for my high school graduation, I declined to attend the ceremony. Seeing my classmates surrounded by their families would have made me sad, so I spent the evening at the movies munching on popcorn. Graduation left me at a crossroads. For the first time in my life, I was not a ward of the state. Graduation officially severed my ties with Catholic Charities. I was finally unshackled, but I was also scared to death.

Two days later, I packed what little clothing I owned into a nylon bag Lena had given me and said good-bye to the Wilson family. Miss O'Rourke gave me a ride to the Greyhound terminal in downtown Buffalo, and I bought a one-way bus ticket to Boston. I was now officially on my own. Somehow, I had pulled through nineteen years of foster care.

Epilogue

Once I finished this book, I breathed a sigh of relief. So did my friends who struggled along with me as I wrote it. The process was a long, difficult experience, one that dredged up unpleasant memories. But as I sat and pondered over the strides that I have made in my life, I realize that many other foster children did not fare as well. Long-term studies that have followed the outcomes of foster children are scarce. Not every foster child grew up without problems. I am very fortunate that my life took a very different turn.

In the summer of 1973, I left Buffalo for what I hoped would be the last time. The city held too many painful reminders of my past. I trusted that college in Boston would give me a new beginning, the chance to start over again. I embraced the challenge, but I was also scared to death. Other young adults faced similar issues such as what school to attend, where and how to open a checking account and whether to live on or off campus. Once accepting an offer from a college, they had a parent or parents to help guide them in their decisions, but I had to make all of these decisions by myself.

I spent July and August enrolled in a special program for minority students, called the "Black Talent" program. The short courses were geared to prepare students like me who showed promise, but did not always have the best high school grades. It was equivalent to a higher educational version of Head Start and was taught by upper-class black students who had once been enrolled in the program. The student-operated program also introduced us to the rigors that were expected of college students.

Believe it or not, after one year in Boston College, I transferred to SUNY in Buffalo. Was I a glutton for punishment? I felt frightened and alone in a bustling city the size of Boston. Compared to Buffalo, Boston was a huge metropolis, one that I was not quite prepared for. At least in Buffalo, I was familiar with the surroundings. I also had my friendship with Miss O'Rourke to fall back on. To me, that connection was everything.

In my junior year of college, I won a fellowship and studied in Denmark for a year. I lived with a family who tried to make me feel at home in their country. I was impressed by the social welfare system in Denmark and how it took care of more vulnerable citizens. This experience helped me decide to further my education in the field of planning, with an emphasis on housing policy.

I graduated with honors with a bachelor's degree in sociology. At the University of Michigan I earned a master's degree in urban planning. I worked in the private and public sectors in several different planning jobs. My ultimate academic dream began in 1989. Accepted by Harvard University, I received a doctorate in design in 1991. This book is published ten years after that momentous occasion.